MACRO ACCOUNTING
AND
MODERN MONEY
SUPPLIES

MACRO ACCOUNTING AND MODERN MONEY SUPPLIES

G. A. Swanson

QUORUM BOOKS
Westport, Connecticut • London

Library of Congress Cataloging-in-Publication Data

Swanson, G. A.
      Macro accounting and modern money supplies / G. A. Swanson.
         p.   cm.
      Includes bibliographical references and index.
      ISBN 0-89930-794-9 (alk. paper)
      1. Money supply.   2. Monetary policy.   I. Title.
   HG226.3.S93   1993
      332.4'14—dc20   92-38001

British Library Cataloguing in Publication Data is available.

Library of Congress Catalog Card Number: 92-38001
ISBN: 0-89930-794-9

First published in 1993

Quorum Books, 88 Post Road West, Westport, CT 06881
An imprint of Greenwood Publishing Group, Inc.

Printed in the United States of America

The paper used in this book complies with the
Permanent Paper Standard issued by the National
Information Standards Organization (Z39.48-1984).

10 9 8 7 6 5 4 3 2 1

Contents

Illustrations

TABLES

MACRO ACCOUNTING AND AND MODERN MONEY SUPPLIES

1

Introduction and Overview

Economies are physical phenomena. They are built by humans, may be destroyed by humans, and can be examined by empirical scientific methods. No mystical unseen hand guides them.

Modern market societies have emerged as predominately debt-monetary systems. They combine trade behavior, the artifacts money-information markers, and law in dynamic motivative systems. Those systems are capable of supporting large magnitudes of economic activity while providing an extensive degree of individual freedom.

Debt-monetary economies are systems that arise from accounting documentation. As systems, they are bounded. That is to say, they have certain discoverable interrelationships and interactions that make them work. Modern economic analysis generally neglects the accounting basis of debt-monetary economies and, thus, certain interrelationships and interactions.

The purpose of this book is to develop a frame of reference, methodology, and methods for examining the influence of money-information markers on economic production and distribution. Those accounting documents can be introduced in a manner that impedes or complements the fundamental trade process. Because modern economies provide the best combination of controls and freedom devised to date, attempts to complement their processes should be made. The ideas in this book can be used by societal policymakers as well as economic participants to improve current economic policies and activities.

Macro accounting is a set of concepts, theory, and procedures that may be used to investigate the concrete processes of higher-order human systems such as societies and supranational systems. The framework focuses attention on concrete (physical) processes. Such processes are the ultimate objects of empirical science.

The seminal idea of macro accounting concerns economic exchanges. Modern economic processes, although extremely complex, are combinations of one fundamental type of process, the exchange. No purely economic dynamic exists for initiating a transaction. Reciprocating transactions in an exchange initiate each other. Consequently, the exchange is the irreducible unit of modern economic processes.

THE EXCHANGE

The irreducible unit of modern economic processes is the exchange, not the transaction. Although the words *exchange* and *transaction* are commonly used synonymously, they have different technical meanings. The word *action* means any change over time. A *transaction* is an action that moves something across the boundaries of interacting systems. In concrete systems, transactions consist of movements of various forms of matter, energy, and information across physical boundaries. An *exchange* consists of a set of reciprocating transactions.

Exchanges obviously may be divided conceptually into their component transactions. No dynamic exists, however, in the concrete processes of modern economies to activate individual transactions. On the other hand, the dynamic of mutual benefit activates reciprocal transactions in an exchange.

Every exchange may be divided conceptually into two fundamental types of transactions: the outflow from one entity is the inflow to another and the inflow to one entity is the outflow from another. The two types would be a single type were it not for the coupling relationship of the dynamic of mutual benefit. The concrete economic exchange process does not exist without the coupling relationship.

Consequently, economic processes consist of three basic elements: a transaction, a reciprocating transaction, and a coupling relationship. Modeling a basic unit of such processes requires a minimum of four accountings: the outflow of a transaction from an entity, the inflow of that transaction to another entity, the outflow of a reciprocating transaction from an entity, and the inflow of that reciprocating transaction to another entity. The minimum accounting requirement imposes a constraint on the models that fully map concrete economic processes, termed the *quadratic constraint*.

Possibly because the component transactions of exchanges are easily observed, modern economic investigations often focus on them. Transaction-based investigations may constitute incomplete research designs. Such designs at best result in incomplete research and at worse provide no rational information.

Partial observations like those are different from the ones imposed by such data reduction techniques as sampling. Sampling is a proven useful means of investigating extensive populations. Sampling procedures are used to select a part of a population from which the results of an investigation may be inferred to the entire population. Successful inference depends upon the selection of a sample composed of elements that are distributed in some pattern in the population. Transaction analyses leave out important elements and their distribution patterns. If a sample involves processes, its elements must also persist over time in some order. The transactions and reciprocating transactions of trade exchanges are often separated by different periods. Transaction analyses do not observe those orders.

Observing transactions without imposing the quadratic constraint neglects the coupling relationship in economic processes. That observation focuses on an action disconnected from the dynamic that causes the action. If an investigator is trying to understand what causes a complex process and neglects the basic dynamic that causes the simplest component process, human ingenuity likely rationalizes an endless set of possible causes for the observed actions.

Higher-order human systems such as societies and supranational systems are distinguished by certain emergent properties. Those emergent properties do not exist in their component lower-order systems such as groups and organizations. Because of such emergents, higher-order concrete systems are not entirely reducible to their component lower-order systems. That is to say, higher-order concrete systems simply would not exist without certain emergent physical properties. In the absence of such emergents, lower-order concrete systems would be unconstrained by higher-order systems and would function according to lower-order relationships.

The exchange is an inherent societal-order emergent concrete property of modern economic processes. It is not simply an accounting or economic analysis concept or model. The quadratic constraint incorporates the exchange property in economic models.

Living systems theory (LST) (Miller 1978) views all concrete systems from the vantage of living systems. LST identifies certain forms of life, termed *living systems,* on a hierarchy differentiated by levels of complexity and related by the common cosmological origin and development of all life. The different levels are cells, organs, organisms, groups, organizations, communities, societies, and supranational systems. All of those types of living systems are concrete systems composed of various forms of matter and energy. Emergent properties distinguish each higher-level type system from the lower-level ones. Systems at each level include both structures and processes in a steady state of flux. If process is emphasized, the time-intensive term *higher order,* instead of the term *higher level,* better describes the progression of the hierarchy. LST provides the backdrop for discussing macro accounting.

On the LST hierarchy, societal emergents distinguish societies from other types of living systems. Although societies might be viewed conceptually from the perspective of cells, doing so would not explain much about those higher-order systems. Cells function similarly in a head of government and a janitor. Yet the two types of individual function very differently in societies. Consequently, it is important to identify critical emergent properties of societies and to analyze them using models that consider those emergents. The exchange is a societal emergent. The quadratic constraint takes that emergent into consideration.

The historical development of economic processes supports the idea that exchanges are the irreducible units of such processes. The progenitors of modern production and distribution processes likely were ancient administrative and commercial processes.

Administrative procreators were tax collection and goods-distribution systems in which goods and services were rendered to a ruling class in exchange for a receipt. Commercial antecedents were trading processes in which individuals traded different kinds of goods that they valued equally. The administrative processes were motivated by the perceived authoritative pronouncements of a ruling class. Trades, on the other hand, were self-motivated. The parties to a trade each had a self-interest in consummating the trade. As the administrative and commercial processes merged over time, the commercial motivator became the fundamental dynamic of economic processes. The accounting artifacts of the administrative systems evolved into various forms of monetary artifacts termed *money-information markers*.

TRADES

Trades are the foundational exchanges of modern economic processes. A *trade* is a set of reciprocal transfers of matter and energy forms commonly termed *goods* and *services*. This fact is often overlooked in macroeconomic analyses.

Commerce and industry should not be confused. The progenerative processes of modern economies were trade oriented, not production oriented. Excess production was a result of trade, not the other way around.

An exchange environment makes it possible for individuals to specialize their production activities. Specialization produces efficiencies that increase overall production. As commercial skills develop increasing demand for products and services, that demand provides incentive for additional production as well.

The process works because, in a particular trade, the parties involved believe that they are exchanging goods and services of equal economic value. Otherwise, no trade would occur, and there would be no specialization, no efficiencies, and no incentives to increase production. Rational people simply will not give up voluntarily more production than they receive in return.

THE ACCOUNTING BASIS OF MONEY

Discussion of the accounting basis of money is clarified by assigning technically precise meanings to certain words that are sometimes used synonymously. *Exchanges* are composed of reciprocal transactions. *Transactions* are economic actions across the boundaries of two higher-order living systems. Transactions are usefully subclassed as transfers and transmissions. *Transfers* are matter-energy (goods-services) transactions, and *transmissions* are money-information marker and other information marker transactions. A *flow* is the action of crossing the boundary of a single higher-order living system (a concrete entity). The words *inflow* and *outflow* indicate direction of action with reference to a particular higher-order system. Every transaction consists of both an inflow and an outflow, each with reference to a different higher-order system. The words *inflow* and *outflow* generally correspond to the words *inputs* and *outputs*, respectively, in LST. The root word *flow* is chosen because it seems to emphasize process rather than structure.

Early administrative processes likely introduced accounting instruments (documents) into commercial processes. Administrators collected taxes at intervals of time, and common stores of goods were accumulated over one period for distribution over another one. Receipts documenting the satisfaction of individual obligations were issued by administrators (Schmandt-Besserat 1979, 1982; Swanson and Miller 1989: 37–53).

Receipts may take on economic value in the hands of holders. If holders believe that a series of advantageous exchanges might be made prior to administrators demanding proof of satisfaction of the individual obligation documented by a receipt, they exchange the receipt for goods and services. The value of the receipt is the value of the taxes or goods and services it certifies that have already been delivered to the administrators. Such an action introduces an accounting artifact (the receipt) of an administrative system into a commercial process.

The condition that gives rise to negotiability of receipts is a time lag between the delivery of a receipt and a demand for proof of satisfaction of individual obligation. The condition introduces a period during which the receipt may be substituted for actual delivery of goods and services to the administrators.

The negotiable instrument (the receipt) is an accounting document. Its economic value lies in its legal representation of an actual economic transaction—more precisely, a particular type of transaction, the transfer of goods and services. The value is imputed to the document by its exchange for stipulated economic goods and services.

Money-based economies likely arose from such interactions of administrative and commercial processes. A transition from receipts to loan instruments occurred early in the development of money-information markers. All types of such artifacts, however, introduced lags and leads between the reciprocal transfers of goods and services in specific trades of commercial processes. During the lag-lead periods, such accounting instruments became negotiable, exchangeable for goods, services, and other accounting documents.

The debt accounting instruments were able to introduce time lags and leads because they documented executory contracts enforceable by law (formal or informal). The development of money-information markers is closely related to the development of commercial law.

As modern economies matured, executory contracts documented by many different types of negotiable accounting instruments increasingly were transmitted in exchanges. Today, virtually all exchanges contain a transmission of some form of accounting instrument.

In that resulting process, a fundamental trade is divided into two exchanges, one occurring at the inception of an executory contract and the other at its termination. An accounting instrument is an integral part of the process. Its transmissions between the trading entities provide the two additional transactions needed to satisfy the exchange property at both the inception and the termination of an executory contract. Those actions make it possible for the reciprocal goods-services transfers of a trade to be separated on the time continuum.

During the period of an executory contract, an accounting instrument may be negotiated in numerous other exchanges because of the goods-services it can command at a future certain date. Notably, the instrument must be exchanged, not only transmitted, in every economic iteration. Otherwise, no incentive to relinquish it exists. And just as notably, such a fundamental accounting process provides the basis for modern money—the basis for debt money.

WHY IS THE ROLE OF ACCOUNTING LARGELY IGNORED?

By recognizing both the fundamental accounting basis for money and the exchange emergent of modern economic processes, understanding why economists have not used the accounting double-entry model extensively to analyze economies is difficult. Some economists have recognized the importance of accounting and the double-entry model.

Marx (Eastman 1932: 236) discussed the role of accounting in economic process in the following statement.

> There is nevertheless a certain difference between the costs arising out of the process of bookkeeping and those arising out of the process of buying and selling. The latter arise solely from the fact that the product is a commodity, and would consequently disappear as soon as the process of production assumes another social form. Bookkeeping, on the contrary, in so far as it controls the process and epitomizes it in an ideal manner, becomes all the more necessary in the measure in which the social scale of production develops, and in which the process of production loses its individualistic character. Bookkeeping is, therefore, more necessary in the capitalist system of production than in the split-up systems of handicraft and peasant production—and still more necessary in a system of production by the community itself, than in the capitalist system. But the costs of bookkeeping diminish simultaneously with the increased concentration of the process of production.

That statement recognizes accounting as a fundamental factor of production in higher-order human systems.

Sombart (Most 1979: 251) describes the double-entry model as a powerful instrumental reasoning devise. He states,

> If its (double-entry bookkeeping) significance is to be correctly understood, it must be compared with the "knowledge" which scientists have built up since the sixteenth century, concerning relationships in the physical world. Double-entry bookkeeping came from the same spirit which produced the systems of Galileo and Newton, and the subject matter of modern physics and chemistry.
>
> By the same means it organizes perceptions into a system, and one can characterize it as the first cosmos constructed on the basis of mechanistic thought. . . . Double-entry bookkeeping is based on the methodological principle that all perceptions will be manipulated only as quantities, the basic principle of quantification which has delivered up to us all the wonders of nature.

Although the writings of those economists describe to a degree accounting's fundamentally important role in modern economies, Western economics has all but ignored that role. Why? Perhaps the answer lies in two developments in professional accountancy: the failure of accountants to develop comprehensive theory that clearly establishes accounting as a discipline of thought and accountants' neglect of distinguishing clearly between measurements taken on concrete economics processes and interpretative adjustments of those measurements in public reports.

The first development provides only a circular explanation because economists have generally provided the basic theory for modern accounting research, which possibly explains why accountants also generally neglect the fundamental role of accounting in modern economies. The second development, however, may contribute to economists' neglect in recognizing that role.

Modern accountancy has increasingly followed an eclectic approach to accounting theory. That approach has combined many specific-purpose theories, some of which overlap and conflict with each other. In the absence of a comprehensive guiding theory to delimit the applications of such theories, each vies for expression in accounting reports. The degree of expression each receives is determined by political process, not by a prevailing logic—although some appeal to objectivity enters that process. The specific-purpose theories generally are justified on the basis of decision usefulness, not on the basis of measurement theory.

The consequence of this situation is that accountants themselves do not know what many derived accounting variables mean in terms of the concrete systems they monitor. Seldom, if ever, does an accounting textbook make a clear connection between assets, liabilities, revenues, expenses, and the like and the various forms of matter-energy flows in the concrete processes of modern economic entities. Leading accountants, having given up efforts to impute meaning, now describe the variable "net income" as a conventional score that business actors accept for evaluation purposes.

In view of the conventionalized confusion in accounting numbers, economists might be expected to reject conventional accounting data for economic analysis. The condescension of Boulding (1962: 55) expressed in the following statement is possibly as close to accounting as most economists want to come. He states

> A known untruth is better than a lie, and provided that the accounting rituals are well known and understood, accounting may be untrue but it is not lies; it does not deceive because we know that it does not tell the truth, and we are able to make our own adjustment in each individual case, using the results of the accountant as evidence rather than as definitive information.

DEVELOPING A MACRO ACCOUNTING FRAMEWORK

Notwithstanding its neglect of accounting, modern economic analysis for policy, administration, and operational decisions may be enhanced by recognizing the fundamental accounting nature of modern economies. Such recognition clarifies the following point. Analyses that do not consider the exchange characteristic with the quadratic constraint analyze partial processes, not whole ones.

Such analyses, by their focus, involve special-purpose theories. Although economic theorists have brought together several such theories in theoretical systems, they have done so generally at the expense of empiricism.

Recognizing that certain aspects of modern economies are human constructions, not mystical expressions that cannot be empirically confirmed or denied, provides the mind-set for an empirical science (concrete systems science) of economics. Such a science restricts its assertions to those that may be empirically demonstrated.

That empiricism leans as heavily on measurement theory and research design as do the natural and biological sciences. The data gathered are counts made on various measurement scales. Those numbering systems include nominal, ordinal, and ratio scales as well as a distinctive accounting scale.

The accounting scale incorporates a monetary scale into a spatiotemporal scaling process. Time is included in the scale itself. The movements of different forms of matter, energy, and information transmissions in modern economies are mapped on that scale. The attribute measured is specific exchange value. That value is stated in terms of monetary units. Using the accounting scale, organizations and other human systems are able to view the many different forms of matter-energy that compose them on a common attribute—thereby achieving a global view of the entity.

Important concepts and procedures are revealed throughout this book for analyzing modern economic processes, mainly from the macro perspective—the society perspective. Together, they form a conceptual framework based on the following four essential ideas:

1. The irreducible unit of economic process is the exchange.

2. Complex modern economic processes are combinations of exchanges.

3. Within modern economic processes, monetary processes emerge from executory contracts documented by accounting instruments that separate the reciprocal transfers of trades on the time continuum.

4. Accounting instrumentation of debt is the basic form of modern money.

The framework is termed *macro accounting* because it incorporates double-entry bookkeeping methodology. The methodology was developed to account for the inflows and outflows of exchanges from the perspective of organizations (social components), termed the *micro perspective*. The framework generalizes the double-entry model to the society perspective.

AN OVERVIEW

Over the last half century, social sciences have developed broad theories substantiating their empirical content. Those theories generally have only vaguely concerned concrete systems. Consequently, empirical science in the view of many social scientists differs from the view incorporated in macro accounting.

People's views of empirical science influence greatly their theories of measurement. The prevalent social science view of measurement theory also differs from that of macro accounting.

Discussing both empirical science and measurement theory before discussing macro accounting is useful. Those discussions delimit the domain of macro accounting. The following paragraphs overview the development of the text.

Chapter 2, Empirical Science—Observing Concrete Systems, discusses types of systems identifying concrete ones; overviews living systems theory; and develops measurement theory emphasizing isomorphism, proximate location, and differing orders of magnitude in physical, biological, and social systems.

Chapter 3, Accounting Measurement of Concrete Processes, identifies the particular aspects of social processes that concern macro accounting and discusses the following important ideas: what accounting is, double-entry and double classification, homomorphic expressions of concrete measurements, the ratio monetary scale, the spatiotemporal accounting measurement scale, and the basic double-entry measurement model.

Chapter 4, Macro Accounting, extends the basic accounting discussed in chapters 1 through 3 to the higher-order human systems termed *societies* and *supranational systems*. It discusses differentiating higher-order living systems on concrete economic processes, why money economies require double-entry mapping, debt money, and a macro accounting analysis method.

Chapter 5, Basic Economic Processes, analyzes basic economic processes within societies. The macro accounting methods developed in Chapter 4 are used to study the effects of various ways of introducing money-information markers into economies. The chapter demonstrates how accounting documents of debt obligations form the fundamental money-information markers and how societies introduce currency money-information markers based on the debt markers. Chapter 5 illustrates these actions with fourteen different situations.

Chapter 6, Fundamental Dynamics of Interest, Taxes, Rent, Royalties, Dividends, and Profit, discusses dynamics introduced into modern economies that provide motives to accelerate economic activity. It demonstrates that their influences can either compound or mitigate the effect of the basic trade dynamic. The chapter illustrates the introduction of these dynamics with ten different situations.

Chapter 7, Recurring Effects of Certain Dynamics, presents simulations of dynamics of introducing different motivators in various ways. Because the systems are complex and interacting, the results are sometimes counterintuitive.

Chapter 8, Supranational Systems: Intersocietal Exchanges, extends the macro analysis to multiple societies and emerging supranational systems. It discusses the basic foreign exchange circuit, the effect of a price increase in one society, limitations of freely fluctuating foreign currency exchange rates, the unequal treatment of members of societies permitted by supply-demand–controlled foreign currency exchange rates, a world order, foreign reserves (a moderating influence?), and supra-money and private debt-initiated trade.

Chapter 9, Conclusions, presents various insights for policy decisions that were developed throughout the book.

REFERENCES

Boulding, K. Economics and Accounting: The Uncongenial Twins. In *Studies in Modern Accounting Theory,* eds. W. Baxter and S. Davidson. Homewood, IL: Richard D. Irwin, 1962.

Eastman, Max. Ed. *Capital, the Communist Manifesto, and Other Writings by Karl Marx.* New York: The Modern Library, 1932.

Miller, James Grier. *Living Systems.* New York: McGraw-Hill, 1978.

Most, Kenneth. Sombert on Accounting History. In *The Academy of Accounting Historians Working Papers Series, Vol. 2,* ed. Edward N. Coffman. Atlanta, GA: The Academy of Accounting Historians, 1979, pp. 244–62.

Schmandt-Besserat, Denise. "An Archaic Recording System in the Urak-Jemdet Nasr Period." *American Journal of Archaeology* 83, no. 1 (1979), pp. 23–31.

Schmandt-Besserat, Denise. "The Emergence of Recording." *American Anthropologist* 84, no. 4 (December 1982), pp. 871–78.

Swanson, G. A., and Miller, James Grier. *Measurement and Interpretation in Accounting: A Living Systems Theory Approach.* New York: Greenwood Press, 1989.

2

Empirical Science—Observing Concrete Systems

Words are wonderful inventions. They make it possible for humans to communicate complex ideas among themselves. Through them, synthesizing and analyzing powers of many different brains are focused on particular problems in explicit detail.

Nevertheless, words may be ambiguous. Particular words often have multiple meanings. As a result, combinations of words may compound ambiguity. Ignorance as well as knowledge can be conveyed by words. That is to say, words can be used to hide certain information as well as to reveal it.

If complex matters are to be understood, the communications of investigators must be as unambiguous as possible. Economic processes are complex. Consequently, it is important to clarify at the outset the aspects of economic processes discussed in this book. The main concern of this discussion is the universe of concrete systems. What those systems are and how they are observed is the focus of this chapter.

SYSTEMS

The universe of all existing things may be viewed as a universe of systems. The word *system* means any set of related and interacting elements. The idea of a system is general but powerful. It may be used both to relate and distinguish the elements of a heterogeneous universe in an orderly and detailed fashion.

THREE BASIC TYPES OF SYSTEMS

The knowledge that concerns empirical science may be usefully divided into three basic and mutually exclusive types of systems: concrete, conceptual, and abstracted. *Concrete systems* are structured matter, energy, and information accumulations of extended physical space-time organized into interrelated and interacting subsystems and components. In such systems, *information* is defined as the patterns of the arrangement of spatially extended and order of temporally extended matter-energy forms. Such information may be communicated in space or retained over time if representations of it are borne on relatively small bundles of matter-energy termed *information markers*. *Conceptual systems* are limited sets of representations of relationships (some of which may be observed to inhere in concrete systems) selected by individual observers and borne on information markers of information-processing subsystems within usually human observers. This definition acknowledges that observers can never be certain that their observations include all aspects of the concrete processes they observe and that how they relate the elements of their observations may differ from how other observers might relate them. *Abstracted systems* are sets of words, symbols, patterns, or numbers borne on various forms of information markers in the human environment. These systems are representations of concrete and conceptual systems. They also may be constructed to represent other abstracted systems.

An *object* is what an observer observes. In concrete systems, objects may be both structures and processes, either of them, or combinations of elements of both.

The definitions of *conceptual systems* and *abstracted systems* given here switch the general meanings that were assigned in the author's previous works. This is done to aline my semantics more closely with the common usage of the root words *concept* and *abstract*. The word *concept* is used to describe a thought or idea originating within a person. The word *abstract* generally incorporates the idea of relative independence with reference to observable objects or even types of objects. The meanings here are also more specific to clarify that the definitions describe mutually exclusive subsets of the universe of systems that concern empirical science.

A brief discussion of the three basic types of systems in the context of a scheme of three ideas attributed to the Stoics by Mattessich (1978: 90) may clarify how the three types of systems are differentiated and related. He states that "the Stoics were the first to express clearly the difference and relationship between three fundamental notions of (1) the *sign* (sound, written symbol, etc.), (2) the *conceptual idea* ('lekton; meaning) communicated by sign, and (3) the actual *object* or *event* behind the concept."

The perspective of the Stoics' scheme differs from that of systems. The notions of the Stoics are differentiated beginning with the signs that represent concepts that, in turn, represent objects or events. The perspective of the systems scheme differentiates from the perspective of objects being observed, moving to conceptual reductions of those objects and finally to specific symbolic systems representing both objects and concepts.

If the Stoics' scheme consists of notions that describe mutually exclusive types of systems, the systems scheme is contained in that of the Stoics. In that case, a single general qualifier can distinguish the two schemes. Concrete systems are a subclass of the notion of objects and events.

The systems scheme concerns a particular kind of object, concrete systems. That kind is a subclass of the class of all kinds included in the Stoics' notion of objects or events. The qualifier precipitates a distinction among types of conceptual ideas as well. Information is narrowly defined in concrete systems. Consequently, it is useful to acknowledge that the notion *conceptual ideas* includes both concrete information observed (arrangements and orders of the matter-energy elements of a concrete system) and the private arrangements and orders given representations of that information by the information-processing subsystems of observers in their concepts (the information's meaning to observers). The Stoics' notion, almost certainly, also includes kinds of concepts that do not concern actual concrete systems such as those believed to originate in religious revelation. The Stoics likely did not distinguish the concrete system-based concepts as defined here, so let conceptual systems be a subclass of the Stoics' class of conceptual ideas.

Although in a technical sense particular observations may be arranged and ordered by observers without actually processing the information through human nervous systems, observation instruments used for that purpose are built by humans who design particular patterns into them. Observations of concrete processes, therefore, are never quite completely independent of the influence of individual observers. Both types of information should be considered in research designs. Consequently, distinguishing conceptual systems within the broader notion of conceptual ideas is important.

The concrete systems qualifier also affects the notion of signs. It places on this notion the restriction that signs are concrete system elements consisting of matter-energy forms termed *information markers*. Such markers might be chemical or electric processes of brains as well as communication media in the human environment. The systems scheme, however, classifies conceptual systems and abstracted systems as mutually exclusive. Information markers (signs) in brains are consequently classified as conceptual systems, and those in environmental media are abstracted systems. It is likely that the Stoics' class of signs did not overlap their class of conceptual ideas, which could include some sort of ideas existing in non-physical reality. So the systems classifications parallel that of the Stoics. Spatially separated spirits and humans might communicate with language in the Stoic scheme. Spirits are not included in abstracted systems. Abstracted systems, therefore, are a subclass of the class of signs. Figure 2-1 diagrams the relationship between the two schemes.

The foregoing discussion assumes mutually exclusive classes in both the Stoics' scheme and the systems scheme. The information perspective of the Stoics' scheme, however, might leave open the question of exclusivity. In fact, a forthright reading of the sentence identifying the three notions defines them as they relate one to another, not as they might exist as integral entities (stand-alone elements). From the local perspective of particular signs (symbols), the notion of objects or events might include both other signs and conceptual ideas as well as concrete systems and other things such as ultimate reality. Indeed, in philosophy the word *object* has come to mean anything that can be known or perceived by the mind. Without the exclusivity assumption, the notions of the Stoics' scheme are ambiguous. That ambiguity is indicated by the overlap areas of the diagram in Figure 2-2.

Figure 2-2 also illustrates that the classes in the systems scheme are defined as exclusive categories. The areas representing concrete systems, conceptual systems, and abstracted systems do not overlap one another. The area representing objects and events overlaps all three, as well as those areas representing the Stoics' notions of conceptual ideas and signs. The overlap occurs because signs may concern (be constructed to represent) all six classes, and objects or events are what signs concern. Overlap instead of circumscription occurs because elements of the classes may exist independently—of no concern to signs.

Such ambiguity does not advance effective communication among researchers. To avoid ambiguity, the systems scheme forthrightly asserts the exclusivity of its classes. Concrete systems are integral systems. They are regarded as existing outside the conceptual systems of the mind.

The ambiguity problem elucidated here illustrates a common pitfall when solutions to problems are attempted from an information perspective instead of from an object perspective. The information perspective too easily views conceptual ideas and signs as legitimate aspects of the domain of empirical scientific discovery—a view that stops short of discovering the physical systems underlying the ideas and signs. Observing that situation, Einstein wrote that "perfection of means and confusion of goals seem, in my opinion, to characterize our age" (1950: 113). The goal of empirical science ought to be discovering how concrete systems work and how they may be made to work better—not to study means by means.

EMPIRICAL SCIENCE

The object perspective of the trichotomy of the universe of systems clearly identifies the discovery of concrete systems as the goal of empirical science. That goal is achieved by observing concrete systems through measurement methodology and building abstracted systems to study observers' concepts of them. Whitehead wrote of the origins of science, "It grounded itself upon what every plain man could see with his own eyes, or with a microscope of moderate power. It measured the obvious things to be measured, and it generalized the obvious things to be generalized" (1967: 114).

The term *empirical science* has many different meanings. Here its use does not correspond to the empiricist atomism of the behaviorist movement in psychology. At the other extreme, neither does it correspond to Durkheim's positive idealism (1915: 321, 526). Instead, the term *empirical science* is used to describe a positive science that concerns concrete systems. It recognizes the ideas of both the organic whole and the part. The properties of both are determined by their interrelationships and interactions. Such an empirical science denies neither the Gestalt nor the part.

Refusing to ignore the part while recognizing the Gestalt at once makes the Gestalt a system composed of related and interacting subsystems that themselves may be viewed as systems in a suprasystem. Then the Gestalt is not a mystical whole, an impenetrable black box. Rather, it is one more system-subsystem in a hierarchy of complexly related and interacting elements of a universe.

Furthermore, such an empirical science recognizes that a Gestalt perceived by observers is subject to various observation errors, including those consequent to the spatiotemporal location of an observer relative to an object. Although the goal orientation of its driver generally dominates the pattern of a moving automobile, for example, the size of its fuel tank or any faulty part can dominate the pattern in a particular period. Furthermore, societal components such as the road system or road repair crews can also dominate at times.

Various degrees of macroscopic views of concrete system elements, consequently, should be evaluated in the context of other such views. Measurement theory, itself a macroscopic view, may be used to identify and map properties of fundamental explanatory elements of concrete processes. The resulting measurements, in turn, may be used to validate different macroscopic views.

Parsons (1968) influenced the social sciences to adapt a view of empirical science that included "empirical generalizations." Arguing the importance of grand theory and general theoretic structure in empirical science, he viewed methodology as a middle field between science and philosophy. Such methodology was not viewed eclectically, as disjointed conglomerations of theoretical and empirical systems, but rather as an organic whole. The organic whole was a special interpretation, however, one that virtually ignored the existence of its parts. Generalizations, consequently, were asserted to be empirical despite the acknowledged truth that they arose in the theoretical system aspect of the organic whole.

Although the idea of generalized theoretical organon is an important aspect of empirical science, how that abstracted system is constructed is also important. Using Parsons' structure of social action as a justification for philosophizing societies in the name of science does not encourage empirical investigations of societies. Parsons advocated building theory on general perceptions of social processes that were not connected in any significant way to measurements of the matter-energy processes occurring in societies. He (1968: 71) wrote

> The only respect in which the facts of the situation are affected by the theory of action is that the action frame of reference requires that they be stated in such a form as to bring out their relevance to its problems, that is, as means and conditions of action, not as aggregates of atoms, cells and the like.

The complexity of social systems and the relative infancy of social science possibly justified such a strong philosophical influence during a certain period of its development. The aim of science, however, is to move away from a purely philosophical approach to a set of problems toward an empirical approach. Abstractly analyzing organic wholes into critical parts certainly continues to provide a source of information about our existence. Concrete processes are one part of social existence, and global limits on the behaviors of such processes may be discovered by scientific operationalization.

Although he attempts to distinguish between his concept of empirical generalizations and Plato's reification of general concepts, Parsons misplaces concreteness (as Whitehead conceived misplaced concreteness) in the direction of idealism in a manner that allows the reification of concepts such as roles, opinions, and intuitions. Measurement theory, long proven useful in the natural and biological sciences, may be used to judge the empirical utility of such reified concepts.

LIVING SYSTEMS

The "concrete," "conceptual," and "abstracted" trichotomy of systems defines the concept of concrete systems and may be used to explain how empirical science observes those systems. Economic processes emerge in concrete systems. All concrete systems do not give rise to economies, however. Only living ones produce those emergents. Furthermore, economic processes themselves involve conceptual and abstracted systems as well as concrete elements.

Living systems comprise a subclassification of concrete systems. Living systems theory (LST) views the class of all concrete systems from the perspective of that subclassification (Miller 1978). LST identifies twenty critical subsystems that include both structures and processes and must function for living systems at eight hierarchical levels of complexity to survive. Table 2-1 defines those levels as cells, organs, organisms, groups, organizations, communities, societies, and supranational systems. Table 2-2 defines the twenty critical subsystems. All systems and subsystems carry out concrete processes composed of different matter-energy forms.

LST provides a handy conceptual framework for discussing details of living systems. The eight by twenty subsubclassification matrix shown in Table 2-3 helps investigators localize particular problems and move step by step through important relationships from the local perspective to the global. The body of the table provides an example of subsystem elements for each level. Living systems at all of the eight levels exhibit behaviors that might be termed *economic processes* such as inflows and outflows of various forms of scarce matter-energy and information transmissions. What is commonly termed economic process, however, occurs at the higher levels of human systems and involves the one hundred subsubclassifications included in the last five columns of Table 2-3.

A group of symbols has been designed for use with LST. Table 2-4 provides those symbols. They may be used in flowcharting and various other symbolic representations of complex problems.

CONCRETE SYSTEMS OBSERVATION
AND MEASUREMENT THEORY

We are our own worst enemies. That contradiction is an enduring characteristic of possibly all human organization. When organizing empirical data, it forces a constant vigil on those who attempt to discover concrete processes. Organizing empirical data on personal biases can obscure critical insights into the operations of concrete systems. The first line of defense against such biases should be raised at the point of observation.

Trichotomizing the universe of all systems that concern empirical sciences into concrete, conceptual, and abstracted classes focuses attention on the observation problem. All abstracted systems that concern concrete systems, such as this book, various econometric models, and so on, are no more or no less than representations of conceptual systems of observers. The paramount empirical consideration should be establishing that the manner of forming conceptual systems that purport to describe concrete systems minimizes individual observer bias by clearly demonstrating the connection between concrete system elements under observation and the abstracted system elements that represent them. This consideration is the focus of measurement theory.

Measurement theory involves two fundamentally important and interrelated questions. What numbers should be assigned to observations? How should objects be scaled (compared to scale)? The former question is the concern of the idea of isomorphism. The idea termed *proximate location* concerns the latter question. Proximate location is the concrete action that locates information markers bearing the elements of a scale in spatiotemporal proximity to an object being measured.

ISOMORPHISM

Isomorphism is specifically a mathematical term. A mathematical system is an abstracted system consisting of such elements as numbers and other symbols, points, vectors, and so on, that are defined exclusively in terms of specific relationship among themselves. Two mathematical systems are isomorphic if a one-to-one correspondence exists between their elements and if they permit all of the same operations.

More precisely, two algebraic systems, A with the operation * and B with the operation ·, are isomorphic to each other if and only if there exists a one-to-one and onto function f from A onto B such that

$$f(x*y) = f(x) \cdot f(y)$$

for all x and y in A. The "product" x*y is transformed into the "product" $f(x) \cdot f(y)$. In such a case, f is an isomorphism from A to B (Skrapek, Korkie, and Daniel 1976: 201).

Precisely establishing similitude between different concrete systems can provide a means of discovering aspects of such systems that may not be obvious at first glance. The idea of mathematical isomorphism is one way to demonstrate precise similarity between concrete systems. Of this means, Rapoport states, "Isomorphism between two mathematical systems induces a conceptual isomorphism between the concrete systems they represent. In other words, two concrete systems can be said to be conceptually isomorphic to each other if both can be represented by the same mathematical model" (Klir 1972: 46).

Rapoport's statement is part of an effort to tighten analogies between scientific disciplines such as physics, biology, and sociology. Early in the development of general systems theory, theorists recognized that although certain analogies from one discipline provided critical insights into another, many analogies were actually detrimental, obscuring critical insights. Rapoport's idea of induced conceptual isomorphism between concrete systems limits acceptable analogies to those that may be described by a particular mathematical model or by isomorphic mathematical systems. That is to say, all concrete systems that may be described by a particular mathematical model constitute a classification of concrete systems that in turn is a special case of a more general mathematical system consisting of all mathematical models isomorphic to each other. As a consequence, "All the theorems of the mathematical system are applicable to all consequences derived from the definition of the concrete systems" according to Rapoport (Klir 1972: 47).

Such an induction is a useful limitation on loose analogy. While it is abstractly and perhaps conceptually rigorous, the induction need not be empirical because its connection to concrete systems is by definition not by any particular observation process. It is a tautological system. The mathematical model, probability theory, is widely used to induce general characteristics of populations (that might represent concrete systems) from sample measurements or assessments. Whether the conclusion of the induction represents a concrete phenomenon depends on both whether the logic of the mathematical system was valid and whether the sample measurements were in fact taken on concrete processes. Such an observation process involves scaling as well as establishing isomorphic relationships.

In measurement methodology, the idea of isomorphism is used to ensure that a model permits the same operations as those of a scale such as the ratio scale. The ratio scale has been studied for centuries; consequently, the logical meanings of permitted operation are well known. By establishing isomorphism between a particular model and such a scale, empirical data may be manipulated according to the understood operations of the scale to reveal aspects of concrete systems that may not be readily observable through instrumentation alone.

The mathematical trend in general systems theory concentrates on identifying the common properties of all mathematical systems, such as linear systems of differential equations, that are isomorphic to a particular one. That effort provides insights into limitations of particular mathematical systems for modeling concrete processes. Understanding such limitations is important because certain operations permitted broadly by a validly used scale may not validly describe certain concrete processes because the unique interactions of particular concrete elements do not correspond to those particular operations. Essentially, this trend refines the classification scheme of algebraic systems to a much finer grid than that of commonly accepted measurement scales such as ordinal and interval.

Before leaving the subject of isomorphism, it should be pointed out that the more generalized idea of homomorphism might better describe the connection between a particular model and a scale. A homomorphic transformation does not require that the transformation function be one-to-one and onto. Consequently, there may be more than one element in the first system corresponding to the same element in the second system. Corresponding elements are combined, however, in the same way in their respective operations. For example, the function $f(x) = |x|$, where x is a vector, is a scaler function because it maps a vector space *into* a subset of real numbers giving the length of each vector, which is a scaler (a point).

Notwithstanding the fact that an isomorphism is a special case of the generalized homomorphism, the word *isomorphism* is construed more loosely by systems scientists to describe any demonstrable formal parallelism between two or more systems. The word is used in this broader sense to describe one of two fundamentally important actions in measurement methodology—that of assigning numbers. Its meaning insists, however, on proper mathematical rigor for any particular method employed.

By demonstrating that a model permits the same operations as an already understood scale, observers provide for themselves and others a generally understood logic for explaining their various restatements of empirical data. Establishing isomorphism between models and scales substantially answers the question of what numbers should be assigned to observations by restricting the assigned numbers to the elements of a particular scale and the operations of a model to those permitted by that scale. Elements of that scale may then be compared to objects in a manner that independent observers would record the same comparisons within identifiable error limits. Isomorphism, however, does not answer the question of how objects should be compared to scales.

PROXIMATE LOCATION

How a scale is located in spatio-temporal proximity to an object being measured is important. In concrete systems, relocating any information requires that it be borne on relatively small bundles of matter-energy termed *information markers*. Information markers bearing a scale, consequently, must be brought into the spatiotemporal proximity of an object, or of other information markers bearing information about that object, for a scale to be accurately compared to an object.

A scaler may be an element in any region of abstracted space (any field), not just in a field of numbers. However, a scaler field (any real-value function f

defined over a region R of E^n) not consisting of only numbers requires that the set of points in the field be associated with scaler values, thus forming a scaler function of position.

Objective numbering occurs when such scaler values are inherently associated with a set of concrete system elements (matter-energy forms). In that case, the scaler values are inherent parts of concrete systems, and their spatiotemporal proximity can be used to characterize other concrete system elements. That characterization, in turn, can be represented in various communication media and mapped into or onto other useful number systems. Such spatiotemporal proximate location of scaler values is an important aspect of measuring the concrete processes of social systems.

Avoiding ontological questions in analytic science, mathematicians do not typically include association with regions of physical space in the definition of scalers. They often associate such scalers, however, with Euclidean two- and three-space to diagram patterns in fields of scalers. When they do that, they clearly associate scaler values with points that are concrete system elements in a region of physical, not abstracted, space. Those diagrams describe scaler functions of position via the relationship of points in a usually very limited extended physical space.

That action is similar to the inherent association of scalers linked to other points in less limited physical space such as those linked to certain elements in societies. Societies with monetary economies inherently link scaler values with money-information markers.

In dynamic processes, scalers may be inherently associated with elements that change in their relationships to other elements over time. The changing relationships may be traced over time by intermittently mapping functions of position onto or into the set of real numbers. The dynamic processes of monetary economies may be studied by mapping the values of money-information markers into the set of real numbers and manipulating those numbers according to certain models.

Loosely defined, a *point* is an irreducible element in n-dimensional space. What a point represents is defined by the user of the abstracted system. For example, the element (3, 1, 6) is a point in Euclidean three-space defined on three coordinates, each of which may represent any number of different concrete or conceptual things.

Concrete system measurement attempts to identify irreducible elements of various kinds of concrete systems in extended space-time and associate scaler values with them, forming objective numbering systems. The resultant scaler functions of position provide representations of fundamental units that compose the larger concrete systems that more directly concern investigators. The representations of the fundamental units (irreducible elements) may then be manipulated to analyze perceived actions of the larger systems that they corporately represent.

The relative magnitude of the irreducible elements in extended space-time differs significantly for investigators in different sciences. An observer's perception of what constitutes an integral whole determines the relative magnitude of the irreducible elements that compose that whole. What fundamental concrete processes correspond to the fundamental explanatory primitives of the perceived higher-order processes? The relative magnitude of those fundamental processes is an important determinant of observation methodology. An astronomer simply cannot view a galaxy through a microscope. The relative magnitude of irreducible elements consequently poses a problem for investigators attempting to locate measurement scales in spatiotemporal proximity to concrete objects.

ORDERS OF MAGNITUDE

The proximate location action of measurement methodology is more easily accomplished at some orders of magnitude encountered in the physical sciences than at others. The phrase *orders of magnitude* refers to the ranges of sizes and the processing rates of different types of systems. For example, molecular and astronomical systems range very differently in both sizes and processing rates. In the extended space that constitutes the immediate environment of organisms, for example, observers simply place a ruler beside an object and record the number on the ruler that represents the length of the object. At that order of magnitude, even the time dimension may be incorporated with relative ease using such devices as speedometers and common gasoline pump meters.

An additional degree of difficulty is introduced when measurements of objects are attempted at magnitudes of order different from that of organisms. Organism-level observers cannot directly observe those objects. They must instead construct instruments that communicate information from one magnitude of order to another. For example, a microscope magnifies images of processes occurring in minute extended space at the cellular order of magnitude to communicate that information to the organism order.

By using such devices, human observers overcome the added difficulty and are able to use measurement methodology to make observations at different orders of magnitude. Such extended observations are fallible to errors in communicating across different orders of magnitude, however, as well as to basic measurement errors. The probability of those communication errors occurring increases as extended observation machines become more complex. A microscope, for example, is subject to errors resulting from such problems as flawed lenses and dust in a shaft or on a lens. When computer imaging is used to enhance an observation, the logic of the digital programs used may introduce additional biases and errors.

Another way that observations may be made indirectly is to calculate derived measurements. When discovering relationships that persist in repeated observations is possible, derived measurements of certain elements may be calculated using measurements taken on other elements. This method, however, requires information about the position of observers (including observation instruments) relative to that of the other elements. For all systems of a greater order of magnitude than the organism level, that information must locate the observer *within* the system. Such additional information increases the difficulty of derived measurement over that of straightforward indirect observation. Derived measurement is subject to logic errors in the conceptual and abstracted systems used to relate elements of the observed concrete system as well as errors in measuring and communicating.

MEASURING BIOLOGICAL SYSTEMS

Comparing units of a scale or standard to an object is an obvious aspect of measurement in the physical sciences. Such comparisons are more difficult in the biological sciences. Nevertheless, they are made and have contributed dramatically to advancing those sciences.

Different orders of magnitude have made locating the units of a scale in spatiotemporal proximity to objects difficult. As technological advances provided instrumentation to accomplish indirect observation, however, subdisciplines such as molecular and cellular biology emerged, as had subdisciplines in the physical sciences.

The difficulty of measuring biological systems is compounded by their characteristics as open systems. According to the second law of thermodynamics, physical systems are relatively closed systems that are degrading. That is to say, their elements are moving from an improbable state of organization toward one of random disorder. Living systems are relatively open systems that overcome that propensity by taking in forms of matter-energy having higher negative entropy, breaking them down for growth and repair, and putting out matter-energy forms having lower negative entropy.

The input-throughput-output process extends the survival of living systems indefinitely. That very process is a fundamental emergent that generally distinguishes living systems from other concrete systems. Important characteristics of biological systems consequently concern both processes and structures. All processes occur over time and, thus, their measurements involve temporal comparisons as well as the spatio comparisons of measuring structures.

Furthermore, at each higher level of living systems, more processes exist, and those many processes are integrated one with another. More processes exist because all of the processes of component systems continue to exist along with the emergent processes of higher-order systems. That increasing complexity extends the difficulty of locating units of a scale in spatiotemporal proximity to explanatory objects in biological systems. Nevertheless, the ingenuity of biological scientists continues to produce evermore accurate means of comparing the fundamental units of biological processes to units of scales that may be used to assign numbers in useful models.

MEASURING SOCIAL SYSTEMS

Few, if any, scientists deny that a measuring device is placed in spatiotemporal proximity to an object being observed in the physical and biological observations being discussed. Nor do they doubt that such an action increases the confidence of nonparticipating scientists that the restatements of measurements in observers' models in fact represent some aspect of concrete systems. The importance of this action is so obvious, so fundamental, that it is taken for granted. Almost everybody knows some brand name of automatic dishwashers. Nearly nobody knows a brand name of kitchen sinks. The function of kitchen sinks needs not be justified to modern homeowners. Justification was likely necessary, however, during the period when kitchen sinks were being introduced. Apparently, a need exists to justify using basic measurement ideas to investigate concrete processes of social systems such as economies.

Comparing objects to measurement scales is accepted as a fundamental and obviously important aspect of empirical observation methodology in physical and biological sciences. It is commonly neglected by social sciences. Possibly two important reasons for that neglect are the compounded complexity of the processes studied and the relative dependence of objects with reference to observers.

Among other things, the compounded complexity of social systems is related to the changing characteristics across orders of living systems of what Miller terms the boundary subsystem. The *boundary,* according to Miller (1978: 3), is "the subsystem at the perimeter of a system that holds together the components that make up the system, protects them from environmental stresses, and excludes or permits entry to various sorts of matter-energy and information." In living systems from cells to organisms, boundary subsystems are continuous with many gaps. Many boundaries of higher-order systems are the limits of the channels over which those systems communicate, and such information processes are often dispersed to other systems. Observers consequently must sort out many boundaries of higher-order living systems.

Many accepted experimental procedures of physical and biological scientists are designed around laboratory controls. Those controls allow observers to construct physical boundaries that permit entry of only certain matter-energy and information transmission forms. Experimenters then may vary the inputs and measure covariances on hypothesized related variables, confirming or disconfirming those relationships.

Such ingenious relocation of physical boundaries generally is not possible in social science studies. To study concrete social processes, scientists must discover the physical boundaries that exist in social systems, measure inputs and outputs containing information about important processes at those boundaries, and ingeniously sort the measurements into those concerning variables being observed and those reflecting the many other related and interacting variables of such processes. Accomplishing that task is momentous. The procedure makes social science studies particularly sensitive to errors in the logic of statistical models employed in the sorting process. Such errors are similar to those that may be encountered in computer imaging. They both arise in a process of communicating across different orders of magnitude and introduce into the measured data a bias of particular abstracted system logic.

Discovering the boundaries of concrete social systems is far more difficult than similar discoveries at the biological and physical science levels. The compounded difficulty of finding what to measure is itself further compounded by difficulties similar to those in the physical and biological sciences in locating units of a scale in spatiotemporal proximity to those objects.

While increasing complexity in systems being studied may explain why some social scientists neglect comparing objects to scales, the more important reason is that objects being observed are relatively dependent on observers. Significant differences exist between astronomers or space scientists and various types of social scientists. Both kinds of observers are located within the systems they investigate. It is unlikely, however, that the studies of an astronomer or a space scientist can affect the processes of a solar system or a galaxy in any important way. The spatiotemporal order of magnitude of information processed in a space science study is an insignificant part of the information processes that arrange and order those parts of the physical universe. On the other hand, the studies of social scientists are important parts of the information processed in social systems. The information processed in those reports is at a similar spatiotemporal order of magnitude to that of the fundamental information transmissions arranging and ordering social systems. The attainable observer independence in the social sciences, therefore, is considerably less than in biological and physical sciences.

That condition increases the need for vigilance in raising a defense against individual biases at points of observation. Basic measurement ideas developed in the physical and biological sciences can be used to raise such a defense when investigating concrete processes of societies. Those ideas clearly distinguish between measurements and interpretations of those measurements.

THE IMPORTANCE OF DISTINGUISHING BETWEEN MEASUREMENT AND INTERPRETATION IN SOCIETAL STUDIES

Distinguishing between measurements and interpretations of those measurements is especially important in social process studies. Interpretation is certainly as important as measurement. The two actions are clearly different, however. They are validated on two different bases. An observer's measurements are validated by the empirical confirmation of other observers. An observer's interpretation is validated on the basis of consensus of a scientific discipline.

Confusing measurements and interpretations is directly related to the problem of observing across different orders of magnitude. As procedures incorporate more and more levels of abstracted systems to observe concrete processes indirectly, the objectivity of the resulting information is increasingly imperiled. This happens because the original observation is biased in turn to conform to the unique relationships of each successive abstracted system, compounding bias upon bias. Observing concrete processes of social systems across magnitudes of scale as human observers must consequently has a tendency to confuse measurements and interpretations in an observation procedure itself. Tightly analogizing measurement procedures developed in the physical and biological sciences may provide insights for mitigating that propensity.

The problem of independence of observers with reference to objects further compounds the problem of distinguishing measurements and interpretations at the social science level. Because social science reports are at a similar spatiotemporal order of magnitude to that of the fundamental information transmissions arranging and ordering social systems, those reports themselves, including interpretations, affect the processes scientists are observing.

That dependent relationship between observer and object makes it very difficult for influential observers to limit their observations to those constrained by basic scientific methodology. Realistically, it is unreasonable to expect them to do so considering the Second Law of Thermodynamics. A log burnt cannot be unburnt and a life lived cannot be unlived. Science simply does not concern all of life, and no life should be lived less than fully. As social scientists become influential, they may be expected to affect society by their casual observations and intuitions as well as by observations formed by measurements taken on concrete processes.

A consequence of that situation is that the field of inquiry of social scientists likely overlaps both philosophy and science to a greater degree than do the fields of physical and biological sciences. By explicitly recognizing that consequence, basic measurement methods analogous to those of the physical and biological sciences should be extended to the social sciences but only as one form of inquiry among others. A strong and persistent argument for the application of basic measurement methodology is certainly not an argument to discontinue indirect methods of observation. Neither is it an argument to limit the field of inquiry of the social sciences to concrete processes.

Despite the many obvious benefits produced by empirical scientific methodology, science is not the only beneficial form of human inquiry. After all, civilizations rose and fell long before scientific methodology developed. Life would be dull indeed if the human mind reached no further than observations that can be scientifically demonstrated.

Nevertheless, the intrigue of human curiosity in tandem with individual biases can create science fiction with relative ease. Limiting personal bias to discover how concrete processes function is much more difficult. Consequently, commitment to empirical scientific observation should be continually reaffirmed if we are to reap the obtainable benefits of this method at the social science level.

Societal objects that can be measured in the manner being discussed should be. The resultant measurements should be clearly distinguished from their various interpretations. Such measurements obviously concern only certain aspects of social processes, the concrete ones. Those measurements, although limited as they might be, may be used to confirm or deny various common perceptions, thus aiding important social policy decisions.

MINIMIZING INDIVIDUAL OBSERVATION BIAS

Within the limited scope of studies measuring concrete social processes, the problem of independence of observers with reference to objects is a critical one. The very purpose of measurement procedures can be nullified by procedures that fail to limit the influence of individual observer perceptions in the measurement methodology.

As discussed previously, observers compare concrete objects to units of measurement scales to standardize their observations so that in repeated, similar observations similar measurements are obtainable within identifiable measurement error limits. This action effectively biases the conceptual systems being formed by the observers to the relationships understood to exist among the elements of the measurement scale. A consensus bias, that of the measurement scale, is imposed on observations.

The benefit of that bias over individual biases is that common understanding of the relationships among the scale's elements exists. Consequently, the proposed meanings of any restatements of the measurements in models built by individual observers can be evaluated by other observers.

This procedure removes observers' individually biased conceptual systems from each individual observation action itself. It does not remove those biases from the design of a study generally or from that of any models used in a study to restate measurements. Minimizing individual biases in those aspects is accomplished through research design and demonstrating isomorphism, respectively. The procedure has the effect of mechanically constructing an abstracted system using the relationships of a measurement scale to bypass individual observer conceptualizations. That is to say, individual observers do not observe, conceptualize, and then abstract those concepts in a communication medium. Rather, they observe, abstract through the assignment of numbers by comparing objects to a measurement scale in a communication medium, and conceptualize their observations by studying the abstracted systems. The same elements are involved in both procedures. The order is different, and that order is critical.

Minimizing individual observer bias is the purpose of measurement procedures. That bias is minimized by bypassing, in a mechanical fashion, the direct conceptualization of individual observations. The bypass mechanism is the measurement scale. Comparing objects to a scale placed in spatiotemporal proximity to them is the bypass process.

Procedures that apply the measurement scaling mechanism after individual observations are conceptualized completely circumvent the purpose of measurement. Abstracted systems that are constructed from such applications are science fictions. They translate individually biased observations into the quantitative language of science. When these data are restated by models designed to make the observation of certain global aspects possible, the restatements are some sort of corporate observation bias not necessarily any closer to discovering how concrete processes occur than the individual observations.

MEASURING CONSENSUS PERCEPTIONS

Again emphasizing that this immediate discussion concerns a limited aspect of social science, the study of concrete social systems, is important. It is quite possible to study various aspects of social systems by discovering corporate perceptions. As with reports of social scientists, those perceptions are transmitted at the same spatiotemporal order of magnitude as that which arranges and orders society-level systems. As a result, corporate perceptions affect social systems.

Quantifying such perceptions in a manner analogous to that used to quantify concrete processes may provide useful information that can be compared across the two types of systems, conceptual and concrete. Such comparisons may be necessary for interpreting measurements of concrete processes. For example, one country may use spy satellites to map a military buildup in another country. Discovering certain corporate perceptions of the ruling class is likely required before the measurements taken on concrete processes by the spy satellite can be correctly interpreted.

Quantifying both types of information is important. The distinction between the two types, however, is easily obscured in their numerical form. Important aspects of societies are assessed in both cases. The two types of information, nevertheless, are different and consequently should be distinguished one from the other.

A discipline that does not recognize what elements of its abstracted systems are measurements of concrete processes and what elements are assessments of consensus perceptions, notwithstanding the quantification of both types of elements, likely is more philosophical than scientific. On the other hand, a discipline that does not recognize that society-level concrete processes are not independent from corporate perceptions is likely more technical than scientific. Neither measurements of concrete processes or assessments of corporate perceptions alone can explain social processes. Both are necessary. This book, however, mainly concerns measurements of concrete processes.

When observing concrete processes, therefore, bypassing individual perception biases by comparing objects to measurement scales is important. The measurement process provides a means for separating scale-biased information obtained at some level of basic explanatory elements from information biased by individual perceptions typically based on various different aggregates of such elements (macroscopic views). That separation of information obtained at two levels of observation makes it possible to demonstrate which general perceptions are commensurate with the relationships discovered at the level of basic explanatory elements. This action provides one means of validating generalizations of various sorts.

SUMMARY

This chapter has discussed important aspects of observing concrete systems. It has explained what concrete systems are and how science observes those systems. Macro accounting fundamentally concerns the concrete processes of modern debt-based economies. Consequently, clarifying what is meant by concrete systems is important for understanding the discussion of macro accounting in the following chapters.

REFERENCES

Durkheim, Émile. *Les formes élémentaires de la vie religieuse.* Paris: Bibliothéque de philosophic contemposaire, 1912; *The Elementary Forms of the Religious Life.* Trans. by Joseph Ward Swain. New York: Macmillan, 1915.

Einstein, Albert. *Out of My Later Years.* New York: Philosophical Library, 1950.

Klir, George J. (ed.). *Trends in General Systems Theory.* New York: Wiley-Interscience, 1972.

Mattessich, Richard. *Instrumental Reasoning and Systems Methodology.* Dordrecht, the Netherlands/Boston, MS: D. Reidel, 1978.

Miller, James Grier. *Living Systems.* New York: McGraw-Hill, 1978.

Parsons, Talcott. *The Structure of Social Action.* New York: Free Press, 1968.

Skrapek, Wayne A.; Korkie, Bob M.; and Daniel, Terrence E. *Mathematical Dictionary for Economics and Business Administration.* Boston: Allyn and Bacon, 1976.

Whitehead, Alfred North. *Science and the Modern World.* New York: Free Press, 1967.

Figure 2-1
The Relationship between the Stoics' Scheme and Systems Scheme

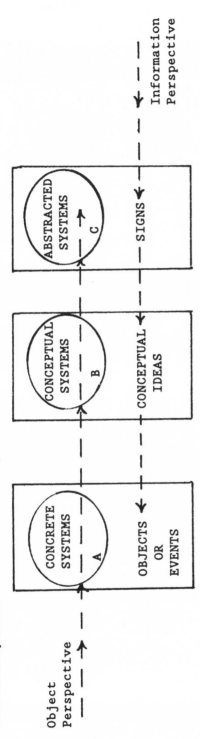

A--Objects or events that are composed of matter-energy and
   information.

B--Conceptual ideas that are borne on information markers within
   organisms and may represent arrangements and orders of the matter-
   energy forms in concrete systems.

C--Signs that are borne on information markers in the environment of
   organisms and may represent (1) arrangements and orders of matter-
   energy forms in concrete systems, (2) conceptual systems, (3) other
   signs, or (4) any combination of the three.

Figure 2-2
Relationships without the Exclusivity Assumption

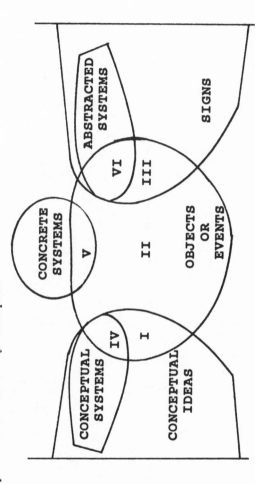

I.   Conceptual ideas that are objects or events

II. Objects or events that are neither conceptual ideas, signs, concrete systems, conceptual systems, or abstracted systems

III. Signs that are objects or events

IV. Conceptual systems that are objects or events

V.   Concrete systems that are objects or events

VI. Abstracted systems that are objects or events

Table 2-1
Hierarchy of Living Systems

1.	Cells	Minute unitary masses of intricately organized protoplasm. "All living systems either are free-living cells or have cells as their least complex living components" (Miller 1978: 203).
2.	Organs	Organism subsystems that are formed from tissues. Tissues are collections "of adjacent cells of like origin and structure which carry out similar, specialized processes" (Miller 1978: 315).
3.	Organism	Any animal or plant with organs and parts that function together to maintain life.
4.	Group	"A set of single organisms, commonly called members, which, over a period of time or multiple interrupted periods, relate to one another face-to-face, processing matter-energy and information" (Miller 1978: 515).
5.	Organizations	Concrete living systems with multiechelon deciders whose components and subsystems may be subsidiary organizations, groups, and (uncommonly) single persons (Miller 1978: 595).
6.	Communities	Higher-order human systems prominently composed of both organizations and individual persons as subsystems. They have governmental organizations that are given special powers to control their components.
7.	Societies	"Large, living, concrete systems with organizations and lower levels of living systems as subsystems and components" (Miller 1978: 747).
8.	Supranational Systems	Concrete, living systems "composed of two or more societies, some or all of whose processes are under the control of a decider that is superordinated to their highest echelons" (Miller 1978: 903).

Source: James G. Miller, *Living Systems,* McGraw-Hill, 1978. Used with permission.

31

Table 2-2
The Twenty Critical Subsystems of a Living System

SUBSYSTEMS THAT PROCESS BOTH MATTER-ENERGY AND INFORMATION

1. REPRODUCER. The subsystem that carries out the instructions in the genetic information or charter of a system and mobilizes matter and energy to produce one or more similar systems.

2. BOUNDARY. The subsystem at the perimeter of a system that holds together the components that make up the system, protects them from environmental stresses, and excludes or permits entry to various sorts of matter-energy and information.

SUBSYSTEMS THAT PROCESS MATTER-ENERGY

3. INGESTOR. The subsystem that brings matter-energy across the system boundary from the environment.

4. DISTRIBUTOR. The subsystem that carries inputs from outside the system or outputs from its subsystems around the system to each component.

5. CONVERTER. The subsystem that changes certain inputs to the system into forms more useful for the special processes of that particular system.

SUBSYSTEMS THAT PROCESS INFORMATION

11. INPUT TRANSDUCER. The sensory subsystem that brings markers bearing information into the system, changing them to other matter-energy forms suitable for transmission within it.

12. INTERNAL TRANSDUCER. The sensory subsystem that receives from subsystems or components within the system markers bearing information about significant alterations in those subsystems or components, changing them to other matter-energy forms of a sort that can be transmitted within it.

13. CHANNEL AND NET. The subsystem composed of a single route in physical space or multiple interconnected routes over which markers bearing information are transmitted to all parts of the system.

14. TIMER. The clock, set by information from the input transducer about states of the environment that uses information about processes in the system to measure the passage of time and transmits to the decider signals that facilitate coordination of the system's processes in time.

15. DECODER. The subsystem that alters the code of information input to it through the input transducer or internal transducer into a "private" code that can be used internally by the system.

6. PRODUCER. The subsystem that forms stable associations that endure for significant periods among matter-energy inputs to the system or outputs from its converter, the materials synthesized being for growth, damage repair, or replacement of components of the system, or for providing energy for moving or constituting the system's outputs of products or information markers to its suprasystem.

7. MATTER-ENERGY STORAGE. The subsystem that places matter or energy at some location in the system, retains it over time, and retrieves it.

8. EXTRUDER. The subsystem that transmits matter-energy out of the system in the form of products or wastes.

9. MOTOR. The subsystem that moves the system or parts of it in relation to part or all of its environment or moves components of its environment in relation to each other.

10. SUPPORTER. The subsystem that maintains the proper spatial relationships among components of the system, so that they can interact without weighing each other down or crowding each other.

16. ASSOCIATOR. The subsystem that carries out the first stage of the learning process, forming enduring associations among items of information in the system.

17. MEMORY. The subsystem that carries out the second stage of the learning process, storing information in the system for different periods of time, and then retrieving it.

18. DECIDER. The executive subsystem that receives information inputs from all other subsystems and transmits to them outputs for guidance.

19. ENCODER. The subsystem that alters the code of information input to it from other information processing subsystems from a "private" code used internally by the system into a "public" code that can be interpreted by other systems in its environment.

20. OUTPUT TRANSDUCER. The subsystem that puts out markers bearing information from the system, changing markers within the system into other matter-energy forms that can be transmitted over channels in the system's environment.

Source: James G. Miller, *Living Systems,* McGraw-Hill, 1978. Used with permission.

33

Table 2-3

Examples of Living Systems and Subsystem Components

CRITICAL SUBSYSTEMS	CELLS	ORGANS	ORGANISMS	GROUPS	ORGANIZATIONS	COMMUNITIES	SOCIETIES	SUPRANATIONAL SYSTEMS
REPRODUCER	DNA and RNA molecules	Upwardly dispersed to organism	Testes, ovaries, uterus, genitalia	NASA officer who selects astronauts for crew	Dispersed upward to society that creates space agency	Space agency that establishes space station	Constitutional convention that writes national constitution	United Nations when it creates new supranational agency
BOUNDARY	Matter-energy and information: Outer membrane	Matter-energy and information: Capsule or outer layer	Matter-energy and information: Skin or other outer covering	Matter-energy: Inspectors of covering of spacecraft; Information: Crew radio operator	Matter-energy: NASA inspectors of contracted equipment; Information: NASA guards who arrest intruders	Matter-energy: Dispersed to builders of habitat; Information: Operators of downlink to Earth	Matter-energy: Customs service; Information: Security agency	Matter-energy: Troops at Berlin Wall; Information: NATO security personnel
INGESTOR	Transport molecules	Input artery	Mouth, nose, skin in some animals	Astronauts who bring damaged satellite into spacecraft	Receiving department of NASA base	Receivers of materials from shuttle	Immigration service	Legislative body that admits nations
DISTRIBUTOR	Endoplasmic reticulum	Intercellular fluid	Vascular system of higher animals	Crew member who distributes food	Operators of conveyor belt in factory that makes parts for space habitat	Food servers in dining facility	Operators of national railroads	Personnel who operate supranational power grids
CONVERTER	Enzyme in mitochondrion	Gastric mucosa cell	Upper gastrointestinal tract	Dispersed to maker of packaged rations	Workers who stamp out parts for space vehicle	Organization that mines moon	Nuclear industry	EURATOM, CERN, IAEA
PRODUCER	Chloroplast in green plant	Islets of Langerhans of pancreas	Organs that synthesize materials for metabolism and repair	Crew members who repair damaged equipment	Doctors who examine astronauts	Medical organization in space community	All farmers and factory workers of a country	World Health Organization
MATTER-ENERGY STORAGE	Adenosine triphosphate	Central lumen of glands	Fatty tissues	Crew member who stows scientific instruments	Workers who store supplies on space vehicle	Workers who put supplies into storage areas	Guards at entrance to launch facility	International storage dams and reservoirs
EXTRUDER	Contractile vacuoles	Output vein	Sweat glands of animal skin	Crew that ejects satellite into orbit	Janitors in NASA buildings	Mine organization that sends minerals to Earth	Export organizations of a country	Downwardly dispersed to societies

CRITICAL SUBSYSTEMS	CELLS	ORGANS	ORGANISMS	GROUPS	ORGANIZATIONS	COMMUNITIES	SOCIETIES	SUPRANATIONAL SYSTEMS
INPUT TRANSDUCER	Receptor sites on membrane for activation of cyclic AMP	Receptor cell of sense organ	Sense organs	Crew member who receives messages from ground control	NASA secretaries who take incoming calls	Operators of downlink to Earth	Foreign news services	UN Assembly hearing speaker from nonmember territory
INTERNAL TRANSDUCER	Repressor molecules	Specialized cell of sinoatrial node of heart	Proprioceptors	Crew member who reports crew's reactions to life in capsule	Representative of employees who reports to executive	Communicator over downlink to Earth	Public opinion polling organizations	Speaker from member country to supra-national meeting
CHANNEL AND NET	Pathways of mRNA, second messengers	Nerve net of organ	Hormonal pathways central and peripheral nerve nets	Astronauts who communicate person to person	Users of NASA internal phone network	Psychologists who report on morale of spacefarers	Telephone and communications organizations	INTELSAT
TIMER	Components not known	Upwardly dispersed to organism	Supraoptic nuclei of thalamus	Dispersed to all members who hear time signals	Office responsible for scheduling flights	Users of communication system in space station	Legislators who decide on time and zone changes	Personnel of Greenwich observatory
DECODER	Molecular binding sites	Second echelon cell of sense organ	Sensory nuclei	Member who explains coded message	Experts who explain specs to contractors	Caretakers of clocks in space community	Cryptographers	Translators for supra-national meetings
ASSOCIATOR	Unknown	None found; upwardly dispersed to organism	Unknown neural components	Dispersed to all members who learn new techniques	People who train new employees	Engineers who interpret building blueprints	All teaching institutions of a country	FAO units that teach farming methods in third world nations
MEMORY	Unknown	None found; upwardly dispersed to organism	Unknown neural components	Dispersed to all crew members	Filing department	Scientists who do research in space	Keepers of national archives	Librarians of UN libraries
DECIDER	Regulator genes	Sympathetic fibers of sinoatrial node of heart	Components at several echelons of nervous system	Captain of crew in capsule	NASA executives	Central computer of space community	Voters and officials of national government	National representatives to inter-national space conferences
ENCODER	Structure that synthesizes hormones	Presynaptic region of output neuron	Temporoparietal area of dominant hemisphere of human cortex	Members who write reports of space experience	Public relations staff	Commanding officer and staff	Drafters of treaties	UN Office of Public Information
OUTPUT TRANSDUCER	Presynaptic membrane of neuron	Presynaptic region of output neuron	Larynx; other components that output signals	Members who report to mission control	Administrator who makes policy television speech	Officer who writes report to Earth station	National representatives to international meetings	Official who announces decisions of supranational body

Table 2-4
Living Systems Symbols

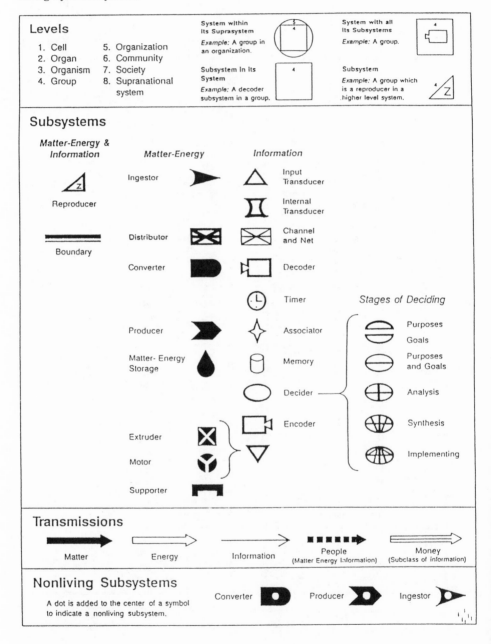

3

Accounting Measurement of Concrete Processes

Chapter 2 identified the particular aspects of social processes that concern macro accounting. This chapter further delimits the subject of this book by defining important ideas about accounting methodology, especially measurements within that methodology, in the context of concrete processes.

WHAT IS ACCOUNTING?

Macro accounting is not based on the common perception that accounting is what accountants do. For clarification and the purpose of this study, let *accountancy* be what accountants do, and let *accounting* be a methodology that maps concrete processes and structures on both objective and abstract numbering systems and reduces the resultant data in an orderly fashion by classifying and aggregating them, providing reports to various deciders in a manner that attempts to minimize information overload. *Objective numbering systems* consist of elements that are not fully abstract. The meanings of the system's elements cannot be separated from the physical information markers bearing them (Swanson and Miller 1989: 37–51).

The difference between accountancy and accounting is discussed by Swanson (1987) and Swanson and Miller (1988). Although accountancy (as practiced by certified public accountants, charter accountants, and others) cannot be described as an applied science, important aspects of accounting information systems exhibit characteristics consistent with those that concern applied sciences. Those aspects taken together form a coherent core of related theory and applications that constitute the template of accounting information systems. The term *basic accounting system* is used to differentiate those core systems that emerge controlled by that template from entire accounting information systems that often involve procedures that cannot be characterized as applied science and do not map concrete processes into either objective or completely abstract numbering systems.

Basic accounting systems are concrete living systems. As such, they are composed of people, machines, electricity, and many other concrete elements as well as abstracted systems including words and symbols in books and accounts, computer memory configurations, and mathematical equations. Those information systems map the concrete processes of corporations and other social entities.

In doing so, the systems perform the vital and sometime inseparable functions of measurement and data reduction. In fact, some aspects of data reduction are collapsed into measurement to form a four-dimensional (spatiotemporal) measurement scale (Swanson 1987; Swanson and Miller 1989).

The spatiotemporal scale is applied in an accounting methodology that includes a double measurement method commonly termed *double-entry bookkeeping*. In tandem, double-entry bookkeeping and the spatiotemporal accounting scale form the pillars of accounting methodology around which basic accounting systems are built. The theoretical framework developed on the following pages is constructed from those central ideas.

DOUBLE ENTRY AND DOUBLE CLASSIFICATION

In a sense, measurements and classifications are the same actions. Measurements are simply numerical classifications on relatively fine grids. Distinguishing the two actions generally has proven to be useful, however.

Such a distinction is useful for differentiating various types of measurements taken on different attributes of a particular object. The different sets of numbers assigned in various measurement and assessment methodologies are different classifications of measurements and assessments. Double measurement in a particular methodology, and double classification involving two methodologies can thus be differentiated. The differentiation can be extended to models, distinguishing between double-measurement models and double-classification models.

The double-entry bookkeeping method is historically a double-measurement method. Double-entry mapping is the consummate form of economic exchange process measurement because it measures both the inflow transaction and the outflow transaction of an exchange. Inflow and outflow fully define the universe of all actions included in an exchange—that is what an exchange is. The set of all excluded actions is not interesting because we can never be sure that all excluded actions have been identified.

Basic accounting systems record all observed entity inflows of concrete elements (various forms of matter, energy, and money-information markers) in the accounts as debit entries and all such outflows as credit entries. The universe of actions included in exchanges consequently can be mapped fully by debit-credit notation.

Double entry is consummate. Recording an exchange requires only two general descriptions, one for inflows and one for outflows. Double classification, on the other hand, is by no means consummate. Classification can be generalized from single classification to the nth degree, with n possibly limited only by the ingenuity of investigators. Different general classifications may include, among other things, measurements and assessments made of various physical attributes on such scales as pounds, liters, and board feet; the attribute arising out of economic exchange itself, specific exchange value measured in monetary units; reorderings of specific exchange values such as book values of depreciable assets; hypothetical values such as current market values or discounted future cash flow values; and different decision models that include or exclude certain specific exchange values. Obviously, such general classifications can easily include both measurements taken on concrete processes and interpretations of those measurements.

Referring to multiple general classifications as multiple entry confuses the structure of the double-entry model and the processes that structure supports. To ameliorate both the process-structure and the measurement-interpretation confusions, the unqualified term *double entry* is restricted to a structural description of the exchange-mapping method (a logical constraint) and to monetary measurements taken on concrete processes (an empirical constraint). If the double-entry model is expanded to include data on more than one scale, the general classifications of multiple attributes measured by multiple scales are termed *multiple dimensions* or *variables*. A particular method might thus be described as a triple-dimension double-entry mapping method.

Selecting the word *dimensions* to describe such *general* classifications is useful because the account-recording method includes both measurements on the global attribute-specific exchange value and models of multiple *specific* classifications based on other, less global characteristics of the flows of an exchange. Such subclassifications of the basic double-entry measurement model may then be termed simply *classifications*.

The term *dual entry* is sometimes used to describe the double-entry bookkeeping method. The term *double entry* is retained here because it better conveys the idea that the same amount is recorded in both entries. The emphasis thus is the measurements made on the common attribute-specific exchange value in terms of a particular monetary unit. That attribute arises in an exchange, and it cannot exist in a transaction alone. The accounting dual entry consequently is a double entry of two measurements of that self-same value.

Nevertheless, the double-entry sameness should not be overstated. The money-information markers being exchanged for value quantify the value of the exchange, and thus their value is assigned to both the inflow and outflow of a particular exchange. The assignment of a same value does not, however, change the fact that two measurements are made, one on the inflow(s) and another on the outflow(s). It only ensures that in every case and in terms of monetary value, inflows will equal outflows.

The monetary assignment, however, is not the only value assignment made.

The less global-specific account classifications of accounting models are integral parts of the accounting measurement methodology. So, although the monetary values of the inflow and outflow transactions of a particular exchange are always the same, the concrete element flows that are the objects on which the attribute-specific exchange value is measured are almost never the same. Specific account classifications are used to differentiate those objects. Schemes that include different specific account classifications of measurements on the common attribute-specific exchange value are termed *double-entry measurement models*.

HOMOMORPHIC EXPRESSIONS
OF CONCRETE MEASUREMENTS

Swanson and Miller (1988) demonstrate that basic accounting systems input measurements of concrete processes into the double-entry model. Outputs of basic accounting systems consequently provide homomorphic expressions of measurements taken on concrete processes.

On the other hand, common accounting systems do not report homomorphic expressions of concrete process measurements. Two types of actions generally distort the reported information. First, values based on certain decision models are introduced into the model (as in lower-of-cost-or-market inventory valuation procedures). Second, representations of concrete inflows and outflows of the entities being mapped occurring in one period are recorded or distributed as having occurred in another period (as in depreciation and absorption inventory-costing procedures).

Such actions generally are rationalized by accountants as providing increased prospective information to deciders. From the perspective of concrete processes, the first action confuses the value being reported by accounting numbers and the second action ignores an ordering function inherent in the accounting measurement methodology.

While the first type of actions obviously distorts data measured on concrete processes, it is not inherently erroneous. Deciding involves biasing a set of data to bear on a particular decision. Consequently, decision models sort relevant and irrelevant data and concern many different value systems, only one of which is specific exchange value. The question of what value emerges when different values are mixed in a particular decision model nevertheless arises. Sometimes that question is not empirically resolvable. The accounting profession generally views the values on public financial statements conforming to generally accepted accounting principles (GAAP) as scores on a report card reflecting economic activities in an agreed-upon manner—not as measurements of concrete processes or any other empirically identifiable value.

In the context of a decision model, the second type of actions likewise is not inherently wrong. Because such actions subtly tamper with basic accounting system measurements taken on concrete processes, however, deciders are more apt to believe erroneously that the introductions of other information are homomorphisms from the algebraic system of raw accounting measurements to the algebraic system of a decision model. They often are not.

The two algebraic systems often are not homeomorphous for the following reason. The accounting scale takes measurements on a four-dimensional process (three dimensions of physical space and one of physical time). As a consequence, two functions are needed to characterize the set of measurements. The two functions are a cardinal mapping function that maps specific exchange monetary value onto the set of rational numbers and an ordering function that maps time "periodaneously" (Swanson and Miller 1989: 84–88) into the set of integers. The cardinal mapping function alone cannot define the set of accounting measurements. Consequently, the measurements are not preserved if the cardinal values are recorded violating the ordering function.

The theoretical framework developed in this study recognizes the dual-function mapping characteristics inherent in accounting measurements. Specific monetary exchange value is recognized as the value measured by the basic accounting methodology. The fact that the ordering function relating the cardinal amounts may limit the types of mathematical manipulations permitted on accounting measurements is also recognized.

THE RATIO MONETARY SCALE

Measurement theory is a major progenitor of modern methods of empirical scientific investigation. Modern measurement theory recognizes that certain limitations are inherent in particular and different methods of observation (Stevens 1946, 1951). Different methods use different forms of sensors and clocks to assign numbers to observations. Some methods permit different or fewer mathematical operations than others.

Several accounting theorists (Ijiri 1967; Chambers 1966; Sweeny 1936) apply measurement theory to accounting. Those applications, however, do not generally accept as given the accounting observation method itself and, therefore, do not attempt to provide rules based on the concrete characteristics of that method. Instead, they attempt to demonstrate that accounting numbers parallel an already defined scale or that accounting methodology does or does not constitute measurement (see, for example, Abdel-Magid 1979).

Other accounting theorists (Belkaoui 1975; Canning 1923; Chambers 1966; Paton 1922; Scott 1941; Sprouse and Moonitz 1962; Sweeny 1936; Zeff 1978) advance the views that accounting *should* assess many different abstractions, for example, purchasing power, capital maintenance, economic income, just or fair information, national economic good, social welfare, and current value. Those theorists generally assume that such abstractions themselves are measurable, perhaps not forthrightly, but through justifying measurable surrogates for them. That justification scheme creates a measurement aura that extends to the principal concepts themselves, in effect reaying nonempirical concepts. Although numbers can be consistently assigned to surrogate concrete objects by comparing those objects to scales, the connections made between the measurements of surrogate objects and the principal concepts are not measurement actions. A principal concept may guide the development of certain useful derived measurements as investigators search for its surrogate. The principal concept itself, nevertheless, is not a measured abstracted system. Its public expression is constructed not through measurement mechanism but, rather, through private conceptualization.

Notwithstanding the theoretic contributions to empirical science it may gender, such surrogation is not measurement. Macro accounting is concerned with measurements and how those measurements may be used to improve our understanding of fundamental concrete social processes. It recognizes limitations inherent in the accounting observation method itself and provides measurement rules accordingly.

The accounting method observes flows of various forms of matter, energy, and information markers as they pass across boundaries of different societal components by exchanging various forms of money-information markers for those products and services. That method is an inherent part of the economic exchange process itself and does not depend on accountants or any other information-gathering system. That is to say, the fundamental information feedback is relatively independent of what is commonly viewed as accounting systems. That feedback, nevertheless, is accounting, and modern economic systems could not exist without it. In fact, they themselves are expressions of the fundamental recording process underlying it.

Money-information markers transmitted in exchanges are stated in monetary units, such as yen or dollars, that are all alike. Those monetary units taken together compose a numeric system that is isomorphic to arithmetic. Even though markers are not constructed representing every possible real number, the mathematical operations commonly performed on monetary amounts clearly recognize that the number system underlying monetary units is the real number set. The monetary scale consequently is a ratio-level measurement scale. That scale fully parallels other ratio-level scales, such as the centimeter and the liter scales.

Such an obvious parallelism would not evoke a defense if what may be termed *the purchasing power dilemma* were not so widely propagated. The notions of the "unseen hand" of the market and the purchasing power dilemma have fostered a nearly mystical order of economics. That order reafies many different concepts and abstractions.

The purchasing power dilemma is stated something like this. Although the monetary system for assigning numbers introduces a unique, comprehensive, and objective quantification of various forms of matter-energy flows, it generates variant exchange values for physically alike units of those flows. The monetary system therefore lacks a necessary measurement scale quality, the invariance of its units.

The dilemma is not real. It results from a fallacy. The units of a scale are not asserted by any science to be variant because they vary with reference to the units of an object of measurement. A scale in internally invariant with respect to its own units. The monetary scale consists of monetary units, not exchange values (purchasing power). Fallaciously confusing the object being measured with the measurement unit creates the purchasing power dilemma.

The numbers of scale units that describe different amounts of an attribute always differ. Independence with reference to the object being measured is a fundamental quality of a scale. The intensity of an attribute being measured may vary, but each unit of a scale remains consistently the same as other units, requiring more or fewer units to describe the varying intensity.

The attribute measured by the monetary scale is specific exchange value, not other physical attributes such as length or weight. It emerges in the process of economic exchange that is, in turn, a higher-order human system emergent. In some sense, specific exchange value itself is therefore a societal emergent. As a result, measurements of specific exchange value would not be expected necessarily to be convertible into physical measurements such as pounds or inches.

Emergents, by definition, are differences across levels of living systems. Even at the same level or when describing similarities across levels, however, inconvertibility of different measurements is not uncommon. Burkhardt (1987) establishes a conceptual frame for the complete coverage of classical physics by dividing all extensive (substance-like) quantities into "constituents" (quantities that cannot be converted into one another) and "components" (quantities that form a part of a constituent). At the physical science level, he identifies seven quantities that cannot be converted into one another as volume "V," mass "M," energy "E," momentum "P," angular momentum "L," electric charge "Q," and entropy "S."

No implicit necessity exists for measurements of specific exchange value to be convertible to other physical measurements. On a particular set of objects, rather, measurements of specific exchange value are likely to vary differently than other physical measurements, such as volume, taken on the same objects. This is so because determinants at the level of societies, not at the level of atoms, influence specific exchange value.

Monetary units do not vary one from another any more than one cubic inch varies from another. Let the volume of one container be 300 cubic inches and that of another be 200 cubic inches. In no situation do we say that the measurement unit cubic inch is variant because in the first measurement action it is 1/300 of a container and in the other it is 1/200 of a container. Why should we say that monetary units vary because more units may be required to cause one person to give up a car than are required to cause another person to do the same thing? The quality of invariance applies to one cubic inch as compared to another. A scale is internally invariant with respect to its own units.

The monetary scale consists of monetary units that are all alike, and it is used to measure the specific exchange values of different economic objects. All of the attributes of a container are not measured when its volume is measured. The exchange value of a container is an attribute, as is its volume, and the quantities of both attributes may change. A dilemma that is empirically unresolvable is created by confusing the attribute-specific exchange value with the monetary scale unit. The dilemma is resolved, however, by recognizing that the monetary scale consists of monetary units. That scale is recognized easily as a well-behaved abstracted system that is analogous to other recognized measurement scales. Swanson (1987) writes:

> The monetary scale is invariant with respect to its units. It is a ratio scale, i.e., zero has meaning and each alike unit measures the same amount of statistical space. For, instance, cross-sectional exchanges of alike monetary units are always made one for one. Nowhere is one amount of dollars exchanged for a smaller or larger amount because the latter was used in exchange for a different amount of a certain commodity. Time series exchanges of alike monetary units cannot be made. Nobody yet has learned how to be in the past or future at a present moment in time.

In sum, money-information markers measure various flows of matter energy such as materials, personnel, energy, and communications. The measurements are made on a ratio scale in terms of monetary units and measure the economic attribute-specific exchange value.

THE SPATIOTEMPORAL *ACCOUNTING* MEASUREMENT SCALE

Recognizing the ratio monetary scale is important. That is only part of the accounting measurement methodology, however. Modern double-entry methodology provides measurements of concrete processes on a much more unique measurement scale.

All processes occur over time. Accountants measure process. The accounting measurement scale consequently is spatiotemporal, providing for measurements in three-dimensional physical space and one-dimensional time. The incorporation of the time dimension is an integral part of the scaling process.

In some ways, the time conscientiousness of accounting has been widely recognized, and in other ways it has been virtually ignored. Accountants, on the one hand, strongly argue for periodicity in ratably spreading the costs of depreciable assets to every period benefitted to match perceived expenses with perceived revenues generated in each particular period. On the other hand, that very procedure violates the period-intensive accounting measurement methodology.

Discussing the period intensiveness of the methodology requires a new term. Swanson and Miller (1989) write that

> the notion of the accounting period is sometimes termed the *periodicity concept*, which may be a subtle misnomer. Periodicity refers to recurrence; and, indeed, some accounting theorists have suggested that the accounting period is defined by dominant accounting cycles. There is little doubt, however, that the modern ac-

counting period generally is arbitrarily defined as one year. The fundamentally important aspect of the meaning of the word *period* with reference to the accounting information system is "a portion of time," that is, extended time. The inflected forms of the word *period* do not include this meaning. We understand instantaneity, but we have no parallel inflection of the word *period*. Perhaps we could term the idea "periodaneity," and thus, a measurement would be made either instantaneously or "periodaneously."

The period conscientiousness of accountants generally focuses on models for interpreting accounting measurements, not on the measurements themselves. Interpretations are certainly as important as measurements. If the two actions are confused, however, important information about the concrete processes of societies may be obscured. The characteristics of periodaneous classification therefore should be identified and recognized as inhering in the accounting measurement scale itself.

Information obtained on the spatial monetary scale is simultaneously obtained on the time dimension. Identifying information with particular entities in space is not enough. Information also should be assigned a time location.

How the time location is identified is important. Without doubt, accountants assign numbers to periods, not to instances. That manner of assignment likely reflects the concerns of society for reliable accounting measurements. The probability approaches zero that a single measurement taken at an instant on the fluxuous processes of societal entities represents in any significant way the population of such measurements. Aggregations of such measurements within properly defined periods, however, represent important aspects of societal concrete processes.

The simultaneous assignment of numbers to both space and time dimensions is a fundamental characteristic of the accounting measurement scale. That spatiotemporal scale uniquely welds the two assignments into one inseparable action. In doing so, it provides a method of obtaining information on concrete processes that cannot be applied in the absence of time.

Accounting process measurements are made in terms of monetary units on the attribute-specific exchange value. By measuring obviously different physical elements on the common attribute-specific exchange value, the accounting scale provides a view of an organization or other societal entity as a coherent whole. That cosmic view is a process, not a structural, view. Measurements of space and time are integrated to form the coherent whole.

In this vein of thought, precise definitions of some related terms may be useful. Living systems theory defines *structure* as the arrangement of the subsystems and components of a living system at an instant. Because the matter-energy elements of concrete living systems interact as well as are related, all structures are fictions. Interaction simply cannot occur in the absence of time. The concept is nevertheless useful because residual measurements at such instants may be calculated from previous inflow/outflow processes. *Process* is defined as all action over time. Reversible changes in structure occurring from moment to moment are termed *functions*. Changes over longer periods and that alter both structure and function are defined as *history*. Process and structure together fully define the *state* of concrete living systems.

An obvious consequence of those definitions is that living systems are in a state of flux. To represent such a state, measurements are taken on important variables that fluctuate within relatively narrow ranges that, in turn, are also fluctuous within some range.

Modern measurement theory permits the construction of scales that are not isomorphic to arithmetic as is the ratio scale. Many different scales have been constructed reflecting various characteristics of empirical data, among them the ordinal and interval scales. The accounting scale is instantaneously (spatially) ratio and periodaneously (temporally) a unique measurement that incorporates characteristics of both the ordinal and interval scales.

The ordinal scale consists of exhaustive subclasses of *assumed* equivalent units of a scaled property that are mutually exclusive and that are ordered by a relationship such as "greater than." The ordering relationship holds *between* subclasses. The relationship *within* subclasses is assumed equivalence. That assumption reflects observers' inability to quantify more precisely the property being measured.

The interval scale consists of exhaustive subclasses of equivalent units of a scaled property that are mutually exclusive and that are ordered by a relationship such as "greater than" with the further qualification that each subclass is the same distance from the next ordered subclass as from the previous one. Rather than being assumed within subclasses, equivalence is determined by the calibration of the continuous number system underlying the scale. Objects belong to the same subclass if the property being measured on them can be described by the same scaler quantity. Because the set of real numbers underlies the interval scale, the distances between subclasses can be divided infinitely. Additional subclasses thus may be introduced to provide a different subclass for every different object up to the degree of precision needed.

The periodaneous aspect of the accounting measurement scale is not fully defined by either the ordinal or interval scales. In periodaneous measurement, all spatial measurements assigned to a period (a subclass) are assumed to have equivalent temporal value as with ordinal scale assignments. Between subclasses (periods), equivalence is required similarly to that of the interval scaling operation. The distance between periods, however, is not infinitely divisible. It is zero. The beginning of a following period is the end of the immediately previous period. On the time dimension, the accounting measurement scale is a sort of connected ordinal scale, ordered by the unidirectionality of the second law of thermodynamics. It *assumes* no time differential within a period although time differences exist there, and it *allows* no time differential between periods. It is a true continuum, discretely divided by single instances into equal-length periods (subclasses).

Every monetary scaled measurement is simultaneously time scaled and, thus, belongs to a specific period. Because no time differential is assumed within periods, the characteristics of the ratio monetary scale dominates there. Across periods, limitations of the unique characteristics of periodaneous measurement should be considered. In every case, however, the accounting scale is spatio-temporal, requiring both a cardinal mapping function that maps specific exchange monetary value onto the set of rational numbers and an ordering function that maps time periodaneously into the set of integers.

The resulting measurement is a process-intensive measurement and only incidentally structural. It nevertheless is a measurement of the state of an entity because it includes both structure and process.

The ordering function that maps time periodaneously provokes a unique characteristic in the set of accounting measurements. Although several to many individual assignments of numbers to objects are made within periods on the time continuum, those individual assignments have no meaning on the accounting scale. The measurements of the accounting scale represent accumulations, totals, over particular periods. The individual assignments may be characterized as measurements on the *ratio monetary scale,* however, and as such may have many uses. Nevertheless, on the *spatiotemporal accounting scale,* decompositions of period totals lack meaning.

Ignoring decompositions of period totals is difficult because individual entries obviously fully constitute measurement on a ratio scale. Those entries assign numerical values without violating the proximate location aspect of measurement. Ignoring them seems to throw away information. That is not true, however.

When physicists measure molecular action, they ignore nuclear action because they are concerned with the higher order of magnitude that influences the actions of molecules. Ignoring nuclear action is relatively easy. Observing nuclear action is much more difficult and requires entirely different procedures. Both molecular and nuclear systems do not include the observer, and they are observed typically in terms of instances. A molecular instant, however, is likely a nuclear period and both are instances at the organism order of magnitude.

The spatiotemporal proximate location of the observer relative to the object being measured makes it difficult to ignore measurements of individual exchanges within periods. Nevertheless, the social "instant" is a fairly large organism "period." Although it may be difficult to ignore many actions obvious to the organism-level observer, that difficulty must be overcome if social-level observations are to be made. The spatiotemporal accounting scale ameliorates the difficulty by accumulating individual exchange entries over defined accounting periods to produce aggregates that are in terms of higher-order living system processes, nondecomposable measurements.

THE BASIC DOUBLE-ENTRY MEASUREMENT MODEL

Accounting observation methodology includes both accounting scale measurements on the global attribute-specific exchange value and classification models composed of different categories (termed *accounts*) based on less-global physical characteristics of objects being exchanged. The models partition the class of all accounting scale measurements into exclusive subclasses that together exhaust that class. They are an integral part of the measurement methodology.

Accounting measurement models effectively introduce a second dimension into the methodology. They measure exchange objects on a dimension of physical characteristics at a nominal (categorical) scale level. Thus, measurements on the dimension "physical characteristics" (e.g., equipment and notes payable) are made on a nonquantitative scale and those on the global dimension-specific exchange value are made on the quantitative spatiotemporal accounting scale. Typical double-entry measurement is also double-dimension measurement. Swanson and Miller (1989: 114) suggest that measurements on the dimension of physical characteristics should be upgraded to ratio scales such as liters and tons.

Double-dimension measurement provides a means of analyzing the total aggregate-specific exchange value of periods into various components based on physical characteristics of economic objects other than monetary value. This dual dimensionality of the accounting measurement methodology provides a flexible system for mapping higher-order living systems that combine various matter-energy forms in almost infinite variety.

Entry operations permitted by the basic double-entry, double-dimension measurement model directly parallel the actions of concrete process exchanges. As discussed in Chapter 1, two actions, inflow and outflow, fully define an exchange. All observed inflows of matter-energy and money-information markers are entered into accounting models as debits, and all such outflows are entered as credits. The irreducible unit of modern economic processes is the exchange, not the transaction. Consequently, every inflow has a corresponding outflow and vice versa. Furthermore, a money-information marker transmission typically quantifies the attribute-specific exchange value in each exchange. The monetary amounts of the inflow and the outflow entries therefore are always the same.

Those operations may be summarized as four fundamental rules for entering amounts into *basic* double-entry measurement models. First, only concrete process exchanges are recorded. Second, all inflows are recorded as debits and all outflows are recorded as credits. Third, inflows and outflows are always recorded for every exchange. Fourth, the same monetary amount is entered for both the total inflows and total outflows of an exchange. Obviously, the total inflows or outflows of an exchange may be classified into several different accounts, with differing amounts being recorded in proper accounts. The total monetary amount of the inflows, however, must always equal that of the outflows. Such multiple classification entries are termed *compound entries*.

The obvious should be emphasized again. The entries are measurements describing processes (exchanges), not structures. The less global physical characteristics classifications identify different processes, the structures of which may be calculated at a moment as residuals of previous inflow-outflow processes. The accounting measurement methodology, however, does not observe those residuals. They are mathematical derivatives of process measurements.

A general basic double-entry measurement model may be represented by the following identity.

$$ME \equiv -MIM \tag{E3-1}$$

where

ME = the union of the set of all classifications of measurements (on the spatiotemporal accounting scale) of forms of matter-energy flows, and

MIM = the union of the set of all classifications of measurements (on the spatiotemporal accounting scale) of forms of money-information marker flows.

Together, ME and MIM exhaust the universe of measurements taken on the spatiotemporal accounting scale of classifications of concrete economic exchanges within a defined accounting period. The inverse relationship of the left-side and right-side terms parallels the typical reciprocal transactions and transmissions that compose concrete economic exchanges.

Amounts are entered into the classifications according to the four entry rules. Positive signs $(+)$ designate a debit entry and negative signs $(-)$ designate a credit entry. Then the following equality is always obtained.

$$MEI - MEO = -(MIMI - MIMO) \tag{E3-2}$$

where

Suffix I = inflows and

Suffix O = outflows.

This general equation adequately represents the different types of concrete processes that may occur—exchanges of matter-energy for matter-energy and money-information markers for money-information markers, as well as the typical matter-energy for money-information markers. The model, including its entry rules, converges on the global-derived process measurement net matter energy (NME). Anything that has entered an entity and has not exited simply is still in it. NME is, therefore, a process (a period) residual, not a structure (an instant) residual. In the incipient period of an entity, period and structural residuals are the same. Thereafter, a structural residual includes all previous period residuals as well as the current period residual.

Accounting scale measurements are additive across accounting periods. Therefore, the following equality holds for more than one period.

$$\sum_{n=1}^{i} MEI_i - \sum_{n=1}^{i} MEO_i = -\left(\sum_{n=1}^{i} MIMI_i - \sum_{n=1}^{i} MIMO_i \right), \tag{E3-3}$$

where

i = accounting period of a specified duration.

The quality holds for any series of consecutive accounting periods. Such a series always converges on a global process residual. It converges on a global structure residual only if the first period of the series is the incipient period of the entity. Such residuals may or may not represent important aspects of societal process. Setting the length of accounting periods is an important aspect of observing economic processes.

A model at that level of generality is useful for describing fundamental relationships. The very reason the basic accounting measurement model is incorporated into the measurement methodology nevertheless is to exhaustively subclassify the class of accounting scale measurements into such detail as needed for analysis. Global measurements are important, but detail is possibly more important. The following model provides broad categories that may be used to classify the measurements at the detail of certain important types of concrete processes. Operational accounting models often contain hundreds of accounts (classifications), so even this model is very general.

$$P + Ma + E + Co = Mo + O + Cr + S = NME, \qquad (E3-4)$$

where in terms of accounting scale measurements

P = personnel (people),

Ma = matter-energy forms commonly identified by their spatial dimensions,

E = energy forms such as electricity and gasoline,

Co = communications such as telephone and television,

Mo = currency money-information markers,

O = time-lagged owner money-information markers,

Cr = time-lagged creditor money-information markers,

S = time-lagged socialization money-information markers, and

NME = net matter energy.

Debits (inflows) are entered as positive amounts and credits (outflows) are entered as negative amounts.

The term *matter-energy* is a duality that describes the extremities of a continuum of physical forms that are commonly termed *goods* and *services*. Whether a particular item is called a good or service is determined by common perception. Together, the transfers of those physical forms are termed the *real economy*.

Concrete elements commonly described by the words *personnel, matter (materials), energy,* and *communications* are not naturally exclusive subclasses of concrete systems. For example, electrical energy transactions involve personnel, materials such as wires and poles, and communications such as numbers on meters. The model, however, consists of exclusive subclasses of accounting scale measurements. The left-side terms P, Ma, E, and C of Equation 3-4 represent measurements of matter-energy forms (concrete elements). Measurement priority should therefore be decided by convention for such models to be comparable so that they may be used for general-purpose reports. Such conventional designations are necessary for all models except the most global and the most specific ones.

Conventionalization is also required to make the middle terms of the model exclusive. Currency money-information markers constitute the accepted ultimate media of exchange and are constructed in such forms as coins, bills, checks, credit cards, and electronic transfers. The time-lagged money-information markers are introduced to create time lags and leads within exchanges of matter-energy forms between their reciprocal transactions. That action basically divides each trade exchange into two exchanges, each containing a money-information marker transmission. Examples of time-lagged money-information markers are promissory notes, the Accounts Receivable account, stock certificates, the account Paid-In Capital in Excess of Par Value, tax receipts, and insurance policies. The various types of these concrete system elements are not absolutely defined. For example, the terms *owner documents* and *credit documents* are a duality that generally describes the extremities of a continuum of legal documents that provide prior private claims on process control and residual claims on period incremental process (income) and terminal structure for owners and just the opposite for creditors. Most documents provide legal claims somewhere between the two—not at the extremes. Using the model for general-purpose reporting thus requires consensus on definitions of the exclusive categories Mo, O, Cr, and S.

This model, as well as those described by equations 3-1 through 3-3, converges on NME. That convergence makes it possible to calculate a global measurement of matter-energy outflow (MEO). That calculation is important because accounting systems typically cannot measure MEO directly. The inability to measure MEO directly is the cost accounting problem. Although the calculation of the global measurement MEO mitigates the cost problem, it does not fully solve it.

The cost accounting problem occurs because organizations specialize by differentiating and synthesizing many different physical processes. When specialization takes place, matter-energy forms observed entering the organization, and recorded in terms of specific exchange monetary values, are not always traceable through the organization to the forms observed leaving the organization. Consequently, the costs (the inflow values) cannot always be associated with the outflows.

Calculating the global measurement MEO provides a benchmark to evaluate the results of the allocation methods used to associate costs with outflows of products and services. It does not eliminate allocation methods because estimates of the costs of individual products are needed for pricing and other management functions.

Operational accounting models partition the general classifications of Equation 3-4 into whatever classifications are needed for particular purposes. Some typical accounts used by accountants are listed in Table 3-1. Some accounts such as Wages Expense are process accounts that aggregate separately the unidirectional transfers and transmissions of exchanges. Others are residual accounts that aggregate both inflows and outflows in the same account, creating a net amount balance. Process measurements are estimated from this latter type of account by calculating the change (Δ) in the balance over an accounting period. Swanson and Miller (1989) suggest that residual accounts should be divided into two accounts, one for inflows and the other for outflows. That simple action would transform all accounts into process-aggregating accounts.

SUMMARY

This chapter describes what accounting measurement scales and models are and how they are used to map the concrete processes of organizations. Chapter 4 introduces a methodology termed *macro accounting* for using similar ideas to examine the higher-order economic processes of societies and supranational systems.

Table 3-1
Typical Accounts and Their Basic Interrelationships

Personnel +	Materials +	Energy +	Communications =
Wages Salaries	Cost of Sales Inventory Δ Buildings Δ Equipment Δ	Utilities Fuel	Telephone Advertising

Currency MIM +	Owner MIM +	Credit MIM +
Cash in Bank Δ Petty Cash Δ	Common Stock Δ Paid in Capital Δ Dividends	Accounts Receivable Δ Notes Payable Δ Interest

Socialization MIM

Insurance Premiums
Income Tax Expense
Insurance Receipts

Δ -- change in

REFERENCES

Abdel-Magid, M. F. "Toward a Better Understanding of the Role of Measurement in Accounting." *The Accounting Review* (April 1979), pp. 346–57.

Belkaoui, A. "The Whys and Wherefores of Measuring Externalities." *The Certified General Accountant* (January–February 1975), pp. 29–32.

Burkhardt, H. "System Physics: A Uniform Approach to Branches of Classical Physics." *American Journal of Physics* (April 1987), pp. 344–50.

Canning, J. B. *The Economics of Accountancy*. New York: Ronald Press, 1923.

Chambers, R. J. *Accounting, Evaluation and Economic Behavior*. Englewood Cliffs, NJ: Prentice-Hall, 1966.

Ijiri, Y. *The Foundations of Accounting Measurement: A Mathematical, Economic, and Behavioral Inquiry*. Englewood Cliffs, NJ: Prentice-Hall, 1967.

Paton, W. A. *Accounting Theory*. New York: Ronald Press, 1922.

Scott, DR. "The Basis of Accounting Principles." *The Accounting Review* (December 1941), pp. 341–49.

Sprouse, R. T., and Moonitz, M. A. *A Tentative Set of Broad Accounting Principles for Business Enterprises* (ARS No. 3). New York: AICPA, 1962.

Stevens, S. S. "Mathematics, Measurement, and Psychophysics." In S. S. Stevens, ed. *Handbook of Experimental Psychology*. New York: Wiley, 1951.

Stevens, S. S. "On the Theory of Measurement." *Science* 103 (1946), pp. 677–80.

Swanson, G. A. "Accounting Information Can Be Used for Scientific Investigation." *Behavioral Science* 32, no. 2 (1987), pp. 81–91.

Swanson, G. A., and Miller, James Grier. "Distinguishing between Measurements and Interpretations in Public Accounting Reports." *Behavioral Science* 33 (1988), pp. 1–24.

Swanson, G. A., and Miller, James Grier. *Measurement and Interpretation in Accounting: A Living Systems Theory Approach*. Westport, CT: Greenwood Press, 1989.

Sweeny, H. W. *Stabilized Accounting*. New York: Hayes & Brothers, 1936.

Zeff, S. A. "The Rise of 'Economic Consequences.'" *The Journal of Accountancy* (December 1978), pp. 17–20.

4

Macro Accounting

As defined in Chapter 1, macro accounting is a set of concepts, theory, and procedures that may be used to investigate the concrete processes of higher-order human systems. It is an extension of the basic accounting discussed in chapters 1 through 3. This chapter develops that extension.

What higher-order systems directly concern macro accounting, how money emerges from debt, and how "supra money" emerges from foreign exchange are discussed. That discussion identifies the elements of societies and supranational systems and their interactions that concern macro accounting models. A method is presented and illustrated for modeling specific subprocesses of economies. Such subprocesses consist of chains of linked exchanges. The method is used in chapters 5 and 6 to analyze ways societies may introduce money into their economies.

DIFFERENTIATING HIGHER-ORDER LIVING SYSTEMS ON CONCRETE ECONOMIC PROCESS

Mixed systems composed of living and nonliving elements are termed *higher-order living systems* in the sense of living systems described by Miller (1978). Among other important characteristics, they are all concrete systems composed of various matter-energy and information transmission forms and, consequently, discoverable by empirical science. The higher five levels of the living systems theory (LST) hierarchy are higher-order living systems.

LST distinguishes hierarchical levels based on identifying unique general properties that emerge at successively higher levels. The levels thus distinguished are supported or denied by a dualistic methodology. Both similarities and orderly differentials across levels are demonstrated. Twenty critical cross-level similarities have been identified and termed subsystems (see Table 2-2). LST asserts that these similarities exist because of the common cosmological origin of life. In a set of related laboratory experiments, Miller and a team of experts, each specializing in a science concerning a different level, demonstrated that information overload may be described on the same function over the first five hierarchical levels. Orderly differentials between levels were demonstrated on the volume of information processed (Miller 1978: 121–202). Miller (1986) describes other cross-level studies.

Three orders of higher-order living systems may be demonstrated by orderly differentials in the minimum number of accounts required to record an economic exchange at successive levels. The orders are societal component, society, and supranational system. Observations at the different orders involve different perspectives because observers or observation devices are contained in systems at each order (are not independent of those systems). The minimum number of required accounts may be orderly differentiated on the geometric progression 2^1, 2^2, and 2^3. Two of the orders, societies and supranational systems, correspond to LST's top levels. The other order, which is termed *societal component*, does not distinguish among organisms, groups, organizations, and communities. Those levels are distinguished on other bases.

Two accounts are sufficient to record an exchange at the societal component level (one for the inflow from another entity and one for the outflow to another entity). A minimum of four accounts is required at the society level, and a threshold of eight accounts is needed for supranational systems.

Figure 4-1 illustrates the minimum requirements. All transactions are recorded in accounts in terms of a particular society's monetary units in both societal components and societies. Consequently, the differential between those levels is immediately a function of the different perspectives of observers. On the other hand, the differential between societies and supranational systems is the immediate result of multiple kinds of monetary units. The supranational differential, thus, is a function of both different perspectives and different monetary units.

MONEY ECONOMIES REQUIRE
DOUBLE-ENTRY MAPPING

Notwithstanding an immediate relationship of observer perspective and multiple monetary units to differentiation of hierarchical orders, double-entry methodology (exchange mapping) itself arises from the properties of money-information markers (MIM).

MIM consist of relatively small bundles of matter-energy that bear monetary information about specific exchange values and are ultimately exchangeable. They are concrete emergents of societies. MIM may be classified as various forms of both currency MIM and time-lagged MIM. Examples of currency MIM are coins and bills, electronic transfers of funds, and checks. Time-lagged MIM consist of such documents as promissory notes, stock certificates, and Accounts Payable accounts.

Currency MIM are the ultimate expeditor of trade in modern economies. Commercial law, however, provides for leads and lags in the transmission of currency MIM related to particular exchanges. Such leads and lags give rise to executory contracts that are evidenced by the transmission of time-lagged MIM in the place of currency MIM. Virtually every exchange that includes a transfer of goods and services also includes a reciprocating transmission of MIM, currency or time lagged. Consequently, a modern exchange is seldom a trade of goods and services for goods and services.

Many time-lagged MIM require reciprocating transmission of currency MIM at a future certain date. Thus, modern exchanges also include reciprocal transmissions of time-lagged MIM and currency MIM.

The differing characteristics of money-information markers are no less important to economic analyses than are those of matter-energy forms. For example, credit MIM and owner MIM may be generally differentiated as the extremities of a continuum with the reciprocal characteristics shown on Figure 4-2. Many points of mixed characteristics exist on that continuum, however. A booklet published by Coopers & Lybrand (1988) describes about 150 different financial instruments (e.g., asset-backed securities and hedging instruments). It states that "lately, hardly a week seems to go by without a new financial instrument being introduced. . . . And for those who don't work closely and frequently with the investment banking community, the LYONs, Tigers, and ZEBRAs of Wall Street can be overwhelming creatures" (1988: 2). By October 3, 1988, John E. Stewart, partner of Arthur Andersen & Co. had accumulated a list of more than 500 types of such documents (1988). All of these are different forms of time-lagged money-information markers.

The patterns in which those many different forms of MIM are processed in economies do not correspond directly to the patterns of any set of matter-energy forms processed. MIM thus require a separate set of mapping classifications.

The need to classify both money-information marker flows and matter energy flows requires double-entry mapping procedures even when goods and services are flowing only one way in an exchange. If MIM flows were only currency, the specific exchange value recorded in the various matter-energy classifications would provide sufficient information about MIM. In that case, a single-entry system would meet the needs of a monetary economy.

That is not the situation, however. Various MIM classifications are important for modeling economic processes. Consequently, double-entry mapping of modern exchanges is required by emergent money-information marker transmissions as well as by the process of trading goods and services.

DEBT MONEY

The accounting basis of money is discussed in Chapter 1. The geniuses condition of negotiable money-information markers is a time lag between the reciprocal transfers of goods and services in a trade exchange. In the most fundamental form, MIM are introduced to document lags and leads between transfers in trades. The typical documentation in modern economies concerns debt. Fundamental MIM provide traceable verification of debt obligations on the part of receivers of goods and services who have not yet reciprocated with goods and services. The condition that requires constructing MIM also requires recording its inflows and outflows.

Currency MIM emerge as certain types of time-lagged MIM increasingly are generically perceived. Eventually, generic units of currency MIM are perceived to have value in exchange by fiat, quite divorced from the debt obligations underlying them. The imputed value, nevertheless, is the value of time-lagged MIM that bear information about debt obligations.

No societal component, society, or supranational system can survive long without a clear record of its debt obligations and rights. That record is borne on MIM. Notwithstanding its being obscured in currency MIM by fiat, this fundamental characteristic of MIM influences the formation of economies.

THE MINIMUM ACCOUNT REQUIREMENTS DO NOT CONSIDER THE ORIGIN OF CURRENCY MIM

When parties enter into debt obligations, MIM are constructed and transmitted (negotiated) in physical channels and nets. The minimum number of accounts required to record the inflows and outflows of those transmissions and of the matter-energy transfers of an exchange is illustrated in Figure 4-1. One entity is involved from the perspective of a societal component, two entities are involved from that of a society, and four entities (two societal components and two societies) are involved from the supranational perspective—one entity, two accounts; two entities, four accounts; and four entities, eight accounts. Figure 4-1 pertains only to ongoing processes. It does not take the origin of currency MIM into consideration. If it purports to, it is empirically flawed. In Part C, the progression presumes that MIM can be mapped in the same manner as other concrete flows, neglecting the different types of monetary units involved in foreign exchange. Only the ingester and extruder subsystem processes of a supranational exchange are illustrated as they can actually occur in a system being mapped. Mapping MIM requires consideration of input transducer, output transducer, decoder, and encoder processes as well.

Ingester and extruder subsystems bring matter-energy forms across a system boundary from and to its environment, respectively. The specific values of those exchanges are recorded in terms of a particular monetary unit (such as the mark or the dollar). Because marks and dollars are exchanged for economic value, the monetary values are connected to the physical information markers and thus are not fully abstract. These monetary values form objective numbering systems. Their values are integrally connected to the physical processes of which they are a part. The values cannot be abstracted into a different monetary system. They must be physically introduced into that system. Such an introduction involves the input transducer, output transducer, decoder, and encoder subsystems of both the giving and receiving systems. So an international exchange consisting of both money-information marker flows and matter-energy flows involves those subsystems as well as the ingester and extruder subsystems.

The specific exchange value in a particular currency of matter-energy flows of ingester and extruder processes is recorded in different accounts (classifications) representing different types of matter-energy (goods-services) flows. Thus, the subclasses (accounts) of a particular society's accounting model partition exhaustively the class of specific exchange value of a particular country's money, not the class of matter-energy forms itself.

Only in relatively closed societies are accounts required to record matter-energy flows at the boundaries of societies in addition to the boundaries of societal components. That is thus a special case, and the two-account-mapping (numbers 5 and 6 in Figure 4-1C) is the general case.

Currency money-information markers are constructed by particular societies. Transmissions across society boundaries require transformation (transducing process) of those markers and restatement of their values into other monetary units (encoder and decoder processes).

The MIM map of Figure 4-1C, however, neglects the processes of input transducer, output transducer, decoder, and encoder subsystems. Those processes involve transforming inflows and outflows of information markers to forms that can be transmitted within a system and in a system's environment and altering a code from public to private and from private to public, respectively.

The society accounts in Figure 4-1C numbered 4 and 5 record inflows in DM (German mark) and outflows in $ (U.S. dollar). That action presumes that the output transducer subsystem of one society is the input transducer subsystem of the other. It is not. How did the $s get into the DM society? Higher-order systems often laterally disperse critical functions to other such systems. Dispersing the MIM input transducer function to another society, however, is very unlikely because in the economic arena that function is critical to the society's survival as a distinct entity.

Neither can the encoder subsystem of one society encode its own MIM into that of another society. How can the DM society restate the DMs into $s? A society may use the name of another society's currency MIM and might even capture some store of that MIM and regulate it internally. That society might expand its money supply by constructing specific transformation equations to restate its own currency MIM into the captured MIM. None of these actions, however, make the captured MIM the MIM of that society. When the captured MIM are released, the information borne on free markers is indiscriminately imputed to them. They assume the value of the free MIM.

Consequently, currency MIM bear information about the continually changing specific exchange value of goods, services, and time-lagged MIM exchanged within the boundaries of higher-order human systems even while captured by other such systems. Outside those boundaries, that value can only be estimated. Such estimates are expressed typically in currency MIM exchange rates. If no exchanges of currency MIM occurred, such rates could not be established. More fundamentally, those rates do not exist without currency MIM.

How do currency MIM originate? As the concrete property money emerges by fiat in the societal debt accounting process, societies construct currency MIM to bear information about the property. The property money is no less physical than the property momentum. While it is mathematically convenient with the calculus to consider momentum at an instant, it can exist only over time. Likewise, money can exist only over time. Its physical basis is time-lagged delivery of goods and services.

Both momentum and money are process emergents. So societies construct currency MIM to be transmitted in exchange for transfers of goods and services and transmissions of time-lagged MIM to measure their specific exchange values at each point of exchange. Monetary-specific exchange value emerges as a process attribute of this measurement methodology in a manner similar to the way length emerges as a structural attribute of the metric measurement methodology.

A similar concrete development may occur in supranational systems. There the concrete property "foreign exchange," a sort of "supramoney," may emerge by fiat in the debt accounting system. Supranational systems could construct supracurrency MIM to bear information about the specific exchange value of the societal currencies internationally. By and large, they have not. Instead, societies mainly have estimated exchange values by referring to a particular type of currency MIM that was perceived to be "stable." This situation is not unlike the incipient emergence of monetary units when such widely traded commodities as grain were used as standards to value other kinds of commodities (Schmandt-Besserat 1984: 57).

Perhaps no fully emerged supranational system exists today. The specific exchange value of supramoney cannot be measured in each exchange without constructing supracurrency MIM. It can be estimated only by societal currency MIM exchange rates. That methodology allows larger information gaps, and thus market manipulation, in foreign exchange than is necessary.

In sum, debt obligations underlie modern money. Both time-lagged MIM and currency MIM are physical markers constructed to carry information about debt throughout a society. Only currency MIM are popularly recognized as money. Economists and some other social scientists, however, have recognized that certain time-lagged MIM have characteristics of money and that debt, indeed, underlies modern money. What may not be recognized so broadly is that the debt foundation may be connected directly to the global supply of currency MIM. Furthermore, this connection should be made. Macro accounting concerns that connection.

A MACRO ACCOUNTING ANALYSIS METHOD

A macro accounting analysis method should be introduced before proceeding with the discussion of how debt, in fact, underlies modern money. Understanding complex systems requires some means of reducing the complexity. The notation method described in this section is based on the double-entry bookkeeping model that evolved for that very purpose as organizations and societies grew more complex.

In modern times, an account is a space divided into left and right areas. The T-account notation is used extensively in textbooks to identify such spaces. The name of the account is written over the horizontal line, any amounts entered left of the vertical line are understood to be debits, and amounts to the right are credits. The name of an account is the nominal classification of the monetary amounts entered into it.

In concrete process mapping, inflows across boundaries of systems are recorded as debits and outflows are recorded as credits. For example, an exchange of $10,000 cash paid for an automobile is recorded by the entry in Figure 4-3. The dollar sign in unnecessary in the notation because all amounts entered into a particular entity's set of accounts are in terms of a particular monetary unit.

Accounts are used to map the concrete processes of higher-order systems. Each account accommodates multiple entries, and the set of accounts can be expanded to meet various needs for detailed classification of flows. Counts of monetary units borne on various forms of MIM in exchanges are recorded in the accounts.

Such a space-consuming notation is unnecessary for certain macro analyses of economic processes. When we are not concerned with mapping particular actual processes, the notation may be abbreviated considerably. Certain aspects of the effects of types of actions on both currency and time-lagged MIM may be analyzed using notation that describes chains of exchanges.

One such notation uses sequence indices in a matrix of types of higher-order systems and concrete processes. A sequence always begins with an outflow. Anything transacted must originate within a societal component. Societies contain no empty space. They exist in space extended over their components. Every transaction consists of an outflow and an inflow. Completing the record of a transaction consequently requires an inflow to follow an outflow. The result of those conditions is that all odd numbers are outflows and all even numbers are inflows.

As discussed previously, the mutual benefits of an exchange motivate transactions. That condition requires a reciprocal transaction for every transaction. Exchanges consequently are represented by four consecutive indices, reciprocal outflow-inflow transactions.

A set of related exchanges is termed a *chain of exchanges* because of its sequential character. The set of positive integers is used for sequence indices. A sequence of actions is indicated by the order of the numbers, forming a chronological index representing a chain of linked exchanges.

That notation incorporates a matrix of spaces representing important economic variables. Types of higher-order systems are represented on the rows, and types of concrete economic flows are represented on the columns. By placing all odd numbers to the right and all even numbers to the left, the left-right positioning convention of inflow-outflow used with debit-credit notation is preserved.

Table 4-1 illustrates the notation with a map of economic processes initiated by a labor-consumption entity accepting an IOU from a production entity for the costs of producing and distributing a consumer product within society. The chain begins in the cell that represents time-lagged MIM flows of production entities. The index 2 is placed in the cell representing time-lagged MIM flows of labor-consumption entities. The index 1 represents an outflow of the time-lagged MIM, and the index 2 represents its inflow. The reciprocating transaction of the first exchange is represented by indices 3 and 4, indicating a transfer of matter-energy forms from labor-consumption entities to production ones. The second exchange in the chain begins with a transmission of the time-lagged MIM from the labor-consumption entities to society. The entire chain of events may be traced by simply following the sequence. Table 4-1 illustrates only the notation method. In-depth analyses are forthcoming in the following pages.

Nevertheless, observing that the chain forms a circuit back to where it started is interesting. The chain of linked exchanges is closed. The particular time-lagged MIM constructed to initiate the chain are destroyed in the end. If they were not, the same "money" could be used again. That secondary use could either initiate additional productive processes or drive up the prices of existing goods-services. This observation becomes an important part of the analyses of several social policy-induced chains of exchanges.

The matrix notation is quite abbreviated. It provides a means of viewing an entire chain of exchanges in a relatively small area. Its two-dimensional space aids in conceptualizing spatially distributed flows. The movement of concrete elements across boundaries in economies is represented by the sequence across matrix spaces.

The information obtained in the matrix notation may be condensed further, however, by using symbols rather than spaces to represent it. Five sorts of information are provided by the matrix notation. They are (1) types of concrete element flows, (2) types of higher-order systems (entities), (3) specific entities, (4) direction of flows, and (5) sequence of transactions and exchanges.

All of that information can be provided with symbols and superscripts. The following symbolic notation describes the chain of exchanges represented in Table 4-1:

$$\text{TLM}^P \ \text{TLM}^c \ \text{ME}^c \ \text{ME}^P \ \text{TLM}^c \ \text{TLM}^s \ \text{CM}^s \ \text{CM}^c \tag{4-1}$$

$$\text{CM}^c \ \text{CM}^P \ \text{ME}^P \ \text{ME}^c \ \text{CM}^P \ \text{CM}^s \ \text{TLM}^s \ \text{TLM}^P,$$

where the main terms represent types of concrete element flows, the superscripts indicate types of higher-order systems, TLM is time-lagged MIM, ME is matter-energy forms, CM is currency MIM, P is a producing entity, C is a consuming entity, and S is a society. When tracing flows among entities of the same type, different numerals may be placed in the superscripts to designate different entities. Additional terms are introduced as analyses become more complex.

Two distinct patterns are evident in Notation 4-1. They are the transaction pattern and the exchange pattern. The transaction pattern is successive pairs of similar main terms. The exchange pattern consists of a superscript term of a particular entity followed by two successive like superscript terms of a different entity followed, in turn, by the first entity's superscript term. Those patterns are highlighted by the underlines (transactions) and overlines (exchanges) in Notation 4-2. Exchanges are obviously composed of reciprocating transactions in the notation.

$$\underline{TLM^P \ TLM^c} \quad \overline{ME^c \ ME^P} \qquad \underline{TLM^c \ TLM^s} \quad \overline{CM^s \ CM^c} \qquad (4-2)$$

$$\underline{CM^c \ CM^P} \quad \overline{ME^P \ ME^c} \qquad \underline{CM^P \ CM^s} \quad \overline{TLM^s \ TLM^P}$$

The analyses that follow are performed at first in both matrix and symbolic notations. Both are provided because macro accounting methodology is not widely disseminated and, being new, may be difficult to follow in detail. By providing two methods for conceptualizing the relationships analyzed, the analyses may be more easily understood. Because the analyses incorporate more and more complex situations, however, efficiency of space requires restricting analyses first to symbol notation and finally to graphic presentations of only important results.

SUMMARY

This chapter discussed important characteristics of modern monetary economies and introduced methods for examining the physical introduction of money-information markers into societies. Chapter 5 uses the methods introduced to examine certain basic economic processes of such economies.

REFERENCES

Coopers & Lybrand. *Guide to Financial Instruments.* New York: Coopers & Lybrand, 1988.

Miller, James Grier. "Can Systems Theory Generate Testable Hypotheses? From Talcott Parsons to Living Systems Theory." *Systems Research* 3, no. 2 (1986), pp. 73–84.

Miller, James Grier. *Living Systems.* New York: McGraw-Hill, 1978.

Schmandt-Besserat, Denice. "Before Numerals." *Visible Language* 13, no. 1 (1984), pp. 48–60.

Stewart, John E. Lecture Notes, Arthur Andersen Accounting and Auditing Symposium. St. Charles, IL, October 17–18, 1988.

Figure 4-1
**Minimum Accounts Required to Record Economic Exchanges from the
Perspectives of Three Types of Higher-Order Living Systems**

A. Societal Component (two accounts required)

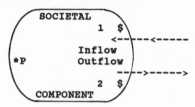

B. Society (four accounts required)

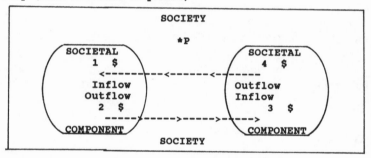

C. Supranational System (eight accounts required)

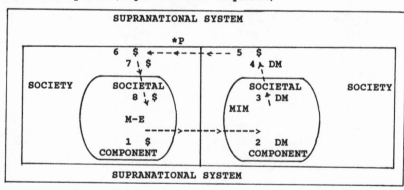

* P is perspective

Note: P is perspective
$ = U.S. Dollars
DM = German Marks

Figure 4-2
Money-Information Marker Continuum

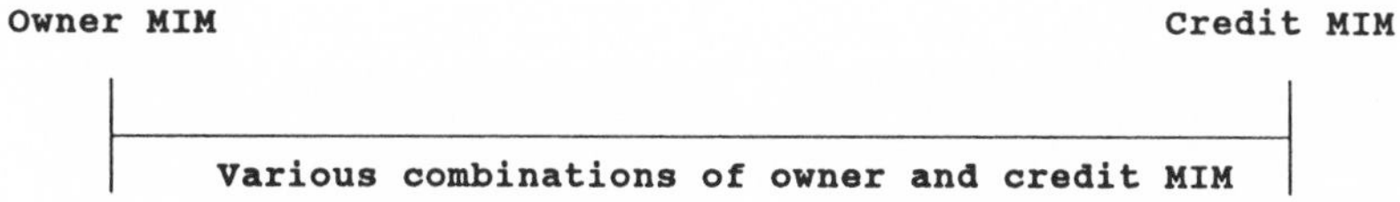

Owner MIM   Credit MIM

```
|                                                      |
|——————————————————————————————————————————————————————|
|      Various combinations of owner and credit MIM    |
```

Private prior claims on control   Private prior claims on
  (process) and negative income.   income and structure.
Private residual claims on   Private residual claims on
  structure and income.   control (process) and
                                           negative income.

Figure 4-3
Information Recorded in T Accounts

```
        Cash                        Automobile
_____          _____
       |                            |
10,000 |                     10,000 |
       |                            |
       |                            |
       |                            |
```

Table 4-1
Chain of Exchanges Matrix Notation

Higher-Order Systems	Concrete Processes	Time-lagged	MIM	Currency	MIM	Matter-Energy	
Society		6	15	14	7		
Societal Components	Production	16	1	10	13	4	11
	Labor-Consumption	2	5	8	9	12	3

5

Basic Economic Processes

An economic system processes various forms of concrete elements to produce and distribute goods and services among different factors of production and distribution in a manner that provides its components more economic satisfaction than they could achieve independently. Viewing economies in that way permits us to study underlying relationships within the systems themselves without confusing them with relationships among elements of moral and ethical conceptual and abstracted systems. That action makes it possible to attempt to build economic systems that are unbiased by particular moral or ethical codes or, for that matter, by particular components.

Such economic systems may provide freedom to their components, or ethical and moral codes may be superimposed on them. In either case, an economic system's influence on particular individual actions may be neutral with respect to any other particular conceptual or abstracted system. Decisions of economic actors, not relationships in the system, can determine the production and distribution of economic goods and services. The system simply facilitates economic activity.

This chapter concerns basic economic processes within societies. The macro accounting analysis methods developed in Chapter 4 are used to study the effects of various ways of introducing money-information markers (MIM) into economies. Different introductions of MIM result in different chains of related exchanges.

Goods and services may exist prior to any form of MIM. Consequently, some chains of exchanges assume preexisting goods and services. None assume preexisting MIM. Currency MIM cannot exist in the total absence of goods and services. The opposite, however, is not necessarily so.

Two types of economic processes are initiated by introducing money-information markers. *Determinate processes* are those that have a definite ending. *Dynamic processes* introduce motives (dynamics) to cause recursive similar processes over time. Determinate processes are mapped by closed chains of exchanges termed *circuits*. Dynamic processes are mapped by open chains of exchanges termed *cycles* that are closed by a following cycle.

As discussed in Chapter 4, every exchange is motivated. A dynamic that causes the exchange to occur exists. All analyses in this chapter construct exchanges that are caused by apparent dynamics.

Economic functions are all interactive. All changes in an economic element affect other economic elements. Economic processes are highly complex and circuitous. Attempts to examine the total effects of an event may degenerate into results that reflect arbitrarily designated probability functions more than they describe or map empirically confirmable patterns of concrete elements.

Examining total effects is not the purpose of the analyses in this book. Their purpose is to examine the initial effects of different ways of generating MIM. Public policymakers should be concerned with initial effects because they are the most predictable.

Public policymakers are not ordinarily constructing a new economy. They are attempting to correct certain imbalances in existing economies (e.g., between consuming and producing processes). Consequently, their actions are designed to achieve certain specific adjustments, not to provide a global set of relationships.

Public policymakers ordinarily rely on the fundamental dynamic of trade to drive the global set of relationships. The *dynamic of trade* is the preference of economic participants for multiple different goods and services. Specialization and the resulting division of labor in modern economies are connected to the phenomenon of separating temporally the reciprocating transfers of goods and services by intervening transmissions of MIM.

Those information transmissions are subject to numerous perils along the circuitous path closing a particular goods-services trade. The sources of the imbalances that concern public policymakers are the periods separating reciprocating transfers. The perils themselves are part of the actions of society to increase production of goods and services. Public policymakers therefore take corrective actions to eradicate imbalances caused by societies' previous actions and not caused by fundamental structural dysfunctions in the process of trade itself.

Chapter 5 analyzes basic economic processes ranging from simple ones to complex ones. The analyses concern sixteen specific situations. Chapter 6 introduces interest and profit to the analyses. Both chapters discuss only processes within a society and couch the analyses in the context of economies that use strictly debt-based currency MIM. Chapter 7 continues the discussion of situations within societies, but those situations are more complex. They model certain types of interactions in economic processes advocated by modern societies. Chapter 8 extends the analyses to supranational systems.

TRADES

Trades are exchanges of matter-energy (goods-services). No money-information markers are required to accomplish trade. Nevertheless, they facilitate it. Trades are the most fundamental commerce. The dynamic that motivates trades is a common human preference for multiple different goods and services. The constraint that limits trades is equilibrium of perceived economic value between parties to particular trades. Together, the dynamic and the constraint form the basis for initiating and consummating trades.

Two situations are analyzed in this section. They are a basic trade and a trade with time-lagged MIM intervening.

Situation 5-1: A Basic Trade

An exchange of goods-services for other goods-services is the most basic economic exchange. The reciprocating transactions of trades are transfers of matter-energy forms. Notation 5-1 and Table 5-1 map such a trade between different societal components (sc).

$$ME^{sc1} \qquad ME^{sc2} \qquad ME^{sc2} \qquad ME^{sc1} \qquad\qquad (5-1)$$

Superscripts 1 and 2 designate different entities.

An exchange is the basic link in what may become very large and complex chains of economic processes. A trade consists of one exchange—the simplest circuit. It is a one-link chain—a determinate process with transfers occurring simultaneously.

A trade is the most condensed and, consequently, simplest chain of economic processes possible. In fact, more complex chains are constructed by splitting a trade into transfers. Any separation of transfers is always temporal and may be spatial as well.

The power released to generate economic action by splitting trades into transfers is roughly analogous to that released by splitting the nucleus of an atom. As long as the nucleus is intact, its influence is orderly and well defined. Being split, it releases enormous power in extended time and space. The influence of that power is less orderly and not so well defined. Nevertheless, the released power is bounded and may be dynamically identified.

The functions of commerce and industry may be separated rationally. No production is necessarily involved in a trade, although it strongly implies some sort of previous or current production. Commerce may occur independently of production. The functions of commerce and industry may be separated rationally.

No money-information markers of any sort are involved in a basic trade. Debt does not enter into the process at all, and society enters only indirectly. A trade is private between the societal components involved. At law, it is an executed private contract. That is to say, the continuation of the changed state resulting from a trade is enforceable by society but only if petitioned by a party to the trade.

Relatively independent entities exchange different goods-services that they perceive to have equal economic value but that provide each receiving entity more economic satisfaction. The dynamic motivating trades is a preference on the part of each entity for different multiple goods-services.

Situation 5-2: A Trade with Debt Intervening

The fundamental trade splitters in debt-based economies are time-lagged MIM. All chains of economic processes are composed of links of exchanges. Each exchange is composed of two transactions that may be transfers of matter-energy or transmissions of money-information markers. Each transaction, in turn, is composed of two accounts. Consequently, every exchange contains four accounts. Accounts and transactions cannot exist independently of exchanges because no dynamic to motivate them exists. Therefore, the transactions of trades are separated by inserting time-lagged MIM transmissions between them—incorporating the basic dynamic of trades in the transmissions of MIM.

A situation may arise, for example, in which an individual societal component has goods-services that it is willing to transfer to another societal component in exchange for a promise to receive other goods-services at a certain future date. Perhaps a merchant passes through a countryside delivering certain jewels upon receiving a written promise of a certain number of bushels of wheat at harvest time. Such a process is mapped in Table 5-2 and in the following symbolic notation:

$$\text{TLM}^{sc1} \quad \text{TLM}^{sc2} \quad \text{ME}^{sc2} \quad \text{ME}^{sc1} \quad \text{ME}^{sc1} \quad \text{ME}^{sc2} \quad \text{TLM}^{sc2} \quad \text{TLM}^{sc1} \quad (5\text{-}2)$$

The transferred debt instrument constitutes debt money. The process chain forms a circuit ending with the retrieval of the debt instrument (time-lagged MIM) constructed to initiate the process.

The willingness of a creditor to accept time-lagged MIM makes the expanded chain of exchanges possible. If that willingness did not exist, no transfer of goods-services could occur because reciprocating goods-services are not yet available for a trade.

Three important characteristics of this chain should be recognized. First, time-lagged MIM are circulated to accomplish only one trade and are taken out of circulation at its conclusion—a fully predictable ending. The chain describes a determinate process. The time-lagged MIM are connected directly to production and distribution of identifiable goods-services. Second, one party to the trade must prefer the other party's goods-services sufficiently to forgo its own goods-services on a promise to receive (at risk of receiving) those goods-services in the future. That preference is an additional dynamic beyond a basic preference for multiple products. It may arise out of any abundance that occurs above subsistence. Consequently, that dynamic is different than the interest dynamic that is discussed in the next chapter. Third, the parties to the exchange originate the money (debt obligation) and construct the time-lagged MIM. In the event of default, the risk taker suffers the loss, and the time-lagged MIM have no further effect on economic activity. No society or supranational system is needed to originate MIM, and its originate form is time-lagged MIM.

That view of money is not necessarily the common view. Money is ordinarily defined by its uses. In the common view, money is what money does. It assigns and stores value and mediates exchange. Historically, many things such as salt, grain, and gold were considered money because they were used to accomplish those actions. A distinction ordinarily is made between such perceived money and debt.

The common view, however, neglects the seminal importance of certification in the development of money-information markers. Swanson and Miller (1989: 37–53) trace the incipient development of money-information markers prior to the emergence of coins. Certification of those markers by higher-order human systems is an important ingredient in their development. The ordinary notion of money refers to some types of currency MIM certified by societies. In modern banking systems, the certification processes (printing and coining money) have been tied to banking systems and their acceptance of debt instruments (time-lagged MIM). Nevertheless, time-lagged MIM are not ordinarily viewed as money. Economists, however, generally include certain types of debt in the money supply.

All analyses in this book assume fundamentally that money originates in time-lagged MIM and that currency MIM originate in societies' direct or indirect certification that such debt instruments have some specified value. In other words, they assume that all money is quite precisely debt-based money.

CURRENCY MIM

Situation 5-2 may be repeated in large volume among many different societal components. During the lag time between the beginning and ending of the chain, the time-lagged MIM may be exchanged for other time-lagged MIM or goods-services of various sorts. Such negotiability, of course, depends on a general trust among participants in the exchange environment. That trust was historically fostered by societies providing legal recourse for enforcing contracts. Currency MIM emerge out of such processes as societies begin to certify debt instruments by accepting them in exchange for their own generic money-information markers.

This section examines five situations. Society provides currency MIM in each situation. How it does that and how time-lagged MIM are originated vary.

Situation 5-3: An Exchange of Existing Goods-Services with Debt and Currency MIM Intervening

Notation 5-3 and Table 5-3 map a chain of exchanges that involve two societal components trading goods-services through an intervening monetary system.

$$\text{TLM}^{sc1} \quad \text{TLM}^{sc2} \quad \text{ME}^{sc2} \quad \text{ME}^{sc1} \quad \text{TLM}^{sc2} \quad \text{TLM}^{s} \quad \text{CM}^{s} \quad \text{CM}^{sc2} \qquad (5-3)$$

$$\text{CM}^{sc2} \quad \text{CM}^{sc1} \quad \text{ME}^{sc1} \quad \text{ME}^{sc2} \quad \text{CM}^{sc1} \quad \text{CM}^{s} \quad \text{TLM}^{s} \quad \text{TLM}^{sc1}$$

The chain consists of four exchanges, eight transactions (six transmissions of MIM and two transfers of matter-energy), and sixteen accounts. Societal Component 1 gives a promissory note to Societal Component 2 in exchange for goods-services in the first exchange. Societal Component 2 exchanges that note for currency MIM with society and uses the currency MIM in an exchange for goods-services with Societal Component 1 in the second and third exchanges, respectively. In the final exchange, Societal Component 1 returns the currency MIM to society, retrieving the promissory note.

Notice three aspects of this situation. First, the money (TLM) still originates with the parties to the trade. Second, in the end, the currency MIM are retrieved by society as the time-lagged MIM are retrieved by their originator(s). Currency MIM are determinately available for no longer than the duration of the executory contract underlying the TLM. Currency MIM, consequently, may facilitate multiple economic exchanges during that period but not beyond it. Third, the conversion of TLM to CM serves no obvious purpose when only two societal components are involved in the chain. The same economic end is achieved in Situation 5-2 with half the exchanges. The purpose of the conversion instead is to increase the negotiability of TLM by providing relatively risk-free MIM that may be easily exchanged with market participants not party to the particular obligations and rights of the executory contract underlying the original TLM. That negotiability facilitates further expansion of the single-link chain of a trade to include exchanges that may contain other trades.

Situation 5-4: An Exchange of Goods-Services between Consuming and Producing Societal Components with Debt and Currency MIM Intervening

Obviously, people both produce and consume. Separating the two actions into distinct societal components, however, provides a means of analyzing the impact of certain monetary policies on each. The separation is not entirely inconsistent with what actually happens in modern economies. Specialization of production among societal components typically ensures that most of the individual consumers of goods and services are not the producers of the particular products they consume.

The following notation and Table 5-4 map a chain of exchanges initiated by a consumer-labor entity (superscript c) accepting debt from a producing entity (superscript p).

$$\text{TLM}^{p} \quad \text{TLM}^{c} \quad \text{ME}^{c} \quad \text{ME}^{p} \quad \text{TLM}^{c} \quad \text{TLM}^{s} \quad \text{CM}^{s} \quad \text{CM}^{c} \qquad (5-4)$$

$$\text{CM}^{c} \quad \text{CM}^{p} \quad \text{ME}^{p} \quad \text{ME}^{c} \quad \text{CM}^{p} \quad \text{CM}^{s} \quad \text{TLM}^{s} \quad \text{TLM}^{p}$$

The chain duplicates the one in Situation 5-3 except that the societal components are designated in a manner that distinguishes consumption-labor entities from production entities and the matter-energy transfers of the chain's first exchange is labor (or other factors of production) to produce a product, and the matter energy of its last exchange is a product.

In this form, the notation clarifies the origin of time-lagged MIM as the willingness of labor to provide its services to produce something in exchange for a promise from a producing entity to pay later. An opposite exchange also can occur if a producing entity has some form of capital and is willing to exchange it for a promise from labor to pay later. Consequently, the initial impetus for production may arise from either labor or capital without any societal action. Society may, however, provide additional impetus by facilitating the exchange of the time-lagged MIM among third parties. That may be accomplished by exchanging its generic currency MIM for the specific time-lagged MIM.

Situation 5-5: Increased Negotiability of Currency MIM
Provides Impetus for Expanded Economic Activity

Notation 5-5 and Table 5-5 map an expansion facilitated by the increased negotiability of currency MIM. The expansion is underlined in Notation 5-5.

$$\text{TLM}^{p1} \quad \text{TLM}^c \quad \text{ME}^c \quad \text{ME}^{p1} \quad \text{TLM}^c \quad \text{TLM}^s \quad \text{CM}^s \quad \text{CM}^c \qquad (5\text{-}5)$$

$$\underline{\text{CM}^c \quad \text{CM}^{p2} \quad \text{ME}^{p2} \quad \text{ME}^c \quad \text{CM}^{p2} \quad \text{CM}^{p1} \quad \text{ME}^{p1} \quad \text{ME}^{p2}}$$

$$\text{CM}^{p1} \quad \text{CM}^s \quad \text{TLM}^s \quad \text{TLM}^{p1}$$

A consumer-labor entity accepts a promissory note from a tool-producing entity P1 for providing the factors of production. It then exchanges the TLM for CM and uses the CM to purchase consumer services from a service producing entity P2. The service-producing entity then purchases the tools from the tool producers, and the tool producer returns the CM to society to retire its promissory note.

Notice that in the circuit only one TLM underlines the currency MIM that facilitate the purchase of both the consumer services and the tools produced in connection with their initiation. A high degree of expansion may occur. The expansion, however, is not unlimited. It is limited by the number of exchanges that can be made during the period of the executory contract underlying the time-lagged MIM accepted by society for the currency MIM. The currency MIM are retrieved by society at the conclusion of that period.

Situation 5-6: A Production and Exchange of Goods-Services
Enticed by Society

Economies are aspects of societies. Economic systems exist to provide more economic satisfaction to components than components could achieve independently. A particular composition of an "economic more" in a society is based on conceptual systems of individual persons and abstracted philosophical, religious, and political systems.

Such monetary injections as those described in situations 5-3, 5-4, and 5-5 are unbiased by any particular component's purpose. They simply pursue the purpose of economies to facilitate economic activity. Such facilitation increases economic activity but is also dependent on societal components to initiate debt. Furthermore, it does not distinguish between industry and commerce.

To further facilitate achieving the "economic more," societies themselves may initiate economic activity by accepting debt from societal components. Different ways of doing that have different initial effects in terms of industry and commerce.

Notation 5-6 and Table 5-6 map a production and exchange process initiated by a society accepting a debt instrument from a producing societal component on the promise to repay the note from the proceeds of the production.

$$TLM^P \quad TLM^s \quad CM^s \quad CM^P \quad CM^P \quad CM^c \quad ME^c \quad ME^P \qquad (5-6)$$

$$CM^c \quad CM^P \quad ME^P \quad ME^c \quad CM^P \quad CM^s \quad TLM^s \quad TLM^P$$

In the first exchange, a producing entity receives currency MIM from society on the transmission of TLM. It uses the currency MIM to purchase factors of production. The currency MIM in the hands of consumer-labor is used to purchase the goods-services produced from the producer who, in turn, remits it to society, retrieving the TLM originated by the producer.

The currency MIM transmissions of Situation 5-3 facilitate the exchange of two existing products but initiate the production of neither. The same action by society (exchanging currency MIM for time-lagged MIM) facilitates in that case only commerce and in this one both production and commerce.

Certain characteristics of the time-lagged MIM accepted by society obviously are important. They can determine the kind of initial effect the introduction of currency MIM has on an economy. Time-lagged MIM connected to industry ensure that the initial effect is production. Connected to commerce, TLM initiate distribution.

In both situations 5-3 and 5-6, only one TLM is introduced. Situation 5-3 leverages the TLM, within the executory contract period, to accomplish twice as much commercial action. Without the CM, both parties to the basic trade would have to accept a debt instrument. The debt accepted by society in Situation 5-6 also doubles the economic clout of the debt money. In this case, however, it initiates both production and distribution of economic products.

Situation 5-7: A Society-Enticed Production and Exchange of Goods-Services and Expanded Economic Activity

The leverage achieved by transmitting the same currency MIM in multiple exchanges may be increased significantly over that obtained in the minimum exchanges required to close the particular circuit illustrated in Situation 5-6. Situation 5-6 may also stimulate third-party activity like that illustrated in Situation 5-5. Situation 5-7 combines the leverage of both situations. Notation 5-7 and Table 5-7 map Situation 5-7.

$$\text{TLM}^{p1} \quad \text{TLM}^{s} \quad \text{CM}^{s} \quad \text{CM}^{p1} \quad \text{CM}^{p1} \quad \text{CM}^{c1} \quad \text{ME}^{c1} \quad \text{ME}^{p1} \tag{5-7}$$

$$\text{CM}^{c1} \quad \text{CM}^{p2} \quad \text{ME}^{p2} \quad \text{ME}^{c1} \quad \text{CM}^{F2} \quad \text{CM}^{c2} \quad \text{ME}^{c2} \quad \text{ME}^{p2}$$

$$\text{CM}^{c2} \quad \text{CM}^{p1} \quad \text{ME}^{p1} \quad \text{ME}^{c2} \quad \text{CM}^{p1} \quad \text{CM}^{s} \quad \text{TLM}^{s} \quad \text{TLM}^{p1}$$

Producer 1 gives a note to society for currency MIM and uses the currency MIM to obtain factors of production. Consumer-Labor 1 receives the currency MIM for supplying the factors and transmits them in exchange for goods-services of Producer 2. Producer 2 uses the currency to obtain factors of production from Consumer-Labor 2 to replenish the goods-services sold to Consumer-Labor 1. Consumer-Labor 2 buys the product of Producer 1 with the currency MIM, and Producer 1 transmits it to society, retrieving its TLM.

In the circuit, one TLM underlies the currency MIM used to produce and distribute two products. A third product, however, must have already existed because the second product replenishes one distributed earlier. That means a second TLM might have been needed to obtain the existing product. It would not have been needed if the product of P2 is a service or good that entity can produce without obtaining independent factors of productions.

Expansions of determinate processes beyond a minimum circuit are not unlimited, but neither are they easily controlled from the society level. How much a circuit expands and what pattern an expansion takes are determined by decisions of societal components. The most direct societal control is influence over the initial effect of introducing currency MIM. That control is exercised by choosing industry-connected TLM, commerce-connected TLM, or both.

DISCRETIONARY CURRENCY MIM

A prominent characteristic of debt-based currency MIM is their introduction to an economy for a discrete period. Their retrieval is predictable. They initiate determinate processes only. The period is established by executory contract. The supply of money is a process (existing over time), not a store. Debt-money normally is not put into an economy and left there in perpetuity.

A way exists, nevertheless, for currency MIM to be disconnected from the time-lagged MIM that, in turn, are connected to the executory contract separating the transfers of a trade. A societal component may default on an executory contract to repay borrowed currency MIM. Such defaults are tantamount to paying off the loan because the executory contract is no longer in force. No currency MIM are retrieved by society from the economy when defaults occur, however. Those currency MIM remain to be used as their holders choose. Currency MIM disconnected from executory contracts initiating them are termed *discretionary currency MIM*. Those disconnected by default on promissory notes held by society itself are termed *global discretionary currency MIM*, and those disconnected by defaults of notes held by various societal components are termed *local discretionary currency MIM*.

Situation 5-8: The Effect of Defaults on Time-Lagged MIM Held by Society

The effect of defaults may be described by using Situation 5-6 as an example and assuming that the producing entity fails to repay society. Notation 5-8 and Table 5-8 map Situation 5-8.

$$TLM^P \quad TLM^s \quad CM^s \quad CM^P \quad CM^P \quad CM^c \quad ME^c \quad ME^P \qquad (5-8)$$

$$CM^c \quad CM^P \quad ME^P \quad ME^c/RSD/TLM^P \quad TLM^s \quad CM^s \quad CM^P$$

where the term /RSD/ means residual transaction(s) follows.

Although the chain of exchanges does not violate the quadratic constraint, the circuit is incomplete. An exchange that could close the circuit is not made before the economic activity stops. The exchange process did not complete itself, and it never will. As the discussion develops, various reasons for defaults will become obvious. Here the focus is on how global discretionary currency MIM are introduced.

The CM^P CM^S TLM^S TLM^P exchange of Notation 5-6 does not occur. The transmission TLM^S TLM^P occurs de facto by default of the executory contract underlying the TLM^P TLM^S transmission. The CM^P CM^S transmission never occurs, leaving the currency MIM in the economy.

Those currency MIM remain in the economy indefinitely, disconnected from any particular activity. They are purposeless. Their power to stimulate additional production depends entirely on how the societal components holding them use them thereafter.

If they are used to buy existing goods, the discretionary currency MIM drive up prices of those goods and, thereby, may loose their power to stimulate further production. A monetary information overload occurs, and the original production information borne on the currency MIM is not necessarily communicated in a recursion of the activity. The monetary amount borne on the discretionary information markers is absorbed into the total amount available for the commerce of existing goods-services, and prices rise.

Held and not exchanged, the currency MIM not retrieved by society are dormant. Their powers to stimulate production, however, may be revived. They may be used in productive processes that maintain the level of production originated by their injection into an economy, or they may later drive up prices. The economy is unaffected by the default only if the abandoned currency MIM become dormant immediately on default of the time-lagged MIM and are never revived. The discretionary currency MIM are wild cards. The use of the loose currency MIM is unpredictable.

The chain of Situation 5-8 assumes that goods-services are produced and distributed and that the producing entity only fails to transmit the currency MIM to society. What causes the failure? Such defaults may be precipitated by customers not buying the goods produced. In that case, the transmission of currency MIM to the producer is limited. The producer thus does not have currency MIM to repay society, and the discretionary currency MIM are in the hands of consumer-labor entities. Those discretionary currency MIM are local until the producer-debtor actually defaults on its note to society.

Therefore, in a strictly debt-based economy, global discretionary currency MIM are produced only on default of a promissory note accepted by a currency MIM–issuing society. Many defaults on loans among societal components may occur without affecting the level of currency MIM in an economy. Only those that cause a societal component to default a loan from society, however, may produce a global increase in the level of currency MIM in an economy.

If the initiation of currency MIM is not in every case connected to specific executory contracts underlying time-lagged MIM, obviously other sources of global discretionary currency MIM may exist. Currency MIM printed in connection with government welfare or military programs, counterfeit currency MIM, and currency MIM connected to specific new discoveries of commodities such as gold, among other sources, may exist for global discretionary currency MIM in mixed monetary economies. On the other hand, private debt transmitted between societal components without contracting with society for currency MIM cannot create global discretionary currency MIM. It nevertheless may provide a ready basis for currency MIM because such debt may be transferred to society for currency MIM.

HOW SHOULD CURRENCY MIM BE INTRODUCED INTO ECONOMIC PROCESSES?

How should currency MIM be used to achieve economic goals? Currency MIM likely would not have emerged if they were not needed in economic processes of the magnitude of modern ones. Currency MIM are here to stay. Consequently, how they are introduced is important.

Debt-money can exist without societies issuing currency MIM as in Situation 5-2. In fact, most modern money is not currency MIM. If trust is established between various producing and consuming entities, patterns of time-lagged MIM that connect dynamic processes in recurring cycles may be established.

Such patterns theoretically may clear each cycle recursively. Empirically, however, uncertain and changing preferences for economic goods-services among entities party to each cycle make it unlikely that every cycle will be completely cleared. Any failure to fulfill an executory contract in a cycle affects some or all parties in the cycle. Thus, defaults in strictly debt-based economies work directly against a mutual trust that undergirds the entire system.

Currency MIM may be introduced at critical points in various cycles to mitigate the effects of defaults on the general trust. Society assumes the risk of default on the time-lagged MIM it accepts in exchange for its generic currency MIM. Currency MIM, consequently, eliminate the risk of specific defaults to societal components.

The introduction of currency MIM, however, is not entirely positive. When societal components default on society-held time-lagged MIM, currency MIM remain in the economy as discussed in the previous section. That process spreads the costs of defaults in some pattern over the prices of goods-services in following production and distribution cycles. It socializes the costs. Many entities bear a little cost, and the default affects their trust a little. Many defaults, obviously, affect their trust more. And some level may be reached at which the cumulative effects of defaults undermine the corporate trust of the system.

How currency MIM may be introduced to most effectively enhance the trust required for more complex economic activity than simple trades is a difficult question. Some guidance, nevertheless, may be obtained by analyzing the global effects of different introductions.

How currency MIM may be used to initiate production and distribution by making them available to producing entities is examined in Situation 5-6. Far more production is initiated by transmissions of time-lagged MIM between societal components than in the manner of Situation 5-6. Over time, producing entities establish a relatively stable relationship with other entities that supply various factors of production and produce certain goods-services within some relatively narrow range of demand. The demand for a particular producing entity's goods-services in a particular cycle, nevertheless, is uncertain in complex economies. In fact, that is typically the major uncertainty confronting producers. Might currency MIM be used to mitigate that uncertainty as well as to initiate production?

In Situation 5-8, failure of demand is passed on to society by defaulting the promissory note that initiated production. The default socializes the cost of the failure. Might the default be avoided?

Situation 5-9: Societal Consumer Loans

Perhaps currency MIM should be made available to increase demand for products directly. Society might make consumer loans, for example. Notation 5-9 and Table 5-9 map a situation in which society initiates demand by accepting time-lagged MIM used by consumers to purchase goods. The goods are already produced by private or societal initiative. The distribution process, however, has faltered, and society wants to take action that will move it along.

$$\text{TLM}^c \quad \text{TLM}^s \quad \text{CM}^s \quad \text{CM}^c \quad \text{CM}^c \quad \text{CM}^p \quad \text{ME}^p \quad \text{ME}^c \qquad\qquad (5\text{-}9)$$

$$\text{CM}^p \quad \text{CM}^c \quad \text{ME}^c \quad \text{ME}^p \quad \text{CM}^c \quad \text{CM}^s \quad \text{TLM}^s \quad \text{TLM}^c$$

Consumer-labor entities receive currency MIM from society to purchase exist-ing goods-services. Producing entities hire consumer-labor entities to produce more products, and consumer-labor entities pay off the time-lagged MIM with the currency MIM received. The action taken accomplishes the goal of stimulat-ing the distribution of existing goods-services. The circuit is complete. The producing entities have not been forced into defaults. The consumer-labor en-tities have been enticed to earn wages by producing more goods-services to repay the consumer loan. On the surface, that seems to take care of the problem.

That action, however, has not actually corrected the entire situation. What is overlooked on such a superficial examination is the fact that two loans are made to accomplish two productions but only one distribution of goods-services. After this successful circuit, the economy is left where it was before society's action was taken. In fact, it may be somewhat worse off as discussed below.

A more complete solution to the problem depends on recognizing how uncer-tain demand occurs in a strictly debt-based economy. If all production were connected to specific time-lagged MIM, all consumption were connected to time-lagged MIM, and all consumption-based time-lagged MIM, in turn, were connected specifically to all production-based time-lagged MIM, the thus-related debt would clear with every circuit of production. Particular participants may suffer fewer goods-services than expected if a particular production process is less successful than expected, but the demand for the process' goods-services always exists. It exists by specific executory contract.

Disconnecting transmissions of time-lagged MIM from transfers of specific-matter energy (i.e., making time-lagged MIM negotiable) permits some pro-ducers to sell their products for more than the price stipulated by executory contracts initiating them. Some customers simply may give some producers more time-lagged MIM for their goods-services than the cost of production. If that happens, all producers may not be able to sell all produced goods-services because money-information markers are not available to purchase them.

The problem of lack of demand for some goods-services apparently arises out of the negotiability characteristic of modern time-lagged MIM. The introduction of currency MIM increases the negotiability of money-information markers. The pattern of currency MIM use typically disconnects the consumer and producer functions almost entirely. That action gives specific consumers the power to change the value of any goods-service from its time-lagged MIM contractual value. In fact, the action ordinarily hides the contractual information from con-sumers. They have little chance of assigning the contractual value.

Society's provision for more currency MIM through consumer loan action, which on the surface seems to be a nice, clean solution to the problem, actually may exacerbate it. The increased negotiability of increased currency MIM further increases the availability to consumers-laborers of products other than the ones they produce, increasing the chance that they will use more of the available money to obtain only part of the production.

Situation 5-9 obscures the fact that twice the amount of currency MIM has been supplied to accomplish the production and distribution expected from Situation 5-6 because it assumes additional production before the consumer currency MIM arising out of the initial production loan is returned to society. If society is unwilling to extend the repayment period on prior production loans to allow time to produce additional goods-services, producers must use the currency MIM received from consumer loans to repay production loans and avoid default on society loans. In that case, no additional goods-services may be produced, and the source of currency MIM for consumer-labor entities to repay their loans is in question. That problem is considered in Situation 5-10.

Situation 5-10: Societal Consumer Loans with No Extension of Production Loans

Assume that producers are required to use the currency MIM received in exchange for their existing goods-services to repay the societal loan initiating the production. Notation 5-10 and Table 5-10 map this situation. Subscripts c and p are consumer and production promissory notes, respectively.

$$\text{TLM}^c_{\ c} \ \text{TLM}^s_{\ c} \ \text{CM}^s \ \text{CM}^c \ \text{CM}^c \ \text{CM}^p \ \text{ME}^p \ \text{ME}^c \hspace{3cm} (5\text{-}10)$$

$$\text{CM}^p \ \text{CM}^s \ \text{TLM}^s_{\ p} \ \text{TLM}^p_{\ p}$$

The currency MIM provided by society in accepting consumer time-lagged MIM are used to retire the original production time-lagged MIM. Where is the currency MIM that should have retrieved the original money-information markers (assuming Situation 5-6)? It is left in the economy as discretionary currency MIM. The action of society in providing currency MIM by accepting consumer debt has doubled the amount of currency MIM associated with one production-distribution cycle. More currency MIM are available. Prices rise generally.

Another interesting thing has happened, however. Although the chain of exchanges in Situation 5-10 is quadratically complete (no transaction exists disconnected from a reciprocating transaction of an exchange) and the circuit at quick glance appears to be closed, the chain of exchanges does not close on itself. Notation 5-10, therefore, is incorrect to the extent that it is incomplete. Although a TLM has been retrieved from society, the TLM that initiated the chain is outstanding. A residual term is needed to complete the notation. Furthermore, the TLM retrieved from society initiated another chain, not this one. A solution to that problem is considered in Situation 5-11.

Situation 5-11: A Societal Production-Distribution Incomplete Chain Connected to a Distribution Chain

Actually, two different but related chains of exchanges have been connected in Situation 5-10. They are (1) the initial but incomplete production-distribution chain and (2) the consumer loan distribution chain. Notation 5-11 and Table 5-11 map Situation 5-11. The term $/y$, $y = 1,2,3 \ldots$ n is used to indicate segments of different interrelated chains. The term $/CON/^{x,y}$, $x = 1,2,3 \ldots$ n and $y = 1,2,3 \ldots$ n, is used to designate exchanges that actually connect two or more chains. The subscripts more explicitly distinguish elements of circuits 1 and 2. In later chapters, subscripts are used to introduce cardinal numbers for quantitative analyses.

$$/^{1}TLM^{P}_{1} \quad TLM^{s}_{1} \quad CM^{s}_{1} \quad CM^{P}_{1} \quad CM^{P}_{1} \quad CM^{c1}_{1} \quad ME^{c1}_{1} \quad ME^{P}_{1} \qquad (5\text{-}11)$$

$$/^{2}TLM^{c2}_{2} \quad TLM^{s}_{2} \quad CM^{s}_{2} \quad CM^{c2}_{2} \quad CM^{c2}_{2} \quad CM^{P}_{2} \quad ME^{P}_{1} \quad ME^{c2}_{1}$$

$$/CON/^{2,1} \; CM^{P}_{2} \; CM^{s}_{2} \; TLM^{s}_{1} \; TLM^{P}_{1} \; /RSD/^{2} \; TLM^{c2}_{2} \; TLM^{s}_{2}, \; CM^{s}_{1} \; CM^{c1}_{1}$$

An incomplete circuit similar to Situation 5-8 has been completed by the connecting exchange. A residual term remains, nevertheless. In the process, the obligation to society has been transferred from producing entities to consuming ones.

That transfer of obligation is important. Producers have no incentive to produce more goods-services when they are holding products they cannot sell. By distributing the goods-services, producers are given incentive to obtain another production loan and try again. On the other hand, consumer-labor entities now have obligations to repay loans. They are thereby coerced to seek ways of obtaining currency MIM. Currency MIM may be obtained by providing factors of production, enabling more production.

Two potentially deterministic process circuits have been connected to produce two dynamic process cycles. Deterministic *processes* are circuits that close on themselves, both introducing and retrieving currency MIM. *Dynamic processes* are made by closing circuits (retrieving currency MIM) as a result of time-lagged MIM from a later circuit, forming processes of connected cycles.

The dynamic process of Situation 5-11 apparently provides specific dynamics for continuing economic activity. Both producing entities and consuming entities are motivated to engage in additional activity. That seems like a win-win situation.

Situation 5-11, nevertheless, is less than an ideal solution. A problem arises in the connecting exchange. That exchange is the signal that initiates the next round of recursive activity. The signal likely is too strong. It doubles the amount of currency MIM used to clear the first cycle. The cycles of such dynamic processes are *overly connected*.

If assurance could be given that numerous cycles described by Notation 5-11 would in fact recursively occur, mitigation of the problem of overly connected cycles would be expected. In that case, the amount of currency MIM of one consumer loan cycle would perpetually remain in the economy. The relative size of the signal to the size of the activity generated would not change.

It is important to recognize that the dynamic process of Situation 5-11 is supported by perpetual debt to society of both consumers and producers. If additional goods-services are to be produced, a producing entity must obtain another production loan. The debt transferred to consumers by connecting deterministic circuits in dynamic cycles is not used to produce more goods. It is used to retire the old production debt. By assuming that no further imbalances such as those caused by consumers paying more for a product than its time-lagged MIM contractual price, the currency MIM earned by consumer-labor entities of a following cycle must be used to retire the consumer loan of a previous cycle, and a new loan must be obtained to purchase the goods-services produced in the following cycle.

So on a perpetual pattern, two loans are required to produce and sell one cycle of goods-services. That makes available more currency MIM than seems to be the case in Situation 5-9. Situation 5-9 erroneously assumes that an extension of the terms of a loan may be treated as though no additional loan is required. The TLM given to society for currency MIM consist of executory contracts. Debt executory contracts are in force over definite periods. An extension of time is tantamount to a new contract.

Recurring patterns, such as those in Situation 5-11, perpetuate a constant level of loans outstanding over time. Situation 5-11 perpetuates a level just double the amount perpetuated by society in making production loans only (Situation 5-6).

A society indiscriminately making both production and consumer loans may be expected to introduce perpetually an amount ranging from that used to initiate its production to just double that amount. Extensive use of consumer loans by society to stimulate distribution moves the required currency MIM toward the 200 percent of production time-lagged MIM level.

At whatever level societies choose to monetize their economies, the processes theoretically can be orderly. Each cycle of recursive dynamic processes can clear, providing full distribution of societies' production.

The introduction of first negotiability of time-lagged MIM and then currency MIM, however, provides a mechanism for inconsistency. No unsold merchandise produced by MIM incentive could have existed if society had not introduced negotiability of debt instruments in the first place. The mutually obligated parties to production TLM would have suffered any failed expectations. Each party's production would have been what the other party received. That is not necessarily the case when negotiable instruments intervene.

As the level of currency MIM moves toward the 200 percent of production time-lagged MIM level, potential inconsistencies increase. The movement provides more and more currency MIM for the kinds of cost-price imbalances that make consumer loans necessary in the first place. That phenomenon combines with consumer loans needed for trading goods and services not requiring production. A consequence of both trades from not requiring production (e.g., secondhand goods) and accelerating inconsistencies between production and consumption is that the amount of currency MIM required to sustain an economy does not necessarily fall between 100 percent and 200 percent of total identifiable production.

Specific dynamics that bring about recurring cycles of economic processes seem to be important ingredients of successful economies. The amount of currency MIM required to sustain them, however, may expand rapidly. Such expansion increasingly destroys the corporate trust as the ratio of total MIM to total goods-services increases. Therefore, the size of a currency MIM signal involved in any connecting exchange should be the smallest that can produce the needed effect.

In essence, a major part of consumer credit provided by societies finances errors made by producers and consumers attempting to balance production and consumption. Those errors are directly related to the negotiability characteristic of time-lagged MIM. Disconnecting individual executory contracts from specific products obscures contractual price information in individual buying decisions. Introducing currency MIM even further obstructs communication of the underlying contractual value of goods-services being purchased. Each society must decide how much error it is willing to finance. Unfortunately, the choices are limited. One hundred percent would likely bring down the economy in hyperinflation. Too little may provide disincentives for further production.

The consumer loan question has another dimension. What is the effect on currency MIM of consumer loans extended by producing entities to sell their products?

Situation 5-12: Producer-Extended Consumer Loans

A producer may attempt to entice demand for its products by offering to accept credit from consumers through open accounts or notes receivable. Notation 5-12 and Table 5-12 map a chain of exchanges for such actions.

$$/^1 \; \text{TLM}^P_1 \; \text{TLM}^s_1 \; \text{CM}^s_1 \; \text{CM}^P_1 \; \text{CM}^P_1 \; \text{CM}^{c1}_1 \; \text{ME}^{c1}_1 \; \text{ME}^P_1 \qquad\qquad (5\text{-}12)$$

$$/\text{CON}/^{2,1} \; \text{TLM}^{c2}_2 \; \text{TLM}^P_2 \; \text{ME}^P_1 \; \text{ME}^{c2}_1$$

$$/\text{RSD}/ \; \text{TLM}^P_1 \; \text{TLM}^s_1, \; \text{TLM}^{c2}_2 \; \text{TLM}^P_2, \; \text{CM}^P_1 \; \text{CM}^{c1}_1$$

Society accepts a promissory note from a producer for currency MIM. The producer gives the currency MIM to a consumer-labor entity for supplying factors of production. For some reason, the producer cannot sell the product and offers credit terms. A second consumer-labor entity delivers a promissory note in exchange for the product. The producer has cleared the inventory but is left with an obligation to society and a promise of a future receipt of currency MIM from a consumer.

The residuals may be directly resolved by society's accepting the consumer promissory note in payment of the producer note. The consumer note is outstanding, but the producer is free to embark on another cycle of production. The societal obligation is transferred to the consumer, providing coercion to earn additional MIM, and selling inventory provides incentive for continued production. Discretionary currency MIM, however, are left in the hands of a consumer-labor entity.

The discretionary currency MIM problem would usually be solved by purchasing another producer's goods-services. Notation 5-13 and Table 5-13 consider that action.

Situation 5-13: Clearing Discretionary Currency MIM with Additional Production

The residual currency MIM term of Notation 5-12 might be cleared by the following chain:

$$/° \ TLM^{po}{}_0 \ TLM^s{}_0 \ CM^s{}_0 \ CM^{po}{}_0 \ CM^{po}{}_0 \ CM^{co}{}_0 \ ME^{co}{}_0 \ ME^{po}{}_0 \qquad (5\text{-}13)$$

$$/CON/^{1,0} \ CM^{c1}{}_1 \ CM^{po}{}_1 \ ME^{po}{}_0 \ ME^{c1}{}_0$$

$$/CON/^{3,1} \ TLM^{p1}{}_3 \ TLM^{po}{}_3 \ CM^{po}{}_1 \ CM^{p1}{}_1$$

$$CM^{p1}{}_1 \ CM^s{}_1 \ TLM^s{}_1 \ TLM^{p1}{}_1 \ /RSD/ \ TLM^{p1}{}_3 \ TLM^{po}{}_3, \ TLM^{po}{}_0 \ TLM^s{}_0,$$

$$CM^{po}{}_0 \ CM^{co}{}_0$$

Another producer (P0) entices the currency MIM from C1 with product in Circuit 0. P_0 lends the currency MIM to P1, and P1 settles its obligation to society. No discretionary currency is left in the economy from Circuit 1. Circuit 1 is closed. P0, however, is unable to repay its production loan from society, and global discretionary currency MIM from that loan remain in the economy. Additional iterations of economic activity do not change the basic situation. Society is holding additional debt to finance consumer debt. The consumer debt, however, has been connected to distribution. That connection may entice additional production.

The chain of Notation 5-13 assumes that P0 is willing to give up its currency MIM for a promissory note from P1. Why should it? An additional dynamic is needed to make that happen. The dynamic needed is interest (discussed in Chapter 6), and that dynamic gives rise to additional economic processes. Notation 5-14 and Table 5-14 consider another chain for resolving the residuals of Notation 5-12. Both chains 5-13 and 5-14 depend on a dynamic beyond the basic trade dynamic of preference for a mixture of different goods and services.

Situation 5-14: Clearing Discretionary Currency MIM with Debt Transmissions among Consumers

A consumer may entice discretionary currency MIM from another consumer. Notation 5-14 and Table 5-14 map such a situation.

$$/CON/^{3,1} \ TLM^{c2}{}_3 \ TLM^{c1}{}_3 \ CM^{c1}{}_1 \ CM^{c2}{}_1 \qquad (5\text{-}14)$$

$$/CON/^{1,2} \ CM^{c2}{}_1 \ CM^p{}_1 \ TLM^p{}_2 \ TLM^{c2}{}_2$$

$$/^1 \ CM^p{}_1 \ CM^s{}_1 \ TLM^s{}_1 \ TLM^p{}_1 \ /RSD/ \ TLM^{c2}{}_3 \ TLM^{c1}{}_3$$

C2 entices currency MIM from C1 with a promissory note and uses the currency MIM to retrieve its promissory note from P. P in turn pays off its promissory note to society. Circuit 1 is complete, and no global discretionary currency remains in the economy. The only residual is a loan between consumers. Production is free to petition society for another production loan based on past success. Society's interventions henceforth are characterized by unconnected but recurring circuits on a process of recurring cycles connected by private debt among consumers.

Each of the three resolutions of discretionary currency provides a different dynamic process. The direct resolution of 5-12 requires society to perpetuate consumer debt and the resulting currency MIM. The resolution of Situation 5-13 requires society to perpetuate producer debt and the resulting currency MIM. Situation 5-14's resolution does not require society to hold debt perpetually. It does require consumers to do so. Debt among consumers, however, does not perpetuate a global discretionary currency MIM.

Apparently, the level of monetization of an economy and, consequently, the risks associated with global discretionary currency MIM may be lessened by encouraging Situation 5-14. Additional dynamics and corresponding additional economic processes, however, are required. Additional processes are discussed in the next section, and additional dynamics are considered in the next chapter. Even this solution is not without pitfalls. As more detailed analyses are developed, it will become apparent that debt obligations of societal components among themselves form distinctive patterns that increasingly transmit more money-information markers from some groups of components than from others. Those patterns may bring about imbalances that work against the corporate trust.

Certain special societal components and money-information markers are likely needed to transmit the information required to bring about productive exchanges of local discretionary currency MIM such as in Notation 5-14. The next section discusses such special societal components.

CURRENCY MIM WITH INTERMEDIARY SOCIETAL COMPONENTS

In most modern economies, currency MIM are not transmitted directly to producing and consuming societal components. Other types of societal components such as governments and banks act as intermediaries.

Those intermediaries function as information transmitters. The information they transmit on money-information markers increases the efficiency of purging the economy of local discretionary currency MIM by enticing or coercing its transmission in exchange for time-lagged MIM connected to production and distribution.

Situation 5-15: Society-Enticed Production and Distribution with an Intervening Societal Component

Notation 5-15 and Table 5-15 map a chain of exchanges that involves an intermediary societal component. Intervening societal components are indicated by the superscript sc. Two interrelated but not connected levels of exchanges are needed. Two interrelated chains map those levels. Each chain begins and ends with a TLM—one transmitted to and retrieved from society by an intermediary and the other transmitted to and retrieved from an intermediary component by a producing component.

$$/^1 \text{ TLM}^{sc}_1 \text{ TLM}^s_1 \text{ CM}^s_1 \text{ CM}^{sc}_1 /\text{CON}/^{2,1} \text{ TLM}^P_2 \text{ TLM}^{sc}_2 \text{ CM}^{sc}_1 \text{ CM}^P_1 \qquad (5\text{-}15)$$

$$\text{CM}^P_1 \text{ CM}^c_1 \text{ ME}^c_2 \text{ ME}^P_2 \text{ CM}^c_1 \text{ CM}^P_1 \text{ ME}^P_2 \text{ ME}^c_2$$

$$\text{CM}^P_1 \text{ CM}^{sc}_1 \text{ TLM}^{sc}_2 \text{ TLM}^P_2 /^1 \text{ CM}^{sc}_1 \text{ CM}^s_1 \text{ TLM}^s_1 \text{ TLM}^{sc}_1$$

Governments and banks are not societies. They are organizations within societies. Thus, a basic analysis of intermediary societal components applies equally to both. Governments and banks differ, however, in the basic dynamic they have traditionally used to affect economic activity. Governments have used the coercion of taxes, and banks have used the enticement of interest. Those differences are discussed in Chapter 6.

The broken line dividing the Intermediary Societal Component of Table 5-15 is important. It represents an information disconnect that may occur within intermediary societal components. Because two different time-lagged MIM are initiated in the interrelated chains, the one transmitted to society may not bear information about the economic activity in which the reciprocating currency MIM will be used. That information disconnect may obstruct societies' knowledge and thus control of the underlying time-lagged MIM. As a consequence, societies may not distinguish between production-connected markers and those used for consumption.

The idea of building pluralistic societies is popular. A *pluralistic society* is one that organizes its economy and its political system so that they are relatively independent of each other. Pluralistic societies depend heavily on minimal connection between banking subsystems and governmental subsystems.

Based on the degree of interrelationship between their banks and governments, different societies organize the process of introducing currency MIM differently. It is unlikely that an ideal process has been achieved yet. Attempts to pluralize societies may exacerbate the information disconnect problem introduced by intermediary societal components. Information disconnects specifically constructed to achieve pluralism may further obscure any information about which time-lagged MIM are based on production.

Banking and governmental subsystems of societies likely cannot be completely disconnected as monetary and real economies cannot be disconnected entirely. The idea of disconnecting governmental and banking subsystems does not mean necessarily that banking systems should be free enterprises, only responding to market conditions for survival. Societies need banking subsystems that can influence global as well as local expansions and contractions in their economies.

Global expansions and contractions concern the entire states of economies and are brought about by currency MIM that originate outside the economy itself. Societies consequently need certain banking functions that are not subject to the ebb and flow of economic processes. Originators of currency MIM should be exogenous to economies but part of a society.

A reminder of the precise definition of the word *state* is appropriate. The *state* of a concrete system includes both its structure and its process. *Structure* is the arrangement of a system's components and subsystems at an instant. *Process* is all action over time. Structure and process integrated together fully define the *state* of concrete living systems.

Global expansions and contractions of states are different from those of processes. By including both process and structure, analyses of processes that simply assume that currency MIM mystically come from somewhere are eliminated. The quadratic construction of debt-based economies requires introducing all currency MIM into an economy from without. Those currency MIM are a societal certification (socialization of the default risk) of private, nongeneric time-lagged MIM accomplished by exchanging the nongeneric for generic currency MIM. Perceived societies that do not have banking functions that originate currency MIM that are exogenous to their economies likely are not free-standing societies.

In such cases, the perceived societies' economies are actually inclusions of components of other societies' laterally dispersed economies or inclusions of components of a supranational system's downwardly dispersed economy. Because economic activity is fundamental to the existence of societies, economic decider components are critical. A perceived society controlled by another society's economic decider components likely is actually a component of that other society.

A banking subsystem that is subject to the ebb and flow of "the market" is likely a component of the system that is characterized by that ebb and flow. The subsystem is a competing element in that economy. It is not an economy-controlling element.

The need for societies to control their economies notwithstanding, societal and commercial banking need not be mutually exclusive. Several echelons may be allowed in processes of distributing currency MIM to producing and consuming components of societies. Societies may disperse downwardly certain currency MIM distribution functions, allowing commercial enterprise banks to prosper or fail on their judgments of whether certain proposed production or commercial activities will be treated favorably by other components of an economy. A society also may disperse laterally to other societies certain aspects of its currency MIM distribution function. If that happens, the society performing the distribution within its own boundaries furthers the purposes of the dispersing society communicated by the information carried on the currency MIM. A dispersion may be both downward and lateral as in the case of multinational commercial banks.

Whatever means of distribution is chosen, societies ordinarily should introduce and retrieve currency MIM in a manner that their initial effect is production, not consumption. In certain specific situations, initiation of commerce may be appropriate. In the final analysis, however, new currency MIM must initiate new production or prices may rise. The relationship between time-lagged MIM connected to production and currency MIM is important for maintaining relatively stable prices. Unstable prices undermine the corporate trust that makes the currency MIM system work.

When intermediary societal components are used to distribute currency MIM, the information disconnect indicated by the broken line in Table 5-15 is of paramount importance. Societies simply cannot control the global expansion and contraction of production in their economies without information about whether the time-lagged MIM accepted by intermediary societal components are connected to production or consumption. Information about whether the executory contract underlying the debt accepted by intermediary societal components exacts production, commerce, neither, or both should be transmitted to societies. Nothing in the basic dynamics of economic exchange compels such secondary transmissions. Legal impetus therefore must be provided through regulation.

Notwithstanding that caveat, commercializing some banking processes may provide additional facilitation of economic activity. Currency MIM provide relatively risk-free money to replace relatively risk-laden time-lagged MIM. A particular organization or person receiving currency MIM is not required to transmit them if subsistence is not imperiled. In fact, an economic participant may choose to save rather than consume. Commercializing certain banking processes introduces organizations that aggressively seek out savings, enticing its recirculation and the corresponding additional economic activity. The other side of recirculation of savings is seeking out commercial and productive opportunities.

Situation 5-16 is a typical purging action accomplished by banking intermediaries. The action does not introduce new currency MIM. Rather, it recirculates existing global and local discretionary currency MIM.

Situation 5-16: A Typical Purging Action of Commercial Banking

Notation 5-16 and Table 5-16 map this situation.

$$/^1 \ TLM^B_1 \ TLM^C_1 \ CM^C_1 \ CM^B_1 \tag{5-16}$$

$$/CON/^{2,1} \ TLM^P_2 \ TLM^B_2 \ CM^B_1 \ CM^P_1 \ CM^P_1 \ CM^C_1 \ ME^C_1 \ ME^P_1$$

$$CM^C_1 \ CM^P_1 \ ME^P_1 \ ME^C_1 \ CM^P_1 \ CM^B_1 \ TLM^B_2 \ TLM^P_2$$

$$/^1 \ CM^B_1 \ CM^C_1 \ TLM^C_1 \ TLM^B_1$$

The bank exchanges a promise-to-pay document (TLM) for currency MIM that are not being circulated (savings). The bank lends the currency MIM to a producer that uses them to purchase factors of production from consumer-labor entities. The consumer-labor entities use the currency MIM to purchase the product. The producer pays off the promissory note to the bank, and the bank, in turn, pays off its note to the consumer-labor entities that hold the original savings.

A similar purging action could be shown for a governmental intermediary. That action, however, is better presented in the context of an expanded analysis.

SUMMARY

Chapter 5 examines basic economic processes of modern economies. The discussions are normative to the extent that they assume strictly debt-money–based economies and do not incorporate dynamics beyond the basic trade dynamic, such as interest. The dynamic that causes trade is the preference of economic participants for multiple, different goods-services. The constraint that consummates trades is equilibrium of perceived economic value between parties to a trade.

An exchange is the basic link of complex chains of economic processes. A trade is a one-link chain—the most condensed and simplest economic process. A more complex chain is introduced by splitting a trade into transfers. The fundamental trade splitters in debt-based economies are time-lagged MIM. All separations of transfers are temporal and may be spatial as well. The complex chains that result from splitting trades are composed of links of exchanges consisting of reciprocating transactions that may be transfers of matter-energy or transmissions of money-information markers. Each transaction, in turn, is composed of two accounts. Every exchange, consequently, contains four accounts. Such accounts and transactions cannot occur independently of exchanges because no dynamic to motivate them exists.

Including all four accounts of every exchange in an economic model is termed *the quadratic constraint.* The constraint should control modern economic studies of exchange economies because the exchange is the most primitive explanatory variable of such economies. Examining elements that compose an exchange independently (without reference to their relation to other elements in the exchange) ignores the fundamental dynamic of exchange economies.

No society or supranational system is necessary to originate debt-money. Money originates in the trust of a recipient in money-information markers, and its original form is time-lagged MIM. Currency MIM originate in societies' direct or indirect certification that time-lagged MIM have some specific value. That certification removes the risk of default from certain specific transmissions and socializes their costs.

Intermediary societal components such as governments and banks are introduced to show that societies may disperse downwardly certain currency MIM distribution functions. Such intermediaries require fundamental dynamics in addition to the trade dynamic. Consequently, the major discussion concerning them is in Chapter 6.

Determinate processes are composed of chains of exchanges that close on themselves, forming complete circuits. Those circuits introduce money-information markers in the first link and retrieve them in the last link. Such processes provide money for a specific set of activities and remove it on completion of those activities.

In strictly debt-based economies, money-information markers may be disconnected from specific activities if time-lagged MIM are negotiable. Currency MIM further disconnect them. If time-lagged MIM given to societies in exchange for currency MIM are defaulted, global discretionary currency MIM are left in economies. That action defeats the closed circuit of determinate processes and fails to retrieve money-information markers on completion of prescribed activities.

Pending defaults may be avoided by initiating a second circuit and connecting the second one to retrieve the time-lagged MIM of the first. Such connected processes are dynamic processes composed of recurring cycles. Debt obligation is a fundamental dynamic working in many such processes in addition to the trade dynamic.

Both determinate and dynamic processes introduce currency MIM into economies over definite periods. To provide indefinitely a particular level of economic activity initiated by currency MIM introduction, some rate of continuous currency MIM introduction is consequently necessary. Dynamic processes ordinarily require a relatively higher rate than determinate processes.

Introducing currency MIM at higher rates though societal loans to consumers may provide signals that are too strong. The resulting monetary information overload may cause hyper-inflation. Therefore, societies possibly should not finance consumer loans directly as a general policy.

Controlling consumer and production loans requires information about the executory contracts underlying time-lagged MIM transmitted to societies. When intermediary societal components such as governments and banks are in place, an information disconnect that obscures such information is generally introduced. Legal impetus through regulatory agency is likely required to provide the secondary information transmissions of executory contract content.

Modern economies typically disperse downwardly certain aspects of currency MIM distribution to intermediary societal components. The receipt of interest commonly functions as an additional fundamental exchange-causing dynamic in those subsystems. The coercive dynamic of taxation may also function. Those dynamics, as well as rent and profit, are considered in Chapter 6.

In the analyses in the following chapters, the matrix notations are not provided. The symbolic notation is space conserving and, ordinarily, is more easily analyzed into subprocesses. The matrix notation, however, provides some benefits that should be emphasized before leaving it. Residuals are obvious in the matrix notation because every inflow or outflow does not have a corresponding outflow or inflow if residuals exist. Determinate processes are signaled by an inflow of time-lagged MIM corresponding to the initiating outflow. And, reflexively, dynamic processes are signaled by no inflow of time-lagged MIM corresponding to an initial outflow.

REFERENCES

Swanson, G. A. and Miller, James Grier. *Measurement and Interpretation in Accounting—A Living Systems Theory Approach.* New York: Quorum Books, 1989.

Table 5-1
Situation 5-1: A Basic Trade

		Products-Services, Matter-Energy	
Social Components	1	4	1
	2	2	3

Table 5-2
Situation 5-2: A Trade with Debt Intervening

		Time-Lagged MIM		Matter-Energy Products-Service	
Societal Components	1	8	1	4	5
	2	2	7	6	3

Table 5-3
Situation 5-3: An Exchange with Debt and Currency Intervening

		Time-Lagged MIM		Matter-Energy		Currency MIM	
Society		6	15			14	7
Societal Components	1	16	1	4	11	10	13
	2	2	5	12	3	8	9

Table 5-4
Situation 5-4: An Exchange of Goods-Services between Consuming and Producing Societal Components with Debt and Currency MIM Intervening

		Time-lagged MIM		Matter-Energy Products-Services		Currency MIM	
Society		6	15			14	7
Societal Components	Producing	16	1	4	11	10	13
	Consuming	2	5	12	3	8	9

Table 5-5
Situation 5-5: Increased Negotiability of Currency MIM Provides Impetus for Expanded Economic Activity

		Time-lagged MIM		Matter-Energy Products-Services		Currency MIM	
Society		6	19			18	7
Societal Components	Producing 1	20	1	4	15	14	17
	Producing 2			16	11	10	13
	Consuming	2	5	12	3	8	9

Table 5-6
Situation 5-6: A Production and Exchange of Goods-Services Enticed by Society

		Time-lagged MIM		Matter-Energy Products-Services		Currency MIM	
Society		2	15			4	3
Societal Components	Producing	16	1	8	11	4 / 10	5 / 13
	Consuming			12	7	6	9

Table 5-7
Situation 5-7: Society-Enticed Production and Exchange with Expanded Economic Activity

		Time-lagged MIM		Matter-Energy		Currency MIM	
Society		2	23			22	3
Societal	Producing 1	24	1	8	19	4 / 18	5 / 21
	Producing 2			16	11	10	13
Components	Consuming 1			12	7	6	9
	Consuming 2			20	15	14	17

Table 5-8
Situation 5-8: The Effect of Defaults on Time-Lagged MIM Held by Society

		Time-lagged MIM	Matter-Energy		Currency MIM	
Society		2				3
Societal Components	Producing	1	8	11	10 / 4	5
	Consuming		12	7	6	9

Table 5-9
Situation 5-9: Societal Consumer Loans

		Time-lagged MIM		Matter-Energy		Currency MIM	
Society		2	15			14	3
Societal	Producing			12	7	6	9
Components	Consuming	16	1	8	11	4 10	5 13

Table 5-10
Situation 5-10: Societal Consumer Loans with No Extension of Production Loans

		Time-lagged MIM		Matter-Energy	Currency MIM	
Society		2	11		10	3
Societal	Producing	12		7	6	9
Components	Consuming		1	8	4	5

Table 5-11
Situation 5-11: Societal Production-Distribution Incomplete Chain Connected to a Distribution Chain

		Time-lagged MIM		Goods-Services Matter-Energy		Currency MIM	
Society		2 10	19			18 1	3 11
Societal	Producing	20	1	8	15	14 4	17 5
Components	Consuming 1				7	6	
	Consuming 2		9	16		12	13

Table 5-12
Situation 5-12: Producer-Extended Consumer Loans

		Time-lagged MIM		Goods-Services Matter-Energy		Currency MIM	
Society		2				3	
Societal	Producing	1	10	8	11	4	5
Components	Consuming 1			7		6	
	Consuming 2		9		12		

NOTE: Broken lines indicate second time-lagged MIM.

Table 5-13

Situation 5-13: Clearing Discretionary Currency MIM with Additional Production

		Time-lagged MIM			Goods-Services Matter-Energy			Currency		MIM	
Society		2		23				3		22	
Societal	Producing 1	1	10	24 17	8		11	4 5		20	21
Components	Consuming 1				7	16		6	13		
	Consuming 2		9			12					
	Producing 2			18			15		14		19

NOTE: Broken lines indicate additional time-lagged MIM.

Table 5-14

Situation 5-14: Clearing Discretionary Currency MIM with Transmissions among Consumers

		Time-lagged MIM			Goods-Services Matter-Energy			Currency MIM		
Society		2		23				3	22	
Societal	Producing	1	10	24 19	8		11	4 5	18	21
Components	Consuming 1			14	7			6		15
	Consuming 2		9	20 13		12			16	17

NOTE: Broken lines indicate additional time-lagged MIM.

Table 5-15

Situation 5-15: Society-Enticed Production and Distribution with an Intervening Societal Component

		Time-lagged MIM		Matter-Energy Products-Services		Currency MIM	
Society		2	23			22	3
Intermediary		24	1			4	21
Societal Component		6	19			18	7
Societal	Producing	20	5	12	15	14 8	17 9
Components	Consuming			16	11	10	13

NOTE: The broken line indicates the two levels of transmissions made by intermediary societal components.

Table 5-16
Situation 5-16: A Typical Purging Action of Commercial Banking

	Time-lagged MIM	Goods-Services Matter-Energy	Currency MIM
Bank	24 1 6 19		4 7 18 21
Consumer-Labor	2 23	16 11	10 3 22 13
Production	20 5	12 15	8 9 14 17

6

Dynamics of Interest, Taxes, Rent, Royalties, Dividends, and Profit

Chapter 5 examines some basic relationships in modern debt-based economies. Those examinations are limited, for the most part, to situations in which preferences for multiple, different goods-services may compose a necessary and sufficient dynamic to drive economic activity. Chapter 6 examines introductions of the additional dynamics interest, taxes, rent, royalties, dividends, and profit.

Those dynamics are additions to fundamental market economies. Their influences can compound or mitigate the influences of the basic trade dynamic discussed in Chapter 5.

Before embarking on a discussion of each additive dynamic in turn, a further clarification of debt-based economies is useful. Debt originates among societal components in such economies. Currency MIM emerge from the negotiability attribute of time-lagged MIM. Negotiability is facilitated by society's providing legal recourse for defaults on executory contracts documented by the time-lagged MIM. Debt-based currency MIM, consequently, are an emergent of societal economic and legal processes. Those processes culminate in society's certification of the economic value of the generic debt documents termed *currency*. The generic documents socialize the risk of default.

The characteristics of such currency MIM processes are quite different from those of currency MIM introduced by societies according to goals of centralized society-level decider subsystems. Goal-oriented subsystems set prices by distributing money-information markers in certain amounts to produce and distribute a certain amount of specific goods-services to particular societal components.

Debt-based currency MIM emerge from what is commonly described as "arm's-length market transactions." That phrase refers to exchanges between relatively independent entities, each vieing for its best self-interest. The exchanges occur between societal components and are characterized by different prices for similar goods-services, depending on the preferences of different components in different exchanges.

Debt-based economies emerge as higher-order systems, being formed from basic processes that are reducible to exchanges. Various relatively independent decider subsystems compete for control of the higher-order systems. That characterizes the higher-order systems as ecosystems. Unlike natural ecosystems, however, they are constructed by humans and may be brought under the control of a particular societal component decider subsystem (such as that of an organization). As such control becomes more absolute, the ecosystem characteristic increasingly diminishes and an organization-level system emerges. In effect, a free enterprise market ecosystem collapses into an organization with a multi-echelon decider subsystem. The grand challenge of early twenty-first century economics is to learn how to organize debt-based economies within societies in a manner that prevents the collapse of societies into organizations.

ECONOMIC PROCESSES WITH INTEREST IMPOSED BY SOCIETIES

Basic economic processes without interest are discussed in Chapter 5. That chapter demonstrates that dynamic as well as determinate processes may be set in motion without using interest as a basic motivator. Interest is not an absolute requirement for extensive economic activity. Nevertheless, it may be required to increase economic activity beyond a certain degree.

The word *interest* is defined as an incremental transmission of money-information markers for the prior transmission of other money-information markers. Time-lagged MIM commonly stipulate, in one manner or another, the amount of interest that they require. When people borrow money from banks, exchanging promissory notes for currency MIM to be used over a prescribed period, they engage in an obvious reciprocating exchange of money-information markers. When they obtain goods-services on credit, the reciprocating exchange of time-lagged MIM for currency MIM is not so obvious. In that case, they may seem to pay interest for the use of goods-services. They do not. They pay interest on the currency MIM that the seller would have received in a cash sale. In essence, the seller made a sale and loaned the proceeds to the customer. The connected exchanges do not require the intervening currency MIM and collapse into a single exchange. The interest is charged on the time-lagged MIM (the Account Receivable of the seller and the Account Payable of the buyer).

This section analyzes processes involving interest. It examines the effects of interest on those processes. It turns out that processes involving interest are mostly dynamic. Determinate processes may be introduced as well, however. Interest charged by societies for using their generic currency MIM is first discussed, followed by interest charged by intermediary components.

Situation 6-1: A Production and Exchange of Goods-Services Enticed by Society by Holding Debt and Charging Interest

This is the same as Situation 5-6 except society charges interest. A society accepts a debt-instrument from a producing societal component on the promise to repay the note from the proceeds of the production. Notation 6-1 maps Situation 6-1. Subscripts p and i indicate the monetary values of principal and interest, respectively. The minus signs indicate outflows, and no signs indicate inflows.

$$\text{TLM}^P_{-pi}\ \text{TLM}^s_{pi}\ \text{CM}^s_{-pi}\ \text{CM}^P_{pi}\ \text{CM}^P_{-p}\ \text{CM}^c_{p}\ \text{ME}^c_{-p}\ \text{ME}^P_{p} \qquad (6\text{-}1)$$

$$\text{CM}^c_{-p}\ \text{CM}^P_{p}\ \text{ME}^P_{-p}\ \text{ME}^c_{p}\ \text{CM}^P_{-pi}\ \text{CM}^s_{pi}\ \text{TLM}^s_{-pi}\ \text{TLM}^P_{pi}$$

Although it seems strange for societies to loan and retrieve currency MIM for interest, that must happen for determinate processes (closed circuits) of production and consumption not to be deflated by the interest charge. Producing societal components cannot produce and sell the total value of CM if they must pay some portion of them to society at the conclusion of a circuit. A society therefore must supply addition CM to cover interest charges if full production promised by an executory contract underlying TLM is to be realized. The additional CM need not be supplied at the beginning of the chain, however.

Situation 6-2: Currency MIM Provided with Interest Charged at End of Executory Contract Period

Notation 6-2 maps this situation. The map consists of two related but unconnected chains of exchanges.

$$/^1\ \text{TLM}^P_{-p}\ \text{TLM}^s_{p}\ \text{CM}^s_{-p}\ \text{CM}^P_{p}\ \text{CM}^P_{-p}\ \text{CM}^c_{p}\ \text{ME}^c_{-p}\ \text{ME}^P_{p} \qquad (6\text{-}2)$$

$$\text{CM}^c_{-p}\ \text{CM}^P_{p}\ \text{ME}^P_{-p}\ \text{ME}^c_{p}\ \text{CM}^P_{-p}\ \text{CM}^s_{p}\ \text{TLM}^s_{-p}\ \text{TLM}^P_{p}$$

$$/^2\ \text{TLM}^P_{-i}\ \text{TLM}^s_{i}\ \text{CM}^s_{-i}\ \text{CM}^P_{i}\ \text{CM}^P_{-i}\ \text{CM}^s_{i}\ \text{TLM}^s_{-i}\ \text{TLM}^P_{i}$$

If Situation 6-1 is strange, Situation 6-2 is even stranger. Situation 6-1 at least provides a producing societal component with the benefit of using the CM_i in the market while the underlying executory contract is in effect. An introduction at the end of a production-distribution chain provides nothing except additional accounting costs. The end-of-chain juxtaposition of the interest chain of exchanges may be introduced, however, in a manner that provides societies a means of changing determinate processes into dynamic ones.

Situation 6-3: Currency MIM Provided for Interest as Part of New Production and Distribution Borrowing

$$\text{TLM}^P_{-pi}\ \text{TLM}^s_{pi}\ \text{CM}^s_{-p}\ \text{CM}^P_{p}\ \text{CM}^P_{-p}\ \text{CM}^c_{p}\ \text{ME}^c_{-p}\ \text{ME}^P_{p} \qquad (6\text{-}3)$$

$$\text{CM}^c_{-p}\ \text{CM}^P_{p}\ \text{ME}^P_{-p}\ \text{ME}^c_{p}\ \text{CM}^P_{-p}\ \text{CM}^s_{p}\ \text{TLM}^s_{-p}\ \text{TLM}^P_{p}$$

$$\text{/RSD/}\ \text{TLM}^P_{-i}\ \text{TLM}^s_{i}$$

In this situation, the initial TLM include an obligation to pay interest to society. Society, however, remits only CM in the principal amount, not the interest. At the expected ending of the chain, the producing component transmits CM in the amount of the principal to society, and society continues to hold its right to the amount of interest.

Another way to write Notation 6-3 is the following:

$$/^1 \; TLM^P_{-p} \; TLM^s_p \; CM^s_{-p} \; CM^P_p \; /^2 \; TLM^P_{-i} \; TLM^s_i \qquad\qquad (6\text{-}4)$$

$$/^1 \; CM^P_{-p} \; CM^c_p \; ME^c_{-p} \; ME^P_p \; CM^c_{-p} \; CM^P_p \; ME^P_{-p} \; ME^c_p$$

$$CM^P_{-p} \; CM^s_p \; TLM^s_{-p} \; TLM^P_p \; /RSD/^2 \; TLM^P_{-i} \; TLM^s_i$$

In this form, that the quadratic constraint has been violated is immediately obvious. No exchange has occurred in Process 2. A producing entity must anticipate some incremental economic value from its production to obligate itself for a future return of more CM than it might expect to receive in a fair exchange.

The ability of societies to charge interest on their currency MIM likely is connected to the profit dynamic to be discussed subsequently. Some activity might arise by trickery or coercion. That activity is unlikely to be as extensive as that of modern economies, however. Currency MIM, being disconnected from specific production executory contracts, make it possible for one producer to sell its goods-services for more than its TLM that initiated those goods-services, as discussed in Chapter 5. Recognizing that much about profits, incremental value from production might be expected by individual producers. Nevertheless, some force other than the trade dynamic likely must exist for such fragmentation of exchange to occur.

The process chains of notations 6-3 and 6-4 are not fully closed. An interest obligation remains with the producing entity. If no incremental value is received in the production-distribution process, the entity must obtain another loan from society for the interest due at the conclusion of the circuit. Society may introduce a dynamic for continuing production-distribution by requiring that the second interest loan be connected to a second production loan. In that manner, a second round of production would be initiated by the second money-information marker transmissions.

Situation 6-5: An Interest Charge Fragmented Exchange Connected to a Following Production-Distribution Cycle

Chain 2 of Notation 6-4 is a fragment of Chain 2 of Notation 6-2. The transmissions required to complete the chain are $CM^s_{-i} \; CM^P_i \; CM^P_{-i} \; CM^s_i \; TLM^s_{-i} \; TLM^P_i$. Notation 6-5 combines the chains of Notation 6-4 with a following production-distribution chain.

$$/^1 \; TLM^P_{-p} \; TLM^s_p \; CM^s_{-p} \; CM^P_p \; /^2 \; TLM^P_{-i} \; TLM^s_i \qquad\qquad (6\text{-}5)$$

$$/^1 \; CM^P_{-p} \; CM^c_p \; ME^c_{-p} \; ME^P_p \; CM^c_{-p} \; CM^P_p \; ME^P_{-p} \; ME^c_p$$

CM^P_{-p} CM^s_p TLM^s_{-p} TLM^P_p $/^3$ TLM^P_{-p} TLM^s_p CM^s_{-p} CM^P_p

$/CON/^{3.2}$ CM^P_{-i} CM^s_i TLM^s_{-i} TLM^P_i $/^3$ CM^P_{-p-i} CM^c_{p-i} ME^c_{-p-i} ME^P_{p-i}

CM^c_{-p-i} CM^P_{p-i} ME^P_{-p-i} ME^c_{p-i} CM^P_{-p-i} CM^s_{p-i} TLM^s_{-p-i} TLM^P_{p-i}

$/RSD/^3$ TLM^P_{-i} TLM^s_i

Chains of Notation 6-5 may repeat indefinitely, forming a dynamic process of recurring cycles. The producing entities must in every cycle obtain other production loans from society to obtain the currency MIM to pay the interest on the loan that financed the previous cycle.

A dynamic for continuing production is thus built into the economic processes initiated by society. To accomplish that dynamic, society has split a money-information marker exchange. That action is similar to splitting a trade. The two actions differ, however, in a very important way. Society's action violates the quadratic constraint. That action is arbitrary with reference to the basic dynamics of exchange processes. It imposes exogenous forces on the economy. That is to say, society has introduced a fragment of an exchange (an economic ion) rather than splitting an existing exchange. The quadratic economic process attempts to supply the missing fragment. To do so, the process completes the necessary exchanges to incorporate the fragment only to leave residual money-information markers for which a similar action must be taken.

The introduced dynamic both assists and impedes the basic purpose of economies to provide more economic satisfaction. It furthers that purpose by coercing repeated production. It obstructs the same purpose by shrinking the currency MIM available for production in recurring production cycles.

For example, an entity produces DM 100,000 (DM = German Marks) of consumer goods, borrowing currency MIM at 10 percent interest per cycle from society to pay for the factors of production. At the end of the first cycle, the entity owes DM 110,000. If society loans in the second cycle only the amount borrowed in the first cycle, the entity can produce only DM 90,000. The entity must remit DM 10,000 immediately to society for payment of interest on the first cycle. The shrinkage stabilizes in the second cycle, however. The entity thereafter can continue recursively borrowing DM 100,000 and producing DM 90,000 indefinitely. Society must hold debt continuously in both the amounts of the continuing production and the interest (DM 100,000), however (Figure 6-1).

An interesting phenomenon occurs if society attempts to maintain the production level at full demonstrated demand (the DM 100,000 in the example) while charging interest. Assume that an entity borrows under the conditions of the previous example. In the second round, however, it borrows DM 110,000 so that it can continue to supply the demonstrated demand. It immediately remits the DM 10,000 interest to society and pays DM 100,000 to consumer-labor entities for the factors of production, duplicating the performance of the first cycle. At the beginning of the third cycle, the entity must borrow DM 111,000 to maintain the DM 100,000 production level. Interest due is now DM 11,000 (DM 110,000

– 10 percent). Progressively, more currency MIM are needed to maintain a particular production level across recursive cycles (Figure 6-2).

That progression follows an ordinary compound interest formula (Equation 6-1).

$$RCMIM_j = P(1+r)^j, j = 1,2,3,\ldots n \qquad \text{(E6-1)}$$

where

$RCMIM_j$ = the monetary amount of currency MIM required to pay the note on the jth cycle,

   P = monetary amount borrowed on initial production cycle,

   r = the interest rate per cycle, and

   j = the cycle ordered on integers from 1 to n.

The interest required by a particular cycle (I_j) is calculated as

$$I_j = RCMIM_j - P \qquad \text{(E6-2)}$$

At 10 percent interest, the total amount of interest charged by society in about eight cycles equals the amount of production it maintains each cycle. Society must supply the currency MIM continually to cover both the constant amount of production and the increasing amount of interest if production is to be maintained at that level.

The obligation of the producing entity to pay interest must be real for coercion to be achieved. A disincentive for production grows as the obligation to society on a constant amount of production progressively increases.

The patterns of dynamic processes differ significantly in the two approaches. The pattern of shrinking production stabilizes very quickly in the first example, and the dynamic for coercing production continues indefinitely. It stabilizes at the incremental production level minus the interest charged. In the second example, production is stable at 100 percent of incremental production from the beginning. The progressive pattern of a producing entity's increasing interest obligation, however, calls into question the number of cycles over which society may support the stability of that production.

The difference in the two patterns arises from the different ways in which producing entities choose to cover the society-imposed interest charges. A one-time cut in production accomplishes that in the first case. In the other case, interest is borrowed, heaping interest on interest.

The increasing progression of the second case might be avoided by society's not charging interest on interest. In effect, simple interest might be charged and discharged by one increment of borrowing, introducing the pattern of Figure 6-3. The interest would still connect two cycles, forming a dynamic process. Interest-free borrowing to cover interest charges would be allowed only in conjunction with a commensurate production borrowing. The forces that permit arbitrarily introducing an economic ion into an exchange economy likely permit the regulation of interest charges. Society could then maintain production at demonstrated demand without causing an unstable pattern.

The closed circuits of determinate processes limit the currency MIM introduced into economies by connecting their duration to definite periods of executory contracts underlying production-distribution time-lagged MIM in these situations. Charging interest on all societal credit nevertheless may circumvent that limitation by introducing an increasingly larger dynamic in recurring cycles. The effect shown in Figure 6-2 does that.

Unlimited introduction of currency MIM might cause hyper-inflation very quickly. Such monetary information overload can destroy an economy. Consequently, limiting currency MIM introduction in a systematic fashion is important.

Economies grow by maintaining previous levels of production and adding more levels. Recurring circuits of successful production-distribution, therefore, should be encouraged for economies to achieve their fundamental purpose of supplying more economic satisfaction than is possible without them. Introducing dynamic processes connecting circuits into recurring cycles is one means of maintaining previously achieved levels of production.

Using interest to connect otherwise independent production-distribution circuits has a distinct advantage over using consumer loans to avoid defaults on production loans for undistributed goods-services (discussed in Chapter 5). The advantage is that the signal connecting circuits into recurring cycles is less intense. Successive chains may be connected using relatively small nonclosures of residual transmissions of interest time-lagged MIM.

The money-information markers of such nonclosures bear signals that are manageable. The amplitude of those signals is small with reference to the amplitude of the money-information marker signals that control economic exchanges themselves. Furthermore, the signals should be communicated only between a society and its producing components. That way, the signals are both quantitative and spatial reductions of the greater information controlling an economy.

Interest imposed by society for using its currency MIM over some period seems to be an ideal way to build a dynamic for continuing production into a system. The act of imposing interest in itself, however, does not activate successful dynamic processes. The vital ingredient of such processes is society's act of continuously holding debt equal to the interest imposed.

If society itself does not hold such debt outside the economy, the dynamic processes activated are degenerative in terms of production and consumption over some determinable number of cycles. The residual transmission of Notation 6-4 perpetually keeps each circuit of a series of recursive cycles open. It also perpetuates the interest debt held by society. Society may either hold that debt perpetually, or it may extract payment from producing components, consumer-labor components, or both. If it extracts payment, the result is obvious. More currency MIM are taken out of the economy than were injected with each cycle.

The amount of currency MIM available to continue a production and distribution recursive process spirals downwardly on the pattern described in Equation 6-3.

$$\text{ACMIM}_j = P \left(\frac{1}{1 + r} \right)^j, \; j = 1, 2, 3, \ldots n \qquad \text{(E6-3)}$$

where

ACMIM_j = available currency MIM in jth period and the other terms are as defined in Equation 6-1.

Clearly, societies cannot charge interest for using their currency MIM without reducing the amount of currency MIM in their economies, other things held constant. Consequently, a society that charges interest on the use of its currency MIM introduces a certain downward pressure on production and distribution. Figure 6-4 illustrates that process.

Situation 6-6: Debt Initiated between Societal Components with Society by Exchanging Debt for Currency MIM and Charging Interest

The deflationary process caused by society by charging interest for the use of currency MIM occurs with every introduction and retrieval of currency MIM. That is the case even if the initial debt is not originated between producing components and societies.

For example, Situation 5-4 subjected to such interest is transformed to Situation 6-6, which is mapped in Notation 6-6. This situation involves a consumer-labor entity's accepting debt from a producing entity to initiate a cycle.

$$/^1 \; \text{TLM}^P_{-p} \; \text{TLM}^c_p \; \text{ME}^c_{-p} \; \text{ME}^P_p \; \text{TLM}^c_{-p} \; \text{TLM}^s_p \; \text{CM}^s_{-p} \; \text{CM}^c_p \qquad (6\text{-}6)$$

$$/^2 \; \text{TLM}^c_{-i} \; \text{TLM}^s_i \; /^1 \; \text{CM}^c_{-p} \; \text{CM}^P_p \; \text{ME}^P_{-p} \; \text{ME}^c_p$$

$$\text{CM}^P_{-p} \; \text{CM}^s_p \; \text{TLM}^s_{-p} \; \text{TLM}^P_p \; /\text{RSD}/^2 \; \text{TLM}^c_{-i} \; \text{TLM}^s_i$$

Without society's introducing currency MIM to cover interest charges, the residual transmission may be satisfied only by reducing the amount of currency MIM available for purchasing the production of a current or following cycle. So regardless of the origin of the time-lagged MIM underlying currency MIM, interest imposed by society is deflationary.

Both avoidance of defaults on societal production credit through societal consumer credit and interest imposed by societies may initiate dynamic processes. The two methods may cause several different conditions, however.

ECONOMIC PROCESSES WITH INTEREST IMPOSED BY SOCIETAL COMPONENTS

Dynamic processes that include societal interest charges such as those described in Situations 6-3 and 6-4 may be dispersed downwardly from a society to some of its components such as governments and commercial banks. Situation 6-7 is an example of such dispersion.

Situation 6-7: A Component of an Economy Imposes Interest for Using Currency MIM That It Has Obtained from Other Economy Components

Notation 6-7 maps the connected chains of a cycle of this situation. The intermediary society component is designated by the superscript sc.

$$/^1 \ TLM^{sc}_{-p} \ TLM^c_{p} \ CM^c_{-p} \ CM^{sc}_{p} \ /^2 \ TLM^P_{-p} \ TLM^{sc}_{p} \ CM^{sc}_{-p} \ CM^P_{p} \qquad (6\text{-}7)$$

$$/^3 \ TLM^P_{-i} \ TLM^{sc}_{i} \ /^2 \ CM^P_{-p} \ CM^c_{p} \ ME^c_{-p} \ ME^P_{p} \ CM^c_{-p} \ CM^P_{p} \ ME^P_{-p} \ ME^c_{p}$$

$$CM^P_{-p} \ CM^{sc}_{p} \ TLM^{sc}_{-p} \ TLM^P_{p} \ /^1 \ CM^{sc}_{-p} \ CM^c_{p} \ TLM^c_{-p} \ TLM^{sc}_{p}$$

$$/RSD/^3 \ TLM^P_{-i} \ TLM^{sc}_{i}$$

Clearly, no currency MIM are introduced by society in Notation 6-7. Discretionary currency MIM must already exist in the economy. The downward dispersion of the dynamic process neither introduces nor retrieves currency MIM from an economy as a whole.

The related chains of exchanges have used only dormant (stored) currency MIM, reactivating them into process. That action can stimulate local growth. It cannot provide additional MIM for the expansion of the state of the entire economy. The state, defined in Chapter 3, is expanded only if the average turnover of currency MIM across similar process chains is accelerated beyond the turnover caused by the original injection of the currency MIM. The word *turnover* refers specifically to expansions of process chains beyond the minimum exchanges needed to close a circuit in determinate processes and to connect a cycle to the next one in dynamic processes.

Consequently, the downward dispersion of dynamic processing described in Situation 6-7 does not include a mechanism for expanding the amount of currency MIM available globally. It might expand processes over some limited period by exciting increased turnover, however.

Alternatively, it may accelerate a downward spiral of production and distribution caused by society's charging interest without introducing an equal amount of currency MIM. Any interest charged a producing entity by a societal component may aggregate with societal interest to increase the downward spiral.

The downward spiral is likely intensified further by a needed motivation for consumer-labor entities to transmit CM to intermediary societal components. What dynamic would cause consumer-laborer entities to give up the discretionary currency MIM they hold?

The dynamic cannot be negotiably based on less risk because that is the prime progenitor of the generic debt embodied in the currency MIM they hold. Currency MIM are the ultimate hedge against the risk of default on specific time-lagged MIM. Any time-lagged MIM received from the societal component are based on an executory contract promising to return the amount of currency MIM involved. In essence, the contract promises to make available the currency MIM at a certain future date. The same end may be achieved by a consumer-laborer entity holding the currency MIM without subjecting itself to the default risk of the specific TLM.

A dynamic that moves currency MIM from the societal component to a producing entity is in place in Situation 6-7. It is interest paid for using the currency MIM. A dynamic must also work to move currency MIM from consumer-labor entities to intermediary societal components. That dynamic may be the coercion of taxation or the enticement of interest.

The coercion of taxation to reactivate dormant currency MIM causes no downward spiral of production and distribution so long as the tax is spent in turn for production and distribution. No additional CM are used to cause the transmission. The enticement of interest, however, introduces a tripartite effect on a producer composed of the following: (1) interest charged by society, (2) interest charged by the intermediary societal component, and (3) interest charged by (in this case) the consumer-labor entity. These factors compound each other. Although interest charged by the intermediary societal component is typically thought of as a unified increment above principal, the second factor refers to the incremental interest above that paid to the consumer-labor entity in obtaining the currency MIM.

Situation 6-8: An Intermediary Component Imposing and Paying Interest

Situation 6-7 is unrealistic to the extent that consumer-labor entities receive no interest to entice them to give up currency MIM. Situation 6-8, described in Notation 6-8, corrects that deficiency. Subscripts 1 and 2 are appended to subscript i to indicate different amounts of interest.

$$/^1 \text{ TLM}^{sc}_{-p} \text{ TLM}^c_p \text{ CM}^c_{-p} \text{ CM}^{sc}_p /^2 \text{ TLM}^{sc}_{-i1} \text{ TLM}^c_{i1} \tag{6-8}$$

$$/^3 \text{ TLM}^P_{-p} \text{ TLM}^{sc}_p \text{ CM}^{sc}_{-p} \text{ CM}^P_p /^4 \text{ TLM}^P_{-i2} \text{ TLM}^{sc}_{i2}$$

$$/^3 \text{ CM}^P_{-p} \text{ CM}^c_p \text{ ME}^c_{-p} \text{ ME}^P_p \text{ CM}^c_{-p} \text{ CM}^P_p \text{ ME}^P_{-p} \text{ ME}^c_p$$

$$\text{CM}^P_{-p} \text{ CM}^{sc}_p \text{ TLM}^{sc}_{-p} \text{ TLM}^P_p /^1 \text{ CM}^{sc}_{-p} \text{ CM}^c_p \text{ TLM}^c_{-p} \text{ TLM}^{sc}_p$$

$$/\text{RSD}/^2 \text{ TLM}^{sc}_{-i1} \text{ TLM}^c_{i1} /\text{RSD}/^4 \text{ TLM}^P_{-i2} \text{ TLM}^{sc}_{i2}$$

The residual transmissions TLM^{sc}_{-i1} TLM^{c}_{i1} and TLM^{p}_{-i2} TLM^{sc}_{i2} may be connected to a second cycle forming interrelated dynamic processes. In fact, they must be connected, or the process collapses. Over the following recursions, the absolute amount paid to holders of discretionary currency MIM (the source of CM_p) in each recursion grows progressively larger even though the interest rate is held constant. The progression follows the formula of Equation 6-1.

The production-distribution downward spiral caused by the two types of interest payment required to move discretionary currency MIM within an economy progresses over recurring production distribution cycles according to Equation 6-4.

$$\text{ACMIM}_j = P \left(\frac{1}{1 - (r1 + r2)} \right)^j , j = 1, 2, 3 \ldots n \qquad \text{(E6-4)}$$

where

r1 and r2 = the interest rates applied to obtain i1 and i2, respectively, and other terms are as previously defined.

This downward spiral compounds that caused by interest imposed by society itself.

Secondary effects may mitigate to some extent the downward spiral caused by interest. Consumer-labor entities and intermediary societal components holding discretionary currency MIM, and increasing them with each cycle, may decide to purchase more production. That action would provide currency MIM for production and distribution. Nevertheless, secondary effects can never mitigate more downward spiral effects than those caused by the interest charged by various societal components. They can never counter the downward spiral caused by a society itself removing from an economy more currency MIM than it injects.

Apparently, an increasing amount of currency MIM dedicated to interest transactions may be required to obtain a constant amount of principal for production over multiple recursions. An additional increasing amount may be needed for societal-component interest transactions. As previously discussed, production may be maintained at the level of subscript p of Notation 6-5 by exempting from further interest any amount borrowed by a producing entity for paying the interest due on a previous production-distribution cycle. No dynamic exists, however, to cause such exemptions among societal components. Therefore, even if societies minimize the interest spiral caused by them, some amount of increasing currency MIM likely is needed to maintain a particular production level.

The use of local or global discretionary currency MIM to initiate production through turnover is limited. Without the introduction of currency MIM from outside an economy, the continuation of a production level eventually depends on enticing currency MIM away from buying products and services produced in a previous cycle. That action reduces the currency MIM available to purchase the previous cycle's production, causing two complications: (1) the product must be sold for less than the amount of currency MIM provided to produce it or inventory accumulates and (2) the producing entity does not receive enough currency MIM to repay the loan initiating its production. Together, falling prices or excess inventories and production loan terminations from defaults may cause an increasingly rapid reduction in the level of production.

In sum, societies likely should provide some level of continuing currency MIM introduction dedicated to the interest dynamic. The level depends on how the dynamic is used by both societies themselves and their components.

ECONOMIC PROCESSES WITH RENT, DIVIDENDS, AND ROYALTIES

In the previous section, effects of the interest dynamic on economic processes were examined. Other dynamics are commonly accepted by societies as legitimate economic motivators. Transactions of the economic values of those dynamics are ordinarily transmissions of currency MIM. Occasionally, they are transmissions of time-lagged MIM and transfers of matter-energy (goods-services). *Wages* are contractual obligations for human services. Wages are virtually universally accepted. For that reason, they are included in the basic economic objects' goods-services. *Rents* are contractual obligations for temporary use of natural resources and matter-energy capital. Rents are almost as universally accepted as wages. *Dividends* are contractual obligations for permanent use of time-lagged MIM that document ownership rights provided by the executory contracts underlying them. Dividends are not always recognized as part of goods-services.

At least one more dynamic has emerged in modern economies. It motivates technological advancement. Contractual obligations for the temporary use of legal instruments that document rights to use technological advancements provided by the executory contracts underlying them are termed *royalties*. This meaning may be more precise than the word's ordinary usage, but not much. An existing body of law underlies a system of license and royalty transmissions that is ordinarily a part of modern economies. Money-information markers are transmitted in exchange for transmissions of information markers such as licenses, patents, and copyrights. Those actions document the economic value of technological advances and demonstrate that royalties compose an additional basic dynamic in modern economies.

Macro effects of each of those dynamics (including wages) are similar. Currency MIM introduced to initiate a production-distribution cycle should be sufficient to cover any dynamics involved in the economic processes. Consumer-labor entities will not have enough currency MIM to purchase the production at cost if all dynamics are not covered.

Wages, rent, dividends, and royalties all must be monetized just as interest must be monetized, or they will introduce a downward spiral in production-distribution. All should be monetized at the micro level to cover the specific prices of successful products—and generally are.

Royalties present a current problem, however. Accounting within organizations for royalties is jumbled—fragmented among research and development, patents, copyrights, and so on. Accounting for the other three (and interest) is quite clear. Royalties are not generally fully monetized because of the ambiguous accounting.

Situation 6-9: Currency MIM–Initiated Production-Distribution When Currency MIM Is Insufficient to Cover Dividends

This situation demonstrates that an accepted dynamic must be covered by the amount of currency MIM introduced for a circuit to close. Multiple dynamics simultaneously existing have a similar but multiple effect.

Situation 6-9 is mapped by Notation 6-9. Subscript p is principal as in previous notation. Interest is ignored. Subscript d is dividends, and the superscripts are as defined previously.

$$/^1 \ TLM^P_{-p} \ TLM^s_p \ CM^s_{-p} \ CM^P_p \ CM^P_{-p} \ CM^{c1}_p \ ME^{c1}_{-p} \ ME^P_p \qquad (6\text{--}9)$$

$$CM^{c1}_{-p} \ CM^P_p \ ME^P_{-p} \ ME^{c1}_p \ /^2 \ CM^P_{-d} \ CM^{c2}_d$$

$$/^1 \ CM^P_{-p-d} \ CM^s_{p-d} \ TLM^s_{-p-d} \ TLM^P_{p-d} \ /RSD/^1 \ TLM^P_{-d} \ TLM^s_d$$

A producing entity borrows from society, producing and selling its product. It pays dividends to its share holders, however, and is unable to repay the credit from society in the amount of the dividend. Paying the dividend introduces an economic ion that becomes a residual. Paying the residual, at least, reduces production and distribution in the next cycle. Whether the reduction spirals depends on the pattern of dividend distribution. A regular pattern produces a downward spiral. A one-time distribution stabilizes at a lower production level in the next cycle. The possible patterns are similar to those discussed in the interest section.

A similar example may be given for the dynamics rent and royalties. Societies should include all legitimatized basic dynamics in the amount of currency MIM introduced to initiate production-distribution.

In essence, societies should introduce 100 percent of the selling price of goods-services being produced and distributed. That statement is made in the context of economic elements introduced thus far, and those elements do not include the ordinary notion of profit.

ECONOMIC PROCESSES WITH PROFIT

The common meaning of the word *profit* is ambiguous. Profit actually is an unexplained incremental value emerging in economic exchange processes.

Over time, more and more parts of the unexplained increment have been explained. Today, the meaning of the word *profit* ordinarily excludes wages, rents, dividends, interest, and royalties. Each explained economic value is accepted by modern societies as a useful basic dynamic that contributes to producing more economic satisfaction for societal components.

Given those exclusions, the word *profit* may be defined as residual unexplained incremental economic value. It may be positive or negative. Local and global profit may be usefully distinguished. *Local profit* is profit at a societal component level. *Global profit* is an incremental global value that is the algebraic sum of all local profits in a society's economy.

As defined, *profit* is any contractual obligation for money-information markers and goods-services except wages, rents, dividends, interest, royalties, and intrinsic value of goods. Local profits may be distributed as local dividends or may be used to increase the money-information marker flows exchanged for particular amounts of matter-energy forms (increasing prices) or to obtain more matter-energy forms at a particular price.

Global dividends and profits ordinarily are not intentionally monetized in modern economies that are guided by popular economic thought. Global wages and rents emerged historically because a quantity of money-information markers dedicated to them was included in the time-lagged MIM documenting fundamental exchanges. Similarly, a quantity of money-information markers dedicated to dividends, interest, royalties, and profit must be introduced for global expressions of those dynamics to occur. Popular economic theory states that dividends are distributions of profits and that global profit should be zero.

In purely debt-based economies, all money-information markers originate as debt. All debt arises from executory contracts in effect over definite periods and are documented by time-lagged MIM. Any transmissions of money-information markers under executory contracts of indefinite duration must be supported by recurring introductions of determinate debt MIM or by defaults on the executory contracts underlying them. Without the introduction of currency MIM, however, defaults cannot perpetuate MIM.

Defaults on all debt contracts in non-currency MIM economies impose penalties on specific creditors. In currency MIM economies, the penalties on society-held defaulted debt contracts are imposed in varying degrees on all economic components. Defaults on society-held time-lagged MIM leave global discretionary currency MIM in economies over indefinite periods. Such currency MIM may allow global expressions of profit to occur. Global profit is commonly accompanied by corresponding defaults on time-lagged MIM transmitted to societies by components or by perpetuated societal credit (both have the same effect).

Why should unexplained currency MIM be transmitted to some societal components? Is profit a necessary basic dynamic in debt-based currency MIM economies? It seems that large and expanding economic activity may be achieved using the basic dynamics of wages, rents, dividends, interest, and royalties. Together, those dynamics entice labor, matter-energy capital, money-information marker capital, and technological advances. What else could economies need?

Notwithstanding the powerful mix of dynamics provided by wages, rents, dividends, interest, and royalties, something is missing. The complex chains of exchanges that incorporate those dynamics emerge by splitting a basic trade. A trade is an exchange consisting of two transfers of goods-services. Both parties to a trade receive and give; they import and export. Both transfers are both exports and imports (Figure 6-5). All of the dynamics mentioned are export oriented with reference to the basic trade being split. An import orientation is missing.

A trade could not occur if either party did not want the goods-services of the other party. The actions separating the transfers of a trade with money-information marker transmissions and other transfers of goods-services introduce at least an information filter and likely a disconnect between the transfers of the basic trade. Wages, rents, and so on communicate information to specialize the export aspect of the basic trade. That specialization is ordinarily termed *production processes*. Production preferences are signaled by those dynamics.

Specialized processes of a basic trade's import aspects are ordinarily termed *consumption processes*. None of the explained and accepted dynamics communicate consumption preferences. They all motivate production-exportation. They communicate the producing preferences of specialized entities, not the consuming preferences of those and other entities. No immediate information about consumption preferences is available because producing-exporting entities are not forced to give wages, rent, and so forth in the forms of goods-services. They give generic currency MIM instead. The signal from consuming-importing entities awaits the attempted sale of the produced goods-services. At that time, only one type of signal is entirely clear. That signal is inventory (residual unsold production)—a signal of decreasing preferences for a product. No clear signal is given by production dynamics if a product is increasingly preferred.

Is profit different from those other dynamics? Does it signal consumption preferences? If it does, profit may no longer be unexplained. It may be explained as a consumption dynamic that motivates the production of wanted goods-services. The answer to whether profit signals changed preferences for goods-services is not simple. Nevertheless, an answer is attempted.

Fundamentally, profit emerges if an entity transmits more monetary value than the value of the time-lagged MIM initiating the production of the goods-services it imports. The monetary value of the time-lagged MIM includes amounts for the basic dynamics of wages, dividends, and so on, as previously discussed. The producing-exporting entity receives the incremental monetary value in the form of currency MIM.

Consequently, profit is made possible by disconnecting specific time-lagged MIM from the specific production-distribution they initiated. Profit is a consequence of the negotiability of MIM, both time-lagged and currency. The disconnect is made possible by the negotiability characteristics. The emergence of currency MIM compounds the negotiability of money-information markers, facilitating the emergence of profits.

Profit, however, perturbs an otherwise orderly system. Some MIM introduced by executory contract for another product are reassigned to the profitable one in the midst of a cycle. A system's negative feed processes work to return a perturbed system to its former state. Consequently, the processes of debt-money economies would be expected to work to reduce the profits (the perturbance).

Disconnected from the production they initiate, money-information markers are used to signal what products are preferred. The signal consists of transmitting an incremental amount of MIM to certain producers of preferred goods-services. Such transmissions are termed *local profits*. Although local profit transmissions are private between particular buyers and sellers, they introduce a public signal as well. The quadratic constraint forces the public signal and initiates a negative feed process. Situation 6-10 demonstrates that fact.

Situation 6-10: Profit in a Non-Currency MIM Debt-Based Economy

Notation 6-10 maps three connected chains of exchanges that include a local profit transmission. Subscripts of the notation are ratio scale quantities. Introducing such subscripts allows analyses of proportionate influences of actions on various variables. The chains close, so the processes form a determinate circuit. Inventory, however, is left in the hand of a producing entity. That matter-energy residual is the result of local profit and likely causes some kind of following economic action.

$$/^1 \ TLM^{p1}_{-1.0} \ TLM^{c1}_{1.0} \ ME^{c1}_{-1.0} \ ME^{p1}_{1.0} \ /^2 \ TLM^{p2}_{-1.0} \ TLM^{c2}_{1.0} \ ME^{c2}_{-1.0} \qquad (6\text{-}10)$$

$$ME^{p2}_{1.0}$$

$$/^3 \ TLM^{p3}_{-1.0} \ TLM^{c3}_{1.0} \ ME^{c3}_{-1.0} \ ME^{p3}_{1.0} \ /CON/^{1,2} \ TLM^{c1}_{-0.5} \ TLM^{p2}_{0.5} \ ME^{p2}_{-0.3}$$

$$ME^{c1}_{0.3}$$

$$/CON/^{3,2} \ TLM^{c3}_{-0.5} \ TLM^{p2}_{0.5} \ ME^{p2}_{-0.3} \ ME^{c3}_{0.3} \ /^2 \ TLM^{c2}_{-0.4} \ TLM^{p2}_{0.4} \ ME^{p2}_{-0.4}$$

$$ME^{c2}_{0.4}$$

$$/^1 \ TLM^{c1}_{-0.5} \ TLM^{p1}_{0.5} \ ME^{p1}_{-0.5} \ ME^{c1}_{0.5} \ /^3 \ TLM^{c3}_{-0.5} \ TLM^{p3}_{0.5} \ ME^{p3}_{-0.5} \ ME^{c3}_{0.5}$$

$$/CON/^{2,3} \ TLM^{c2}_{-0.3} \ TLM^{p3}_{0.3} \ ME^{p3}_{-0.3} \ ME^{c2}_{0.3} \ /CON/^{2,1} \ TLM^{c2}_{-0.3} \ TLM^{p1}_{0.3}$$

$$ME^{p1}_{-0.3} \ ME^{c2}_{0.3}$$

$$/CON/^{2,1} \ TLM^{p2}_{-0.2} \ TLM^{p1}_{0.2} \ ME^{p1}_{-0.2} \ ME^{p2}_{0.2} \ /CON/^{2,3} \ TLM^{p2}_{-0.2} \ TLM^{p3}_{0.2}$$

$$ME^{p3}_{-0.2} \ ME^{p2}_{0.2}$$

$$/RSD/ \ ME^{c1}_{-0.2} \ ME^{c3}_{-0.2} \ ME^{p2}_{0.4}$$

Three different producing entities initiate production by enticing the factors of production on credit from three different consumer-labor entities. Consumer-labor entities 1 and 3 each choose to buy 0.3 of Producers 2's product for half of the TLM each one holds. They spend the other half on the products they produced for Producers 1 and 3, respectively. Consumer 2 buys 0.4 of the produce of Producer 2 and 0.3 each of the products of Producers 1 and 3. Because they each have transmitted a profit of 0.2 of the TLM held to Producer 2, Consumers 1 and 3 can buy only half of the goods-services of Producers 1 and 3. Producers 1 and 3, consequently, sell only 0.8 (0.5 + 0.3) of their products to consumers 1, 2, and 3.

Producer 2 has received excess TLM equal to 0.4 of its production and transmits those money-information markers to the other producers to claim the 0.2 of excess production that each holds. Producer 2 has received a profit signal. The goods-services produced but not purchased by the consumer-labor entities have been transferred to the producer of preferred goods.

The quality of the result of that profit signal is suspect, however. If consumer-labor entities did not purchase the products in the first place, what incentive exists for the successful producer to transmit the TLM in exchange for them? The TLM themselves. The executory contract documented by the TLM requires the transfer of those particular goods at a certain moment. After that moment, the contract is either fulfilled or defaulted. If the successful producer chooses not to claim them, the goods-services remain in the hands of their producers, and the TLM cannot legally claim other goods-services.

Likewise, the quality of the signal to unsuccessful producers is suspect. They transferred all of their product. Why should they not repeat their performance?

That process encourages, to some degree, clearing the production-distribution circuit. It may, but does not necessarily, encourage increased production of successful products and decreased production of unsuccessful ones. Successful producers are given the responsibility of distributing the unwanted goods and services. Unsuccessful producers are left without responsibility for their unwanted products and may initiate a second identical circuit without suffering any inconvenience.

The process does not allow any global increase in the ratio of the quantity of money-information markers to the quantity of goods-services. The MIM used to negotiate profit are removed within a definite period from the economy by either the fulfillment or default of the executory contract underlying the TLM. The redistribution of goods-services, which is the ultimate aim of profit, is accomplished. A producer may or may not be benefited by the redistribution, however. The profit signal is given, and a very powerful negative feedback returns the system to its former state, except that the successful producer has a quantity of goods produced by others.

The feed processes of a currency MIM debt-based economy are not the same as those of a non-currency MIM economy. In fact, the introduction of profit into currency MIM processes causes a positive feedback that moves the system further and further from its previous state.

Situation 6-11: Profit in a Currency MIM Debt-Based Economy

Notation 6-11 maps the same three connected chains of exchanges mapped in Notation 6-10. It transmits the initial TLM to society for currency MIM to further facilitate the negotiability of MIM, however.

$$/^1 \ TLM^{P1}_{-1.0} \ TLM^{c1}_{1.0} \ ME^{c1}_{-1.0} \ ME^{P1}_{1.0} \ TLM^{c1}_{-1.0} \ TLM^{s}_{1.0} \ CM^{s}_{-1.0} \qquad (6\text{--}11)$$

$$CM^{c1}_{1.0}$$

$$/^2 \ TLM^{P2}_{-1.0} \ TLM^{c2}_{1.0} \ ME^{c2}_{-1.0} \ ME^{P2}_{1.0} \ TLM^{c2}_{-1.0} \ TLM^{s}_{1.0} \ CM^{s}_{-1.0} \ CM^{c2}_{1.0}$$

$$/^3 \ TLM^{P3}_{-1.0} \ TLM^{c3}_{1.0} \ ME^{c3}_{-1.0} \ ME^{P3}_{1.0} \ TLM^{c3}_{-1.0} \ TLM^{s}_{1.0} \ CM^{s}_{-1.0} \ CM^{c3}_{1.0}$$

$$/CON/^{1,2} \ CM^{c1}_{-0.5} \ CM^{P2}_{0.5} \ ME^{P2}_{-0.3} \ ME^{c1}_{0.3} \ /CON/^{3,2} \ CM^{c3}_{-0.5} \ CM^{P2}_{0.5} \ ME^{P2}_{-0.3}$$

$$ME^{c3}_{0.3}$$

$$/^2 \ CM^{c2}_{-0.4} \ CM^{P2}_{0.4} \ ME^{P2}_{-0.4} \ ME^{c2}_{0.4} \ /^1 \ CM^{c1}_{-0.5} \ CM^{P1}_{0.5} \ ME^{P1}_{-0.5} \ ME^{c1}_{0.5}$$

$$/^3 \ CM^{c3}_{-0.5} \ CM^{P3}_{0.5} \ ME^{P3}_{-0.5} \ ME^{c3}_{0.5} \ /CON/^{2,3} \ CM^{c2}_{-0.3} \ CM^{P3}_{0.3} \ ME^{P3}_{-0.3} \ ME^{c2}_{0.3}$$

$$/CON/^{2,1} \ CM^{c2}_{-0.3} \ CM^{P1}_{0.3} \ ME^{P1}_{-0.3} \ ME^{c2}_{0.3} \ /^1 \ CM^{P1}_{-0.8} \ CM^{s}_{0.8} \ TLM^{s}_{-0.8} \ TLM^{P1}_{0.8}$$

$$/^2 \ CM^{P2}_{-1.0} \ CM^{s}_{1.0} \ TLM^{s}_{-1.0} \ TLM^{P2}_{1.0} \ /^3 \ CM^{P3}_{-0.8} \ CM^{s}_{0.8} \ TLM^{s}_{-0.8} \ TLM^{P3}_{0.8}$$

$$/RSD/^1 \ TLM^{P1}_{-0.2} \ TLM^{s}_{0.2} \ ME^{c1}_{-0.2} \ ME^{P1}_{0.2}$$

$$/RSD/^3 \ TLM^{P3}_{-0.2} \ TLM^{s}_{0.2} \ ME^{c3}_{-0.2} \ ME^{P3}_{0.2}$$

$$/RSD/^2 \ CM^{s}_{-0.4} \ CM^{P2}_{0.4}$$

Mechanically, little has changed, but an important economic change has occurred. Producer 2 now holds 0.4 discretionary currency—a powerful incentive to increase production of a preferred product. The other producers are left with excess products-services and an unpaid obligation to society.

At first glance, this solution seems very orderly. The preferred product producer is rewarded and the neglected ones are penalized. The rewards and penalties offset each other. The solution is not so orderly, however.

The TLM residuals provide motives for a dynamic process of recurring cycles. Only Circuit 2 has been closed thus far, and that closure resulted in discretionary currency MIM in the hands of Producer 2. Situation 6-12 examines the next cycle.

Situation 6-12: Profit in a Currency MIM Debt-Based Economy—Second Cycle

Notation 6-12 maps a second cycle of Situation 6-11 motivated by the TLM residuals. The producing entities obtain currency MIM with TLM directly from society, however, instead of enticing factors of production from consumer-labor entities. They obtain CM in the amount of their first cycle exports, and they produce product to the extent CM is available. The consumer-labor entities buy product to the extent of their available CM.

$$/^4 \ TLM^{P1}_{-0.8} \ TLM^{s}_{0.8} \ CM^{s}_{-0.8} \ CM^{P1}_{0.8} \ /CON/^{4,1} \ CM^{P1}_{-0.2} \ CM^{s}_{0.2} \qquad (6\text{-}12)$$

$$TLM^{s}_{-0.2} \ TLM^{P1}_{0.2}$$

$$/^4 \ CM^{P1}_{-0.6} \ CM^{c1}_{0.6} \ ME^{c1}_{-0.6} \ ME^{P1}_{0.6} \ /^2 \ CM^{P2}_{-0.4} \ CM^{c2}_{0.4} \ ME^{c2}_{-0.4} \ ME^{P2}_{0.4}$$

$$/^5 \ TLM^{P2}_{-1.0} \ TLM^{s}_{1.0} \ CM^{s}_{-1.0} \ CM^{P2}_{1.0} \ CM^{P2}_{-1.0} \ CM^{c2}_{1.0} \ ME^{c2}_{-1.0} \ ME^{P2}_{1.0}$$

$$/^6 \ TLM^{P3}_{-0.8} \ TLM^{s}_{0.8} \ CM^{s}_{-0.8} \ CM^{P3}_{0.8} \ /CON/^{6,3} \ CM^{P3}_{-0.2} \ CM^{s}_{0.2} \ TLM^{s}_{-0.2}$$

$$TLM^{P3}_{0.2}$$

$$/^6 \ CM^{P3}_{-0.6} \ CM^{c3}_{0.6} \ ME^{c3}_{-0.6} \ ME^{P3}_{0.6}$$

$$/CON/^{4,2} \ CM^{c1}_{-0.3} \ CM^{P2}_{0.3} \ ME^{P2}_{-0.18} \ ME^{c1}_{0.18} \ /CON/^{6,2} \ CM^{c3}_{-0.3} \ CM^{P2}_{0.3} \ ME^{P2}_{-0.18}$$

$$ME^{c3}_{0.18}$$

$$/^2 \ CM^{c2}_{-0.4} \ CM^{P2}_{0.4} \ ME^{P2}_{-0.4} \ ME^{c2}_{0.4} \ /^4 \ CM^{c1}_{-0.3} \ CM^{P1}_{0.3} \ ME^{P1}_{-0.3} \ ME^{c1}_{0.3}$$

$$/^6 \ CM^{c3}_{-0.3} \ CM^{P3}_{0.3} \ ME^{P3}_{-0.3} \ ME^{c3}_{0.3} \ /^5 \ CM^{c2}_{-0.64} \ CM^{P2}_{0.64} \ ME^{P2}_{-0.64} \ ME^{c2}_{-0.64}$$

$$/CON/^{5,4} \ CM^{c2}_{-0.18} \ CM^{P1}_{0.18} \ ME^{P1}_{-0.18} \ ME^{c2}_{0.18} \ /CON/^{5,6} \ CM^{c2}_{-0.18} \ CM^{P3}_{0.18}$$

$$ME^{P3}_{-0.18} \ ME^{c2}_{0.18}$$

$$/^4 \ CM^{P1}_{-0.48} \ CM^{s}_{0.48} \ TLM^{s}_{-0.48} \ TLM^{P1}_{0.48} \ /^5 \ CM^{P2}_{-1.0} \ CM^{s}_{1.0} \ TLM^{s}_{-1.0} \ TLM^{P2}_{1.0}$$

$$/^6 \ CM^{P3}_{-0.48} \ CM^{s}_{0.48} \ TLM^{s}_{-0.48} \ TLM^{P3}_{0.48} \ /RSD/^4 \ TLM^{P1}_{-0.32} \ TLM^{s}_{0.32} \ ME^{c1}_{-0.32}$$

$$ME^{P1}_{0.32}$$

$$/RSD/^5 \ CM^{s}_{-0.64} \ CM^{P2}_{0.64} \ /RSD/^6 \ TLM^{P3}_{-0.32} \ TLM^{s}_{0.32} \ ME^{c3}_{-0.32} \ ME^{P3}_{0.32}$$

The second cycle increases the residual debt to society of the less preferred producers to 0.64. It leaves 0.64 discretionary currency MIM (0.24 more than in the last cycle) in the hands of the preferred producer. The neglected producers hold 0.32 excess inventory (0.12 more than in the last cycle).

The process appears at first glance to be a run-away positive feedback, shifting production and distribution from less wanted products to more desired ones. The full positive feed signal received by Producer 2, however, depends in part on Consumer-labor Entity 2 increasing its appetite for the product it produces. That is unrealistic beyond some magnitude. If Entity 2's appetite were not increasing, Producer 2 would be unable to sell its increased produce because entities 1 and 3 do not have CM to purchase it.

The lack of CM in the hands of consumer-labor entities 1 and 2 is a negative feed signal working to return the production-distribution balance. To the extent that consumers prefer some other product by greater MIM value than the value they receive for producing their own product, they limit successively more and more their ability to buy that product. They initiate the negative feed signal that operates through the quadratic constraint by decreasing demand for their own products—thus decreasing their own income.

SUMMARY

This chapter has examined the introduction of typical motivators in debt-monetary economies. Motivators such as interest, dividends, and profits are introduced into advanced modern economies to increase economic activity beyond that motivated by the basic trade dynamic and the negotiability of time-lagged and currency MIM. Most motivators are production oriented. Only profit is distribution oriented.

The next chapter discusses certain patterns that result from introducing multiple motivators. Simulations of specific situations illustrate the effects of various combinations of motivators.

Figure 6-1
An Effect of Interest on Recurring Cycles of Production

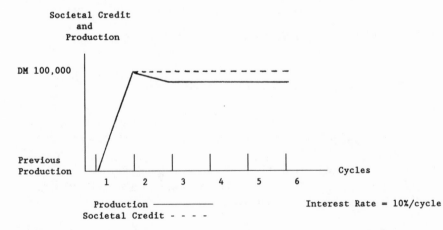

Figure 6-2
An Effect of Interest When Maintaining Production Level

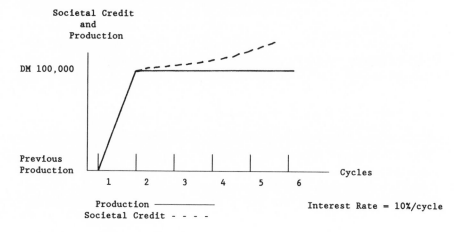

Figure 6-3
The Effect of Simple Interest Charge-Discharge on Production Level

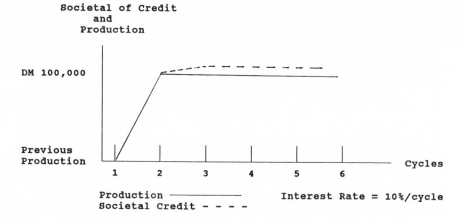

Figure 6-4
**Deflationary Spiral Caused by Societies Charging Interest and Not Carrying
Credit to Cover It**

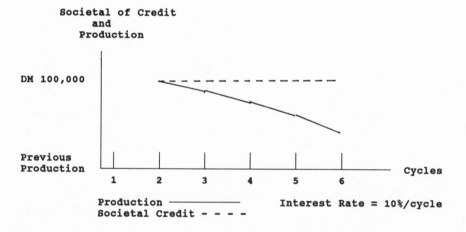

Societal of Credit
and
Production

DM 100,000

Previous
Production

1   2   3   4   5   6

Cycles

Production ————————
Societal Credit - - - -

Interest Rate = 10%/cycle

Figure 6-5
Both Transfers of a Trade Are Both Exports and Imports

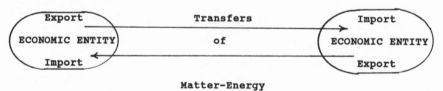

Export   Transfers   Import

ECONOMIC ENTITY   of   ECONOMIC ENTITY

Import   Export

Matter-Energy

7

Recurring Effects of Certain Dynamics

Introducing interest, factors of production price increases, dividends, rents, and royalties into economies can be an orderly process. They may be introduced in a manner that produces determinate circuits that remove all of the process-initiating MIM at the completion of a chain of exchanges. Their introduction may also produce dynamic cycles characterized by residuals of MIM left in the economy by an unclosed circuit. Money-information markers from a following circuit are used to close the unclosed circuit, forming chains of connected circuits termed *cycles*.

Introducing profit is always a disorderly process. Profit is a distribution-oriented motivator. It occurs as a perturbance to a process already set in motion. That characteristic is necessary for importers to signal their preferences for certain already produced products.

This chapter simulates the dynamics of introducing different motivators in various ways. Because the systems are complex and interacting, the results are sometimes counterintuitive.

THE SIMULATIONS

The macro accounting procedure used throughout this chapter traces typical related exchanges from the introduction of currency MIM to their retrieval in each of ten recurring cycles. The notation consists of the following terms, superscripts, and subscripts. The terms are as follows:

TLM, time-lagged, money-information markers (debt instruments).

CM, currency money-information markers.

ME, forms of matter-energy such as people, machines, goods, and services.

Superscripts, indicating the living systems involved in the exchanges, are the following:

S, society.

P1, one producer.

P2, another producer.

C1, one consumer-labor entity.

C2, another consumer-labor entity.

Subscripts indicate amounts in terms of monetary units.

The simulations analyze changes in interest rates, profits, and costs of factors of production in the following situation. Production organizations may borrow from society to produce goods and services. Producers use currency to buy factors of production from one group of consumers-laborers and then sell the product to another group of consumers-laborers. If one group of consumers-laborers has excess currency, it loans the currency to the other group if that group has not bought all the products it normally does. The producers repay society after they sell their products. Society monetizes all changes in interest, profits, and costs of factors of production. Monetization occurs only at the beginning of each cycle, however, when a new loan is made to a producer. Interest rates, costs of factors of production, and profits are varied and the situation is held constant. Those circumstances are modeled by chains of exchanges similar to those of previous chapters.

The Notation 7-1 set of chains constitutes one cycle and is representative of those used for all of the analyses in this chapter. Only the results are given for other simulations. The results are presented in tables and graphs of residuals and tables of production. The acronyms for residuals are RSDS, Residual Debt Society; RSDP1, Residual Debt Producer 1; RSDP2, Residual Debt Producer 2; RSDC1, Residual Debt Consumer-Labor Entity 1; RSDC2, Residual Debt Consumer-Labor Entity 2; RPP1, Residual Production Producer 1; RPP2, Residual Production Producer 2; DCS, Discretionary Currency Society; DCP1, Discretionary Currency Producer 1; DCP2, Discretionary Currency Producer 2; DCC1, Discretionary Currency Consumer-Labor Entity 1; and DCC2, Discretionary Currency Consumer-Labor Entity 2. Residuals can be either positive or negative. Negative is outflow and positive is inflow.

$$/^1 \ \text{TLM}^{P1}_{-1} \ \text{TLM}^{S}_{1} \ \text{CM}^{S}_{-1} \ \text{CM}^{P1}_{1} \ \text{CM}^{P1}_{-1} \ \text{CM}^{c1}_{1} \ \text{ME}^{c1}_{-1} \ \text{ME}^{P1}_{1} \qquad (7-1)$$

$$\text{CM}^{P1}_{-0} \ \text{CM}^{S}_{0} \ \text{TLM}^{S}_{-0} \ \text{TLM}^{P1}_{0}$$

$/^2$ TLM^{p2}_{-1} TLM^{s}_{1} CM^{s}_{-1} CM^{p2}_{1} CM^{p2}_{-1} CM^{c2}_{1} ME^{c2}_{-1} ME^{p2}_{1}

CM^{p2}_{-0} CM^{s}_{0} TLM^{s}_{-0} TLM^{p2}_{0}

$/CON/^{1,2}$ CM^{c1}_{-1} CM^{p2}_{1} ME^{p2}_{-1} ME^{c1}_{1}

$/CON/^{2,1}$ CM^{c2}_{-1} CM^{p1}_{1} ME^{p1}_{-1} ME^{c2}_{1}

$/^3$ TLM^{c1}_{-0} TLM^{c2}_{0} CM^{c2}_{-0} CM^{c1}_{0} CM^{c1}_{-0} CM^{p2}_{0} ME^{p2}_{-0} ME^{c1}_{0}

CM^{c1}_{-0} CM^{c2}_{0} TLM^{c2}_{-0} TLM^{c1}_{0}

$/^4$ TLM^{c2}_{-0} TLM^{c1}_{0} CM^{c1}_{-0} CM^{c2}_{0} CM^{c2}_{-0} CM^{p1}_{0} ME^{p1}_{-0} ME^{c2}_{0}

CM^{c2}_{-0} CM^{c1}_{0} TLM^{c1}_{-0} TLM^{c2}_{0}

$/CON/^{2,1;4,1}$ CM^{p1}_{-1} CM^{s}_{1} TLM^{s}_{-1} TLM^{p1}_{1}

$/CON/^{1,2;3,2}$ CM^{p2}_{-1} CM^{s}_{1} TLM^{s}_{-1} TLM^{p2}_{1}

Residuals

RSDS	RSDP1	RSDP2	RSDC1	RSDC2
0.00000	0.00000	0.00000	0.00000	0.00000

DCS	DCP1	DCP2	DCC1	DCC2
0.00000	0.00000	0.00000	0.00000	0.00000

RPP1	RPP2
0.00000	0.00000

Notation 7-1 shows that the chains of exchange form a circuit when no interest, no profits, and no changes in costs of factors of production are introduced. The full amount of production can be stimulated by repeating the circuit as many times as desired. No residual currency, residual debt, or residual unsold production is left at the conclusion of each circuit. The process is very orderly. It introduces neither inflation nor deflation, excess inventory, nor discretionary currency MIM, nor does it change the level of production from circuit to circuit.

THE INTRODUCTION OF INTEREST

Introducing interest into economic processes produces significant residuals. It changes the orderly return to equilibrium demonstrated in the circuits in Notation 7-1 into cycles of processes connected by the residuals. The condition described in Notation 7-1 motivated economic activity only by introducing debt and currency MIM to facilitate the processes. When a society charges 10 percent interest each cycle, it must lend 1.594 times the value of each producer's product by the tenth cycle to maintain the level of production initiated (Table 7-1). Each producer must bear the increasing burden of debt to produce at a particular level.

Figure 7-1 shows the positive feedback pattern that moves the system increasingly away from equilibrium in terms of the residual debt to society held by producers. The initiated production remains in equilibrium, and no discretionary currency MIM are left in any cycle. The processes are not inflationary or deflationary if society holds debt for the interest it is charging.

The positive feedback driving debt away from equilibrium accelerates rapidly as the interest rate increases. At 50 percent interest each cycle, society must hold residual debt 56.665 times the production initiated for each producer by the tenth cycle (Figure 7-2). Nevertheless, production remains in equilibrium, and the processes are not inflationary or deflationary if society holds debt for the interest it is charging. Although a positive feedback is occurring in the system, it is orderly.

THE INTRODUCTION OF PROFITS

The introduction of profits into economic processes causes positive feedbacks that move production and discretionary currency MIM as well as residual debt away from equilibrium (Figure 7-3). Coincidentally, negative feedbacks that intermittently dampen the positive feedback are initiated. Nevertheless, the dominant feed processes are positive, moving the system away from equilibrium on virtually all measurements. This happens despite society's willingness to monetize the activities fully.

Table 7-2 data indicate that when one producer receives a 10 percent profit, society must hold debt of about 19 percent of the value of the initiated production of each producer by the tenth cycle. The full 37.9 percent of production debt, however, is borne by the non-profitable producer. Discretionary currency MIM of 37.9 percent of production from the unpaid debt to society are in the hands of the profitable producer—signaling preference for its product. The MIM residuals seem to provide proper signals for increasing economic activity.

Production—the activity the monetary signals should increase—nevertheless is not increased. In fact, it is decreased. By the tenth cycle, 37.9 percent of both producers' output remains unsold. Table 7-3 reflects the decline in the overall production of the system from 2.0 in the first cycle to 1.3 in the tenth one.

The quadratic constraint of the exchange process is responsible for this decline in production. Because the profit signal is introduced by individual decision of consumers in the midst of the processes instead of at the beginning (when the processes are monetized by society), the profit signal uses MIM otherwise available for the purchase of another product or for the purchase of the entire production of the preferred product. The profit signal thus sets in motion a negative feedback that drives the production from the incrementally higher level initiated by societal debt and currency MIM back toward its original level. Interestingly, this happens despite society's willingness to monetize any output desired by producers.

The discretionary currency MIM left in the system are potentially inflationary. Society does not retrieve all of the currency money-information markers each cycle, the profitable producer accumulates discretionary currency, and society holds debt to monetize the profit, but the money is not introduced directly for that purpose and not until the next cycle.

If both producing entities make a 10 percent profit, the system is dramatically more orderly. The negative effect on production, however, is increased. No monetary residuals remain after each cycle. Increasingly more residual production is left, however (Table 7-4, Figure 7-4). The overall production in the system decreases from 2.0 to 0.84 (Table 7-5). The decreasing production is again the result of lack of sufficient currency MIM at the place and time needed.

The conventional wisdom is that some producers make a profit and others have a loss in the competitive environment of the market. The profits and losses offset each other in a non-inflationary economy and equilibrium is restored. That wisdom is correct for production. The MIM in the system are not restored to equilibrium, however. Figure 7-5 and Table 7-6 show that a positive feedback moving the MIM away from equilibrium at a constant rate is introduced. By the tenth cycle, the losing producer has a residual debt burden owed to society equal to 100 percent of the initiated increment of production, the profitable producer has discretionary currency MIM equal to 100 percent of the incremental production, and the consumer-laborer entity producing the profitable product and buying the unprofitable one holds debt equal to 100 percent of the production increment. This positive feedback produces significant imbalances in the economy.

INCREASES IN COSTS OF FACTORS OF PRODUCTION

When increases in wages and other factors of production are introduced after the incremental production process is set in motion, a positive feedback on MIM is introduced. Figure 7-6 and Table 7-7 show that debt owed to society by the producer suffering the additional wages increases at a constant rate to 100 percent of incremental production by the tenth cycle. Discretionary currency accumulates in the hands of the benefitted consumer-laborer. Nevertheless, production remains in equilibrium.

If everyone receives a raise, the problem of positive feedback on MIM is compounded. Figure 7-7 and Table 7-8 show the results of 10 percent of cost increases for both producers. By the tenth cycle, society holds debt of twice the value of the incremental level of production, both producers owe debt of 100 percent of the incremental value, and both consumers have discretionary currency MIM equal to 100 percent of the incremental value. The discretionary currency is a strong influence toward inflation of prices. As long as society monetizes the increased costs, however, production remains at the incremental level.

When one producer's costs increase and the other producer's costs decrease by equal amounts, the positive feedback on the MIM has a similar magnitude to that of a cost increase for only one producer. Figure 7-8 and Table 7-9 show that society holds debt and that the producer with increased costs owes debt, the consumer-laborer receiving the increase holds debt, and the producer with lower costs has discretionary currency MIM. All of these imbalances increase at a constant rate to 100 percent of incremental production in the tenth cycle. The production, however, continues at the incremental level. Although the magnitude and pattern of the positive feedback are similar to that of increased costs for a single producer, the pattern of residuals in the system is different. Society holds debt and leaves discretionary currency MIM, and the producer suffering the increased costs owes debt in both cases. The discretionary currency MIM, however, are left in the hands of a consumer-laborer when only one producer's cost increases. It is given to the cost-decreasing producer when offsetting cost changes occur.

COMBINING PROFIT AND INTEREST

The combined effects of introductions of interest, profits, and changes in costs of factors of production are not intuitively obvious. Figure 7-9 and Tables 7-10 and 7-11 present the results of combining a 10 percent interest rate and a 10 percent profit rate. When 10 percent interest is combined with 10 percent profit, the amount of debt society holds and the debt burden of each producing entity decreases dramatically from that required by interest alone (Table 7-1)—from 159.4 percent of incremental production to 67.6 percent.

That seems counterintuitive. Introducing both profit and interest should require monetizing both. What actually happens is that the negative feedback on production introduced by profits is such a drag on the economy that society has less production to monetize. The drag is generated by the unused production (the RPP1 and RPP2 increasing to 0.61 percent of incremental production by the tenth cycle). The process is not inflationary because no discretionary currency MIM are trapped in the system.

Combining offsetting profit and interest has a much different effect. Figure 7-10 and Tables 7-12 and 7-13 show the results of this circumstance at a 10 percent rate. The damper on production is removed, and it remains at the incremental level throughout the ten cycles. The additional production requires society to hold more debt (100 percent instead of 67.6 percent of the incremental production value). The producer suffering negative profits owes debt twice the value of its incremental production, however, and both consumers-laborers hold debt of 100 percent or more of the value of their incremental production/consumption.

CONCLUSION

Effects of introducing motivators into an economy are not always intuitively obvious. In fact, sometimes they are actually counterintuitive. Nevertheless, some general effects have been demonstrated in the simulations in this chapter. They are the following:

1. Introducing interest does not decrease production if society holds debt to cover it fully.

2. Introducing partial profits decreases production even if it is monetized to the extent possible in an exchange system.

3. Introducing full profits decreases production even more.

4. Introducing offsetting profits does not decrease production.

5. Changing costs of factors of production does not decrease production.

6. Introducing interest leaves debt in an economy.

7. Changing cost of factors of production leaves debt and discretionary currency in an economy.

8. Introducing profit can leave debt and discretionary currency in an economy.

9. Combining multiple motivators in a system may produce results that are not intuitively obvious.

The results of this limited simulation do not provide sweeping conclusions about entire economies. They nevertheless raise fundamental questions about the concrete process feedback in modern economies. Questions of particular current importance are the following. Must the debt that society holds continue to increase if interest, profit, and increases in costs of production are allowed? Why is the "national debt" borrowed instead of loaned? If the Federal Reserve Board owes more debt than it holds, where is all the money coming from?

Table 7-1
Residuals When Society Charges 10 Percent Interest

Cycle	RSDS	RSDP1	RSDP2
1	0.2	-0.1	-0.1
2	0.42	-0.21	-0.21
3	0.662	-0.331	-0.331
4	0.928	-0.464	-0.464
5	1.221	-0.611	-0.611
6	1.543	-0.772	-0.772
7	1.897	-0.949	-0.949
8	2.287	-1.144	-1.144
9	2.716	-1.358	-1.358
10	3.187	-1.594	-1.594

Figure 7-1
Residuals When Society Charges 10 Percent Interest

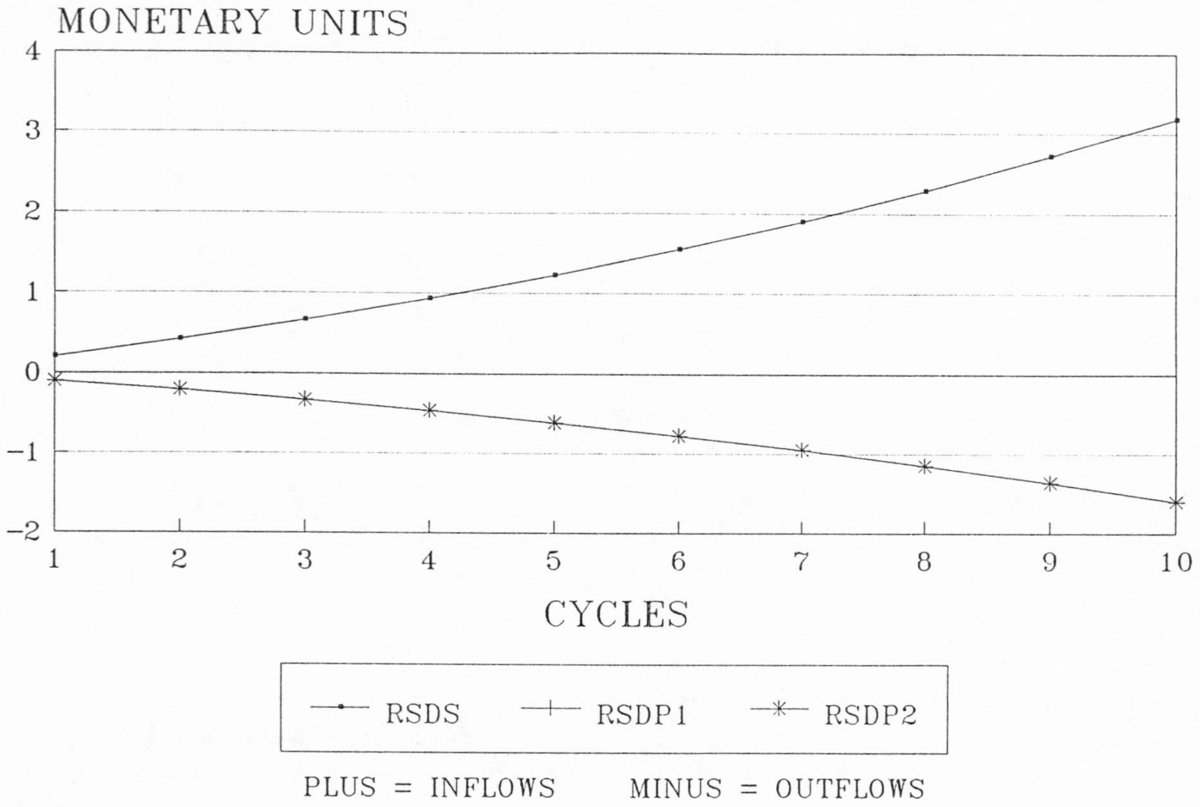
MONETARY UNITS
4
3
2
1
0
−1
−2
1
2
3
4
5
6
7
8
9
10
CYCLES
RSDS
RSDP1
RSDP2
PLUS = INFLOWS
MINUS = OUTFLOWS

Figure 7-2
Residuals When Society Charges 50 Percent Interest

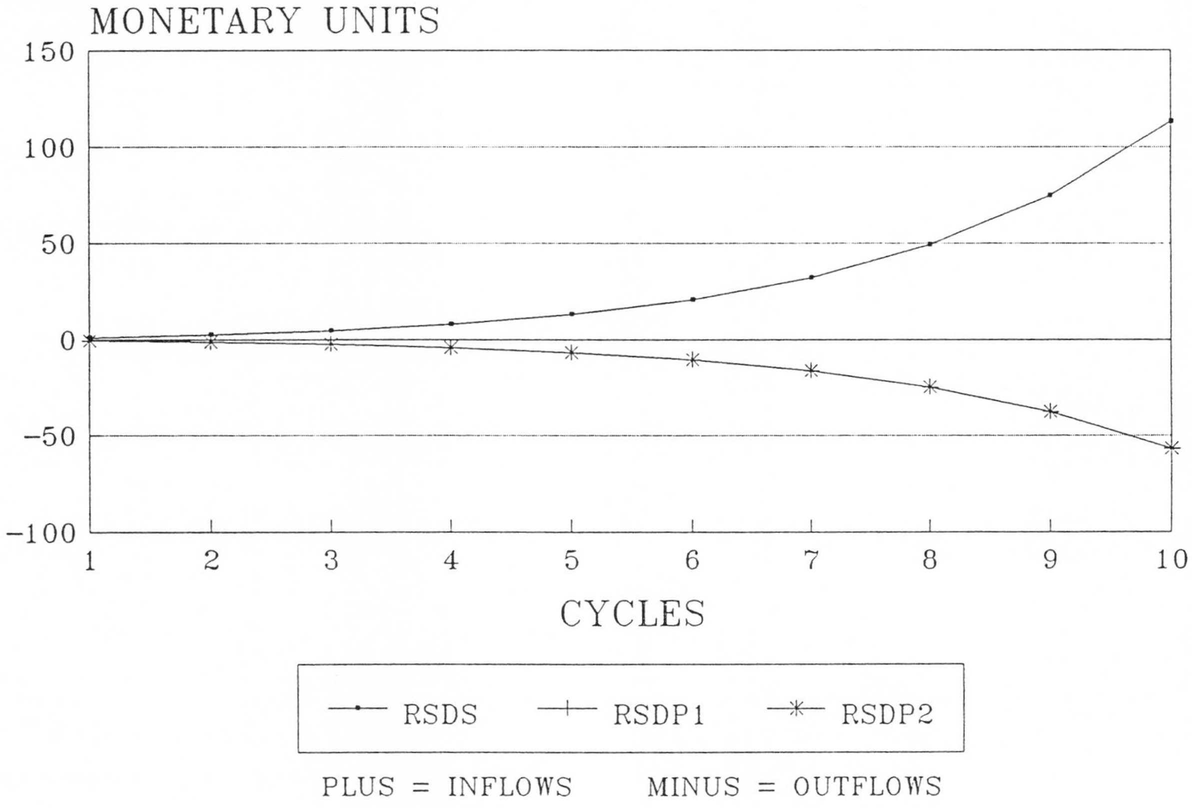
MONETARY UNITS
150
100
50
0
−50
−100
1
2
3
4
5
6
7
8
9
10
CYCLES
RSDS
RSDP1
RSDP2
PLUS = INFLOWS
MINUS = OUTFLOWS

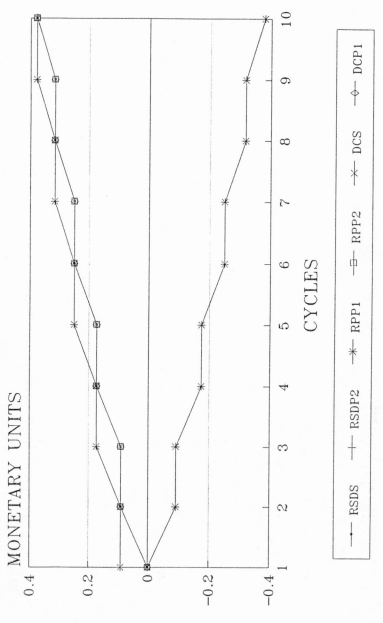

Figure 7-3
Residuals When One Producer Receives 10 Percent Profit

128

Table 7-2
Residuals When One Producer Receives 10 Percent Profit

X Data	RSDS	RSDP2	RPP1	RPP2
1	0	0	0.091	0
2	0.091	−0.091	0.091	0.091
3	0.091	−0.091	0.174	0.091
4	0.174	−0.174	0.174	0.174
5	0.174	−0.174	0.249	0.174
6	0.249	−0.249	0.249	0.249
7	0.249	−0.249	0.317	0.249
8	0.317	−0.317	0.317	0.317
9	0.317	−0.317	0.379	0.317
10	0.379	−0.379	0.379	0.379

X Data	DCS	DCP1
1	0	0
2	−0.091	0.091
3	−0.091	0.091
4	−0.174	0.174
5	−0.174	0.174
6	−0.249	0.249
7	−0.249	0.249
8	−0.317	0.317
9	−0.317	0.317
10	−0.379	0.379

Table 7-3
Production When One Producer Receives 10 Percent Profit

Cycle	Production P1	P2	All
1	1	1	2
2	.91	1	1.91
3	.91	.91	1.82
4	.83	.91	1.74
5	.83	.83	1.66
6	.75	.83	1.58
7	.75	.75	1.50
8	.68	.75	1.43
9	.68	.68	1.36
10	.62	.68	1.30

Table 7-4
Residuals When Both Producers Receive 10 Percent Profit

Cycle	RPP1	RPP2
1	0.091	0.091
2	0.174	0.174
3	0.249	0.249
4	0.317	0.317
5	0.379	0.379
6	0.436	0.436
7	0.487	0.487
8	0.533	0.533
9	0.576	0.576
10	0.614	0.614

Table 7-5
Production When Both Producers Receive 10 Percent Profit

| Cycle | Production | | |
	P1	P2	All
1	1	1	2
2	0.91	0.91	1.82
3	0.83	0.83	1.66
4	0.75	0.75	1.50
5	0.68	0.68	1.36
6	0.62	0.62	1.24
7	0.56	0.56	1.12
8	0.51	0.51	1.02
9	0.47	0.47	0.94
10	0.42	0.42	0.84

Figure 7-4
Residuals When Two Producers Receive 10 Percent Profit

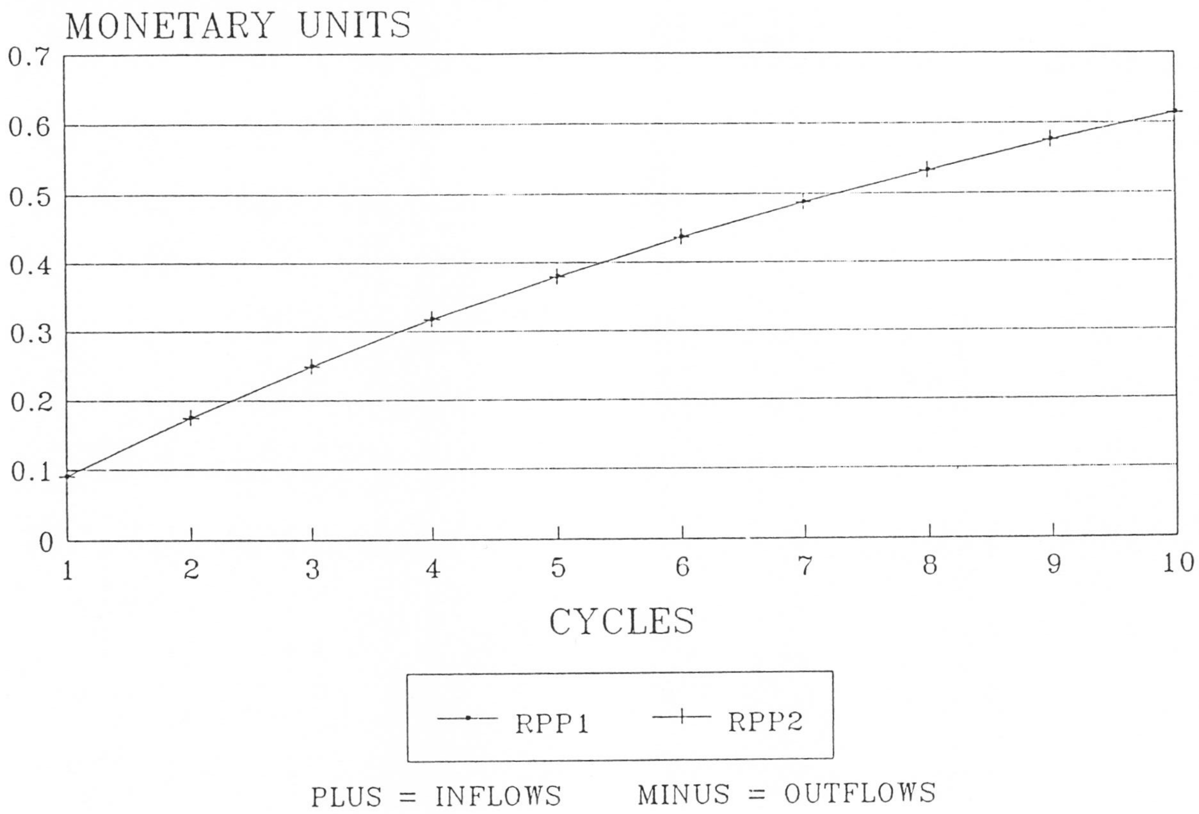

MONETARY UNITS
0.7
0.6
0.5
0.4
0.3
0.2
0.1
0
1
2
3
4
5
6
7
8
9
10
CYCLES
RPP1
RPP2
PLUS = INFLOWS
MINUS = OUTFLOWS

Figure 7-5
Residuals When Two Producers Receive Offsetting 10 Percent Profit

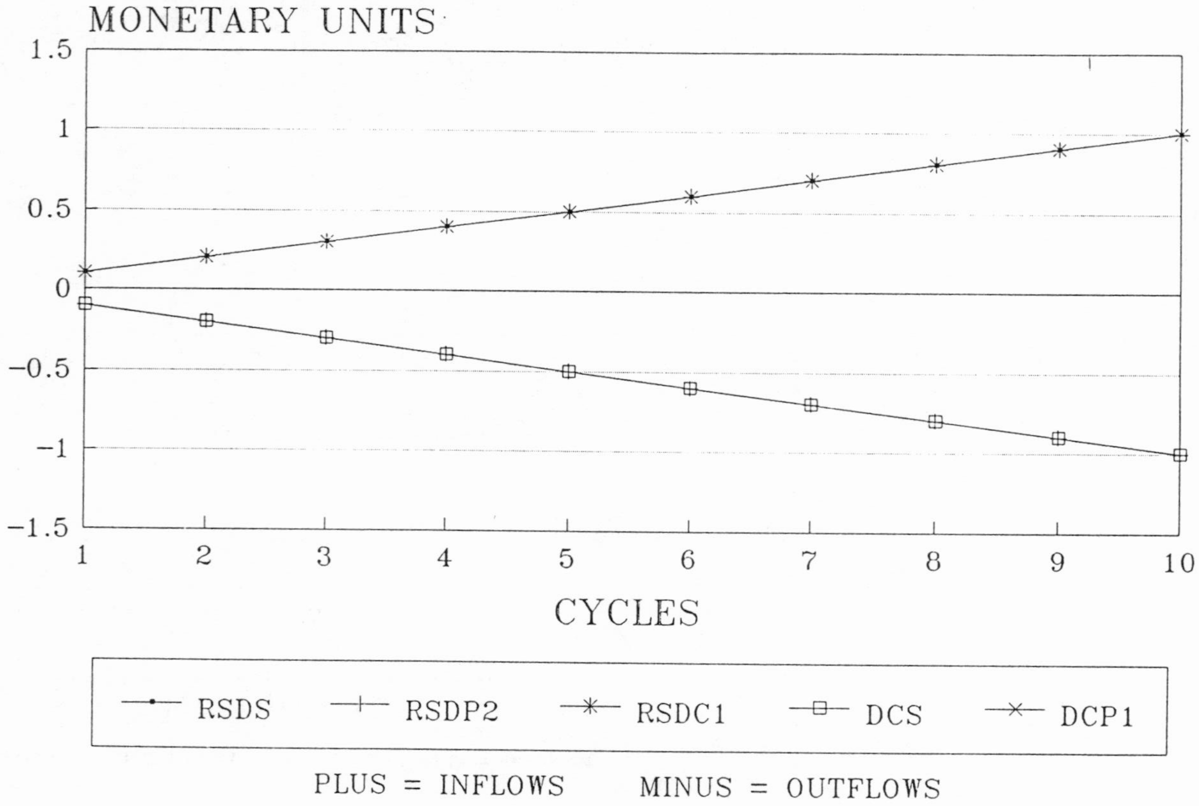

MONETARY UNITS

CYCLES

—— RSDS   —+— RSDP2   —✳— RSDC1   —▣— DCS   —✳— DCP1

PLUS = INFLOWS   MINUS = OUTFLOWS

Table 7-6
Residuals When Two Producers Receive Offsetting 10 Percent Profit

X Data	RSD8	RSDP2	RSDC1	DCS
1	0.1	-0.1	0.1	-0.1
2	0.2	-0.2	0.2	-0.2
3	0.3	-0.3	0.3	-0.3
4	0.4	-0.4	0.4	-0.4
5	0.5	-0.5	0.5	-0.5
6	0.6	-0.6	0.6	-0.6
7	0.7	-0.7	0.7	-0.7
8	0.8	-0.8	0.8	-0.8
9	0.9	-0.9	0.9	-0.9
10	1	-1	1	-1

X Data	DCP1
1	0.1
2	0.2
3	0.3
4	0.4
5	0.5
6	0.6
7	0.7
8	0.8
9	0.9
10	1

Figure 7-6
Residuals When One Producer Receives 10 Percent Increase in Costs of Factors of Production

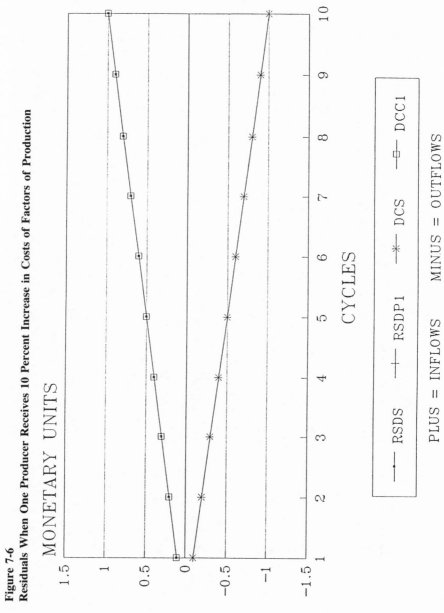

Table 7-7
Residuals When One Producer Receives 10 Percent Increase in Costs of Factors of Production

Cycle	RSDS	RSDP1	DCS	DCC1
1	0.1	-0.1	-0.1	0.1
2	0.2	-0.2	-0.2	0.2
3	0.3	-0.3	-0.3	0.3
4	0.4	-0.4	-0.4	0.4
5	0.5	-0.5	-0.5	0.5
6	0.6	-0.6	-0.6	0.6
7	0.7	-0.7	-0.7	0.7
8	0.8	-0.8	-0.8	0.8
9	0.9	-0.9	-0.9	0.9
10	1	-1	-1	1

Figure 7-7
Residuals When Two Producers Receive 10 Percent Increase in Costs of Factors of Production

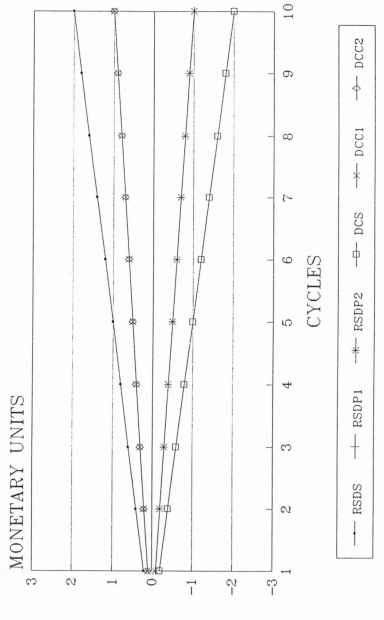

Table 7-8
Residuals When Two Producers Receive 10 Percent Increase in Costs of Factors of Production

X Data	RSDS	RSDP1	RSDP2	DCS
1	0.2	-0.1	-0.1	-0.2
2	0.4	-0.2	-0.2	-0.4
3	0.6	-0.3	-0.3	-0.6
4	0.8	-0.4	-0.4	-0.8
5	1	-0.5	-0.5	-1
6	1.2	-0.6	-0.6	-1.2
7	1.4	-0.7	-0.7	-1.4
8	1.6	-0.8	-0.8	-1.6
9	1.8	-0.9	-0.9	-1.8
10	2	-1	-1	-2

X Data	DCC1	DCC2
1	0.1	0.1
2	0.2	0.2
3	0.3	0.3
4	0.4	0.4
5	0.5	0.5
6	0.6	0.6
7	0.7	0.7
8	0.8	0.8
9	0.9	0.9
10	1	1

Figure 7-8
Residuals When Offsetting 10 Percent Changes in Costs of Factors of Production Occur

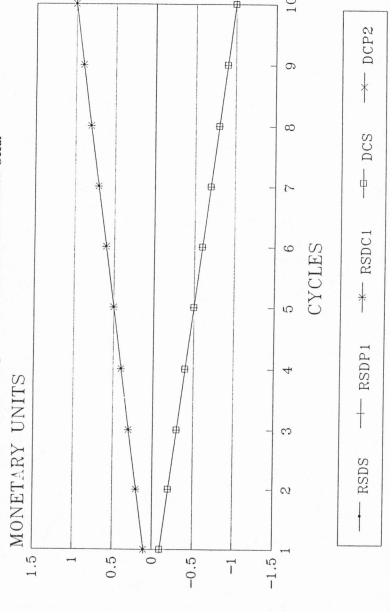

Table 7-9
Residuals When Offsetting 10 Percent Changes in Costs of Factors of Production Occur

Cycle	RSDS	RSDP1	RSDC1	DCS
1	0.1	-0.1	0.1	-0.1
2	0.2	-0.2	0.2	-0.2
3	0.3	-0.3	0.3	-0.3
4	0.4	-0.4	0.4	-0.4
5	0.5	-0.5	0.5	-0.5
6	0.6	-0.6	0.6	-0.6
7	0.7	-0.7	0.7	-0.7
8	0.8	-0.8	0.8	-0.8
9	0.9	-0.9	0.9	-0.9
10	1	-1	1	-1

X Data	DCP2
1	0.1
2	0.2
3	0.3
4	0.4
5	0.5
6	0.6
7	0.7
8	0.8
9	0.9
10	1

Figure 7-9
Residuals When Two Producers Receive 10 Percent Profit, and Society Receives 10 Percent Interest

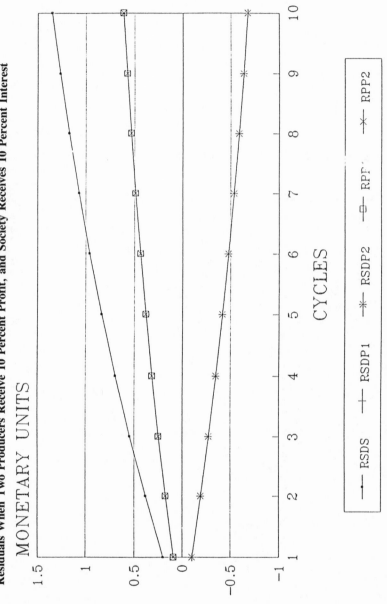

PLUS = INFLOWS   MINUS = OUTFLOWS

Table 7-10
**Residuals When Two Producers Receive 10 Percent Profit and Society Receives
10 Percent Interest**

X Data	RSDS	RSDP1	RSDP2	RPP1
1	0.2	-0.1	-0.1	0.091
2	0.382	-0.191	-0.191	0.174
3	0.547	-0.274	-0.274	0.249
4	0.697	-0.349	-0.349	0.317
5	0.834	-0.417	-0.417	0.379
6	0.958	-0.479	-0.479	0.436
7	1.071	-0.536	-0.536	0.487
8	1.174	-0.587	-0.587	0.533
9	1.267	-0.634	-0.634	0.576
10	1.352	-0.676	-0.676	0.614

CYCLE	RPP2
1	0.091
2	0.174
3	0.249
4	0.317
5	0.379
6	0.436
7	0.487
8	0.533
9	0.576
10	0.614

Table 7-11
**Production When Two Producers Receive 10 Percent Profit, and Society Receives
10 Percent Interest**

Cycle	Production		
	P1	P2	All
1	1	1	2
2	.91	.91	1.82
3	.83	.83	1.66
4	.75	.75	1.50
5	.68	.68	1.36
6	.62	.62	1.24
7	.56	.56	1.12
8	.51	.51	1.02
9	.47	.47	.94
10	.42	.42	.84

Figure 7-10
Residuals When Producers Receive Offsetting 10 Percent Profit and Society Receives 10 Percent Interest

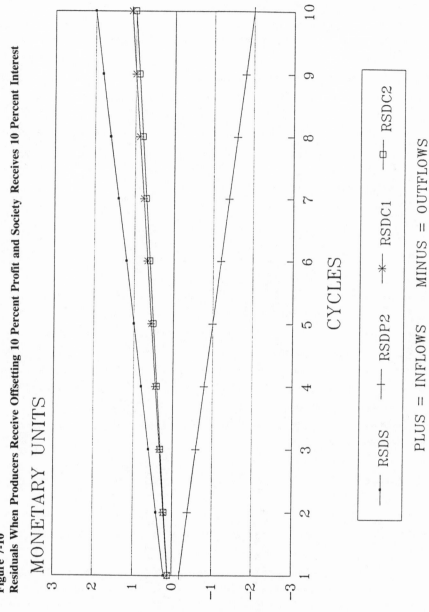

MONETARY UNITS

CYCLES

RSDS RSDP2 RSDC1 RSDC2

PLUS = INFLOWS   MINUS = OUTFLOWS

Table 7-12
Residuals When Producers Receive Offsetting 10 Percent Profit and Society Receives 10 Percent Interest

Cycle	RSDS	RSDP1	DCS	DCC1
1	0.2	-0.2	0.11	0.1
2	0.4	-0.4	0.22	0.2
3	0.6	-0.6	0.33	0.3
4	0.8	-0.8	0.44	0.4
5	1	-1	0.55	0.5
6	1.2	-1.2	0.66	0.6
7	1.4	-1.4	0.77	0.7
8	1.6	-1.6	0.88	0.8
9	1.8	-1.8	0.99	0.9
10	2	-2	1.1	1

Table 7-13
Production When Producers Receive Offsetting 10 Percent Profit and Society Receives 10 Percent Interest

Cycle	Production		
	P1	P2	All
1	1	1	2
2	1	1	2
3	1	1	2
4	1	1	2
5	1	1	2
6	1	1	2
7	1	1	2
8	1	1	2
9	1	1	2
10	1	1	2

8

Supranational Systems: Intersocietal Exchanges

Previous chapters have discussed modern debt money economies in the context of societal processes themselves. This chapter extends the discussion to multiple societies and emerging supranational systems. Supranational systems are higher-order human systems composed of societies. They compose Miller's (Swanson and Miller 1989) eighth-level living systems classification. A macro accounting analysis of exchanges involving the currency money-information markers of two different societies provides interesting insights into the effects of changes in the rates at which societies exchange currencies within supranational systems.

FOREIGN EXCHANGE RATES ARE SUPRANATIONAL SYSTEM EMERGENTS

Foreign currency exchange rates cannot exist within a single society. They are supranational system emergents. They exist because the societies in which currency MIM emerge are components of supranational systems.

A foreign currency exchange rate is composed of a ratio relationship between two ratios. It is a compound ratio ideally consisting of the ratio of all currency in one society to that in another society *to* the ratio of all matter-energy forms in the first society to that of the other (E8-1). The ideal rate likely is unachievable.

$$IR = (DCM \div FCM) \div (DME \div FME) \qquad (E8\text{-}1)$$

where

IR = ideal foreign exchange rate,

DCM = domestic currency MIM,

FCM = foreign currency MIM,

DME = domestic matter-energy forms,

FME = foreign matter-energy forms, and matter-energy forms in both societies are measured on the same attribute.

An example follows:

$$IR = (100D \div 200P) \div (10 \text{ lbs.} \div 20 \text{ lbs.}) = 1D \div 1P$$

Actual exchange rates emerge from actual prices within societies. Prices are ratios of money-information markers to matter-energy forms. The matter-energy forms exchanged between societies are generally measured on the same attribute. The money-information markers, alternatively, are measured in two different currencies. Each society measures them in its own currency. The relationship between the amounts of two different society currencies exchanged for a particular physical amount of a commodity is a foreign exchange rate. It is the relationship between the prices in two different currencies of a certain amount of a commodity.

Societies ordinarily do not export goods and services in the same mixture they produce them. Any average of the prices of the goods and services they export will differ from that average of the total goods and services they produce. Because actual exchange rates emerge from some combination of less than all specific societal prices, the actual exchange rate would not be expected to equal the ideal one.

That emergence process provides a basis for societies to benefit from economic value arising from price differentials among products within their economies. Comparative trade advantages may be identified in such differentials. Ricardo (1817) developed the seminal model for identifying comparative advantage in terms of labor inputs.

Modern economies synthesize in their monetary flows the costs of all legitimatized factors of production by pricing commodities to include them. Additionally, prices include motivators of money-information marker flows. Consequently, prices include distortions and biases that may occur in the markers themselves. The price differentials within economies that may give rise to comparative advantages include both information about matter-energy forms and information about money-information marker forms. Similarly, the exchange rate (differential in the prices of two currencies) contains elements of information about both matter-energy forms and money-information marker forms.

Those two aspects of monetary information are the results of how monetary economies emerge. Modern economies are expansions of fundamental trade processes. Trades are exchanges of matter-energy forms for matter-energy forms. The act of trading determines that the specific exchange values of two different matter-energy forms are equal. That value is imputed to negotiable accounting documents, usually through debt instrumentation. Forms of those instruments become money that carries the value information signal and is exchanged for value.

The monetary value information can be distorted in numerous ways as it recursively moves through a chain of exchanges. The basic motivator (and discipline) of a monetary economy is the one-to-one ratio of the specific exchange value of the matter-energy forms in a trade. The monetary information expands out of that trade information. Therefore, it is important to analyze foreign exchange rates with reference to the discipline of basic trades. Analyzing foreign exchange rates in that manner requires including examinations of price changes within societies as well as rate changes between societies. The supranational emergent foreign exchange rate cannot be understood without reference to its societal emergent components, the prices within societies.

THE BASIC FOREIGN EXCHANGE CIRCUIT

Foreign exchanges present no fundamental problem to debt-based monetary economies despite their involving different currency money-information markers. This assertion is illustrated by the following situation (8-1):

Producer (P1) and consumer-laborer (C1) are in the domestic society, and producer (P2) and consumer-laborer (C2) are in the foreign society. A transaction's value is indicated by subscripts of ratio-scaled numbers. The currencies in which the subscripts are denominated are prefixed to the main MIM terms (D, domestic, and F, foreign). The product is designated similarly. In each society, the producer exchanges a promissory note for currency with its society and uses the currency to entice factors of production to produce a good. The consumer-laborer entities exchange the currency received for the other society's currency and use that other currency to purchase the good produced by the other producer.

$$\text{DTLM}^{P1}_{-1} \ \text{DTLM}^{s1}_{1} \ \text{DCM}^{s1}_{-1} \ \text{DCM}^{P1}_{1} \ \text{DCM}^{P1}_{-1} \ \text{DCM}^{c1}_{1} \ \text{DME}^{c1}_{-1} \ \text{DME}^{P1}_{1} \ (8\text{-}1)$$

$$\text{FTLM}^{P2}_{-1} \ \text{FTLM}^{s2}_{1} \ \text{FCM}^{s2}_{-1} \ \text{FCM}^{P2}_{1} \ \text{FCM}^{P2}_{-1} \ \text{FCM}^{c2}_{1} \ \text{FME}^{c2}_{-1} \ \text{FME}^{P2}_{1}$$

$$\text{DCM}^{c1}_{-1} \ \text{DCM}^{s2}_{1} \ \text{FCM}^{s2}_{-1} \ \text{FCM}^{c1}_{1} \ \text{FCM}^{c1}_{-1} \ \text{FCM}^{P2}_{1} \ \text{FME}^{P2}_{-1} \ \text{FME}^{c1}_{1}$$

$$\text{FCM}^{c2}_{-1} \ \text{FCM}^{s1}_{1} \ \text{DCM}^{s1}_{-1} \ \text{DCM}^{c2}_{1} \ \text{DCM}^{c2}_{-1} \ \text{DCM}^{P1}_{1} \ \text{DME}^{P1}_{-1} \ \text{DME}^{c2}_{1}$$

$$\text{FCM}^{P2}_{-1} \ \text{FCM}^{s2}_{1} \ \text{FTLM}^{s2}_{-1} \ \text{FTLM}^{P2}_{1}$$

$$\text{DCM}^{P1}_{-1} \ \text{DCM}^{s1}_{1} \ \text{DTLM}^{s1}_{-1} \ \text{DTLM}^{P1}_{1}$$

$$\text{FCM}^{s1}_{-1} \ \text{FCM}^{s2}_{1} \ \text{DCM}^{s2}_{-1} \ \text{DCM}^{s1}_{1}$$

$$/\text{RSD}/ \ \text{DME}^{c1}_{-1} \ \text{DME}^{c2}_{1} \ \text{FME}^{c2}_{-1} \ \text{FME}^{c1}_{1}$$

The results of the chain of exchanges are that both societies' currency money-information marker circuits clear, leaving the products in the hands of the consumers. These are clean results that can be repeated time and again without any money-information marker residuals being left in the system.

ACTUAL FOREIGN EXCHANGE RATES

A trade in a free market system equates the goods-services exchanged. They are equal on the attribute-specific exchange value. In two different societies, that value is measured in two different currencies that may not equal each other. For example, the following notation describes an exchange of goods-services when the exchange rate is 1D to 2F.

$$DCM^{c1}{}_{-1} \ DCM^{s2}{}_{1} \ FCM^{s2}{}_{-2} \ FCM^{c1}{}_{2} \ FCM^{c1}{}_{-2} \ FCM^{p2}{}_{2} \ FME^{p2}{}_{-2} \ FME^{c1}{}_{2} \quad (8-2)$$

$$FCM^{c2}{}_{-2} \ FCM^{s1}{}_{2} \ DCM^{s1}{}_{-1} \ DCM^{c2}{}_{1} \ DCM^{c2}{}_{-1} \ DCM^{p1}{}_{1} \ DME^{p1}{}_{-1} \ DME^{c2}{}_{1}$$

Despite the differently denominated measurements, the ME of the first line equals the ME of the second line because they are in fact exchanged. Therefore, the actual foreign exchange rate is given by the following equation:

$$1ME \div 1ME = AR \cdot 1DME \div 2 \ FME$$
$$AR = 2F \div 1D \quad \quad (E8-2)$$

where

AR = actual foreign exchange rate,

DME = domestic currency value of ME, and

FME = foreign currency value of ME.

AR is an algebraic isomorphism that restates one currency in terms of another. When foreign exchange rates are set according to the actual exchange rate of a particular commodity or mix of commodities, an actual exchange rate is used as an isomorphism to map one dynamic system of changing relationships on another. Algebraic isomorphisms apply only to two static (unchanging) algebraic systems. Because money-information marker amounts compose concrete (objective) counting systems, the amounts cannot be fully abstracted from the markers themselves. The ratios between the markers and the matter-energy forms (prices) of different exchanges of similar commodities are not necessarily the same. MIM systems therefore are only dynamically isomorphic to each other. In the nth degree, dynamic isomorphism is the opposite of isomorphism.

Imposing a static condition mapping function (an isomorphism) makes it possible to bias the map toward the self-interests of more knowledgeable or powerful societies or of select individuals within societies. That problem unfortunately cannot be solved completely without removing multiple currencies and their companion benefits. As the amount of trade among societies diversifies and increases, the probability that the actual exchange rate of a particular commodity represents in any significant way the population of the exchange rates of all commodities traded approaches zero. Exchange rates generally should not be set by the exchange of a single commodity or small group of commodities.

PRICE DIFFERENTIALS CAUSED BY DIFFERENCES IN LEVELS OF ECONOMIC DEVELOPMENT

Price differentials can be caused by many different conditions—some acceptable and some unacceptable. Acceptable causes include preferences for different product mixes and availability of natural resources. Price differentials also include several legitimatized economic motivators such as interest, dividends, royalties, and profits. Unacceptable causes of price differentials include certain illegal and internationally unacceptable introductions of currency MIM and unexplained inflation, among others. Most changes in price differentials among societies are caused by introductions of legitimate economic motivators and illegal or unacceptable introductions of currency MIM because such conditions as preferences for products and availability of natural resources do not ordinarily change rapidly.

As they introduce more and more economic motivators, societies must provide more currency MIM to fund them. The currency required is increasingly more than that previously required to produce and distribute a particular amount of goods-services. Consequently, the ratio of CM to ME (price) increases.

Economic motivators increase the overall economic activities of societies. The increase usually improves the technology and quality of life in societies. In terms of cost of production and distribution of goods and services, however, the increasing prices resulting from monetizing economic motivators—that are themselves MIM forms—are increasing monetary inefficiencies as economies develop more complexity. That monetary inefficiency conceivably might be offset by increasingly efficient matter-energy processes made possible by advancing technology, but that does not necessarily happen.

The monetary inefficiency of more developed societies gives an exchange advantage to the less developed societies if the currencies of less developed societies have not been illegitimately inflated. The advantage exists because developing societies are not or should not be funding advanced motivators beyond those needed for their levels of development.

Comparative exchange advantage emerging from differences in the developmental levels of societies is a supranational system emergent. It is a monetary phenomenon that exists because more than one currency exists. Currencies are emergents at the societal level of living systems.

Comparative exchange advantage is different from the comparative trade advantage described by Ricardo and others. Comparative trade advantages are based on differences in preferences and costs among any arbitrarily identified divisions of a producing-consuming whole. They can be identified within societies as well as across their boundaries. Exchange advantages can be realized only when exchanges occur between two relatively independent currency MIM systems.

As they develop, underdeveloped countries increase their monetary inefficiency, approaching the inefficiency level of developed countries. Their comparative exchange advantage diminishes as they develop. Eventually, no comparative exchange advantage remains, and continuing trade must be motivated by such other conditions as comparative trade advantages, some degree of resource monopoly, information distortions, and political power.

Comparative trade advantage arises from commodity price differentials. Prices are forms of information. Comparative trading advantage, therefore, is an information condition. Only when divisions of a producing-consuming whole are societies is comparative trade advantage a foreign trade consequence. Societies have concrete boundaries that consist of both matter-energy and information forms. The most basic concrete information of society boundaries is currency MIM. Comparative trade advantage in foreign trade is a condition of currency MIM. Comparative exchange advantage also is a condition of currency MIM. Although they are distinct and concrete, the two conditions are not necessarily separable in particular exchanges. They are phenomena arising out of relationships of elements that become apparent when observing multiple exchanges (processes).

Notwithstanding the unindirectionality toward a developing society, comparative exchange advantage, if it exists, may be exploited by either partner in a trade. Comparative trade advantage distributes benefits to both parties in a trade by releasing demand constraints of a particular product mix and, thereby, increasing overall production. Comparative exchange advantage can benefit both parties by releasing demand constrained (in this case) by higher prices in one society and, thereby, increasing overall production. The parties compete for distribution of a comparative exchange advantage, however. If a developing nation can negotiate a price that exceeds its domestic price, the price increment can be used to import advanced information and technology without negatively affecting its existing economy. If a price increment cannot be negotiated, the exchange advantage goes entirely to the developed society. Even when that happens, however, trade may continue motivated by comparative trade advantages, abundant resources, political coercion, information distortions, and the like.

FIXED FOREIGN EXCHANGE RATES

Foreign exchange rates may be held constant (fixed), or they may be changing (fluctuating) to reflect certain international exchange conditions. Fixed foreign currency exchange rates pass price increases in one society through to the consuming society. Notation 8-3 is the same as 8-1 except that domestic society increases its product price 100 percent. The foreign currency exchange rate remains the same at 1:1.

$DTLM^{p1}_{-2}$ $DTLM^{s1}_{2}$ DMC^{s1}_{-2} DCM^{p1}_{2} DCM^{p1}_{-2} DCM^{c1}_{2} DME^{c1}_{-1} DME^{p1}_{1} (8–3)

$FTLM^{p2}_{-1}$ $FTLM^{s2}_{1}$ FCM^{s2}_{-1} FCM^{p2}_{1} FCM^{p2}_{-1} FCM^{c2}_{1} FME^{c2}_{-1} FME^{p2}_{1}

DCM^{c1}_{-1} DCM^{s2}_{1} FCM^{s2}_{-1} FCM^{c1}_{1} FCM^{c1}_{-1} FCM^{p2}_{1} FME^{p2}_{-1} FME^{c1}_{1}

FCM^{c2}_{-1} FCM^{s1}_{1} DCM^{s1}_{-1} DCM^{c2}_{1} DCM^{c2}_{-1} DCM^{p1}_{1} $DME^{p1}_{-0.5}$ $DME^{c2}_{0.5}$

FCM^{p2}_{-1} FCM^{s2}_{1} $FTLM^{s2}_{-1}$ $FTLM^{p2}_{1}$

DCM^{p1}_{-1} DCM^{s1}_{1} $DTLM^{s1}_{-1}$ $DTLM^{p1}_{1}$

FCM^{s1}_{-1} FCM^{s2}_{1} DCM^{s2}_{-1} DCM^{s1}_{1}

/ RSD/ $DTLM^{p1}_{-1}$ $DTLM^{s1}_{1}$ DCM^{s1}_{-1} DCM^{c1}_{1} DME^{c1}_{-1} FME^{c2}_{-1}

$FME^{c1}_{1} DME^{c2}_{0.5}$ $DME^{p1}_{0.5}$

The results of the domestic price increase are the following:

1. The domestic producer is left holding inventory worth D0.5.
2. The foreign consumer-labor entity receives product worth only D0.5.
3. Discretionary currency MIM in the amount of D1 are left in the hands of the domestic consumer-labor entity.
4. The domestic society is left holding debt owed by the domestic producer in the amount of D1.

Assuming that the domestic consumer-labor entity desires some of its own product, the residuals from the first three results can be eliminated. The final results in that case are that the domestic consumer-labor entity receives product worth F1 and D0.5 while the foreign consumer-labor entity receives product worth only D0.5.

This situation seems to apply the fundamental discipline of the market in the most efficient manner. The end consumer decides to accept or reject the increased price of the product. All purchases are not fully discretionary, however. Economic coercion may be introduced by higher-level systems (through monopoly, for example). Such coercion violates the 1:1 specific exchange value assigned to products in a free trade. It introduces a higher-level bias on what specific participants in a trade can negotiate. Even though they tolerate extensive violations within their own boundaries, societies usually attempt to protect their participants from economic coercion originating in other societies.

Price increases certainly pay off for the country introducing them if foreign exchange rates are fixed. The reason the increases are introduced does not matter. Consequently, the other society attempts to filter out increases by changing foreign exchange rates.

CHANGING FOREIGN CURRENCY EXCHANGE RATES

Changing foreign currency exchange rates can keep the effects of price changes occurring in one society from being transmitted to another. Changes in exchange rates can remove entire price changes or only those considered unacceptable. Changing foreign currency exchange rates can also introduce price changes in an importing society that did not occur in the exporting society.

If a domestic society has introduced currency MIM in an internationally unacceptable manner (inflating its currency by monetary policy or lack of control), a foreign society would like to protect itself from the negative effects it would suffer from the price increase. To do so, the foreign society must decrease the amount of its currency it is willing to give in exchange for domestic currency. The decrease must be proportionate to the domestic society's price increase (8-4).

$$DTLM^{p1}{}_{-2} \ DTLM^{s1}{}_{2} \ DCM^{s1}{}_{-2} \ DCM^{p1}{}_{2} \ DCM^{p1}{}_{-2} \ DCM^{c1}{}_{2} \ DME^{c1}{}_{-1} \ DME^{p1}{}_{1} \ (8\text{-}4)$$

$$FTLM^{p2}{}_{-1} \ FTLM^{s2}{}_{1} \ FCM^{s2}{}_{-1} \ FCM^{p2}{}_{1} \ FCM^{p2}{}_{-1} \ FCM^{c2}{}_{1} \ FME^{c2}{}_{-1} \ FME^{p2}{}_{1}$$

$$DCM^{c1}{}_{-2} \ DCM^{s2}{}_{2} \ FCM^{s2}{}_{-1} \ FCM^{c1}{}_{1} \ FCM^{c1}{}_{-1} \ FCM^{p2}{}_{1} \ FME^{p2}{}_{-1} \ FME^{c1}{}_{1}$$

$$FCM^{c2}{}_{-1} \ FCM^{s1}{}_{1} \ DCM^{s1}{}_{-2} \ DCM^{c2}{}_{2} \ DCM^{c2}{}_{-2} \ DCM^{p1}{}_{2} \ DME^{p1}{}_{-1} \ DME^{c2}{}_{1}$$

$$FCM^{p2}{}_{-1} \ FCM^{s2}{}_{1} \ FTLM^{s2}{}_{-1} \ FTLM^{p2}{}_{1}$$

$$DCM^{p1}{}_{-2} \ DCM^{s1}{}_{2} \ DTLM^{s1}{}_{-2} \ DTLM^{p1}{}_{2}$$

$$FCM^{s1}{}_{-1} \ FCM^{s2}{}_{1} \ DCM^{s2}{}_{-1} \ DCM^{s1}{}_{1}$$

Societies can protect against foreign inflation by adjusting their exchange rates according to the following equation (E8-3):

$$NER = PER \cdot \frac{1}{(1 + FIR)} \tag{E8-3}$$

where

NER = new exchange rate,
PER = previous exchange rate, and
FIR = foreign inflation rate.

The new exchange rate should vary inversely with the foreign inflation rate. Of course, inflation or deflation is usually occurring in both societies. The following equation (E8-4) provides a just conversion for both societies:

$$\frac{NDP}{NFP} = \frac{PDP}{PFP} \cdot \frac{(1 + DIR)}{(1 + FIR)}, \tag{E8-4}$$

where

NDP = new domestic price,
NFP = new foreign price,

PDP = previous domestic price,

PFP = previous foreign price,

FIR = foreign inflation rate, and

DIR = domestic inflation rate.

The new exchange rate for the situation described in Notation 8-4 is:

$$\frac{NDP}{NFP} = \frac{1}{1} \cdot \frac{(1 + 1)}{(1 + 0)} = \frac{2}{2}$$

Societies manage foreign currency exchange rates both directly and indirectly. Developed societies mostly manage their rates indirectly by their general monetary policies and by trading in foreign currencies. As a result, changing foreign currency exchange rates is not an easy solution to problems of currency manipulation by individual societies. No inherent reason for not directly managing foreign currency exchange rates exists, however, in debt-based monetary systems.

LIMITATIONS OF FREELY FLUCTUATING FOREIGN CURRENCY EXCHANGE RATES

Leaving changes in foreign currency exchange rates to supply-demand market forces imposes certain limitations on what individual societies can do to influence changes in exchange rates. Because currency money-information markers are introduced on demand of economic participants and are retrieved upon the complete execution of an executory contract, societies ultimately have discretionary power only to issue currency, not to retrieve it. The matrix in Figure 8-1 outlines how societies can react to inflationary/deflationary (price change) conditions. When domestic society is deflationary and foreign society is inflationary, domestic society can issue D. When domestic society is inflationary and foreign society is deflationary, foreign society can issue F. The remedies available are internally-externally consistent. They provide negative feedback, working to reverse the change in product transfers. They are always inflationary, however.

Figure 8-2 configures the information on what actions societies can take and have incentive to take in a 2 × 2 matrix.

The cells represent situations, and the symbols in the cells represent critical reactions to those situations. F_L means that foreign society can issue and has incentive to issue its currency. D_L means that domestic society can issue and has incentive to issue its currency.

The critical reactions all loosen monetary policy. They move in an inflationary direction. While they provide a negative feedback on the matter-energy flows (goods-services), they provide a positive feedback on the information signal (money-information markers), working to increase the change in money transmissions. The original ratio of traded goods-services is achieved by raising the price of goods in other societies to equal any change in a particular one. That action, at the limit, maintains both the original ratio of traded goods and the original foreign currency exchange rates. At the limit, the NDP/NFP of the situation in notation 8-4 would be $1/1 \cdot 2/2 = 2/2$, reduced to $1/1$. That result seems to indicate that the system has returned to its original state. It has not. A new equilibrium maintained by twice the amount of monetary signal has replaced the previous state. To the extent that changes in the money supply did not influence changes in the foreign currency exchange rate, the limit is not achieved, and the result falls somewhere between a NDP/NFP of $2/1$ and one of $2/2$.

SUPPLY-DEMAND CONTROL OF FOREIGN CURRENCY EXCHANGE RATES PERMITS UNEQUAL TREATMENT OF MEMBERS OF SOCIETIES

How the current processes change foreign currency exchange rates is interesting. Both the domestic money supply and that used for foreign exchanges are involved. Speculation on changes in foreign exchange rates is the mechanism that most often motivates the changes. Speculators (including central banks of societies) trade various currencies as commodities. They merchandise money. That action introduces supply-demand price-changing forces into the process of setting foreign currency exchange rates. The rates become the prices, and changes in them are influenced by supply-demand forces. The supply-demand forces are directly influenced by the offers to buy and sell various currencies at a particular moment. They are indirectly influenced by information about the domestic money supplies of the currencies involved. The direct influence is by far the stronger signal.

The consequence of that process is that societies may attempt to break with the internal-external consistency of reasonable global action to achieve a less global effect favoring some faction of the economy or some perceived social purpose or goal. Notwithstanding the benefits to the U.S. economy in terms of goods and services of a dollar inflationary money supply and the incentive for Japan to loosen the yen to offset the inflated dollar, for example, the United States may issue dollars on the foreign exchange market to lower the yen-dollar ratio so that fewer yen will buy more American products. The action is justified on the basis of increasing the number of jobs in the United States and ostensibly to balance America's trade deficit with Japan. The jobs argument has great political appeal, so it apparently does not matter that the trade deficit (a monetary phenomenon) argument is completely illogical. How can an imbalance of too many dollars being exchanged for too few yen be brought into balance by increasing the number of dollars being given in exchange for yen? The action succeeds because the increased dollars in the foreign currency exchange market is a very strong signal, completely obscuring the weaker signal of information about the inflationary condition of the general dollar supply.

The political popularity of the jobs argument also obscures other important consequences of this process. The dollars being dumped in the foreign exchange market go to speculator-investors who can buy products-services or ownership-credit in the United States. Because the dumped dollars are targeted to achieve an incremental inflation, the speculator-investor can use them to purchase in the United States at a great advantage. A particular purchase requires fewer yen than otherwise. Domestic participants are placed at a distinct disadvantage. In essence, the U.S. economy is giving dollars to participants of the Japanese economy to buy elements of the U.S. economy at will. Because the incremental inflation is fed through foreign exchange and no restrictions are placed on the foreign purchases of ownership-credit, foreigners are *given* an increasing amount of ultimate control of the American economy. They need not earn it in fair competition. They need not be efficient. They need only to be foreign. Their rise to power, and the consequent fall of the American worker and businessperson, is a result of money-information marker manipulation, not of superior foreign production.

This example, of course, can be reversed with U.S. economy speculators-investors buying elements of the Japanese economy if such purchases are unrestricted. A similar set of examples may be given to show that a milder form of the same kind of advantage is given foreign investors when foreign currency inflationary conditions exist and domestic currency does not inflate proportionately and vice versa. The advantage is that shown in the situation described by Notation 8-3. Incremental inflation of a speculative foreign currency market amplifies the milder form.

Why would such a thing happen? All civilization is a phenomenon that hierarchically organizes humankind. Individual humans organize into groups, and groups form organizations, and organizations form communities, and communities form societies, and now societies are forming supranational systems. The process now working makes it possible to form a world order by introducing an international privileged class that is privy to the most powerful form of information available: money information. The formulation of the privileged class is the process that is motivating the subprocesses. That motivating process is completely logical.

A WORLD ORDER

The unique historical question at the turn of the twenty-first century is whether the ultimate civilization will be a world order organized and controlled by a privileged class or a world order organized and controlled by a distributed supranational decider subsystem. Although humans have progressively attempted to reject privileged class control over the long development of civilization, an alternative form of control has not been adequately understood or developed.

Only in the twentieth century have societal institutions emerged that portend a final rejection of the privileged class cycles of economic boom and bust and political benevolence and despotism. If these emergents can mature at the society order, a pattern for similar incipient supranational order may emerge. The grand catastrophe of the twentieth century could be the development of a world order controlled by a privileged class when the societal order is so close to developing distributed societal subsystem control.

Strong pressures for the rapid development of a world order exist. World population increase, ecological destruction, weapons of total annihilation, and many other mega-problems cry out for world solutions. The standard answer of most philosophers, scientists, educators, and politicians is to develop one more level of human organization—this time a world order.

With every new order, we naively believe that those humans who occupy it will somehow act justly and responsibly. Before long, we are proposing a new higher order to correct the less-than-ideal behavior of the last developed order. Human systems are only that—human. A system will never be more just or responsible than the humans that compose it.

Scientists have recognized that we humans are our own worst enemies and have devised methodologies, methods, and procedures to overcome our individual biases in observing physical reality. Auditors have begun to develop methodologies, methods, and procedures to overcome individual deviant behaviors and systemic inadequacies and malfunctions. In both science and auditing, distinguishing measurements from interpretation and distributing control functions among different individuals and system units are important.

A decider subsystem functions in every living system, from cells through organs, organisms, groups, organizations, communities, societies, and supranational systems. It is the most critical function because it cannot be dispersed to other living systems and it determines the composition, arrangement, and order of the living system. The organization level of human systems has repeatedly travailed in birth, producing communities and societies only to have them mature and collapse into larger organizations. The most important characteristic of the organization level of human systems is the hierarchical structure of its decider subsystems. Organizations have multi-echelon decider subsystems. As relatively independent elements of communities and societies are brought under the control of a multi-echelon decider subsystem of an organization, the communities and societies collapse into that organization.

The organization level is more limited than communities and societies in the complexity that it can tolerate. That is why the higher-order communities and societies continue to emerge. Emerge as they will, a strong propensity to collapse to the organization level apparently exists. Discovering how to disrupt that propensity is the grand quest for the fountain of youth. Inventing community, society, and supranational systems that incorporate information filters that prevent an organization, political or economic, from capturing distributed elements of higher-order decider subsystems should be the supreme scientific objective of the twenty-first century. World boom followed by bust and world benevolence followed by despotism is certainly less appealing than the society-level rendition of the same we are now rejecting.

FOREIGN RESERVES—A MODERATING INFLUENCE?

The situations described by both notations 8-3 and 8-4 assume that both domestic and foreign currency money-information marker circuits are closed. That is to say, the domestic and foreign societies retrieve their currencies from each other—thus retiring them. That does not always happen. In fact, it is quite common for a particular country to hold certain amounts of foreign currencies in reserve to be exchanged, hoping for advantageous situations. This practice makes it possible for a particular country to introduce foreign currency into the foreign currency exchange market process as well as to issue its own currency. Thus, a country is provided a means of influencing the market in the opposite direction.

That seems to take some of the edge off of the unidirectional inflationary response of being able only to issue, not to retrieve, currency. The moderating influence, however, is mostly illusionary. Little incentive exists for societies to loosen foreign currency. Loosening their own currency provides the trade advantage. So they likely dump foreign reserves when the general inflation of that currency is so bad that exchange agreements pretty well revert to trade agreements, essentially removing the money information signal from the exchange process. Speculator elements, of course, buy and sell the currency based on the chance of movement in the rates, and that may provide some moderation.

Foreign currency reserves nevertheless have become an important factor in international trade. The degree to which trade may occur between a developing nation with weak currency and a developed nation with strong currency is often determined by the amount of the stronger currency the developing nation holds in reserve. Furthermore, deficit financing by a foreign government is often connected to its foreign currency reserves.

FISCAL DEFICIT FINANCING

Governments often use foreign funds to finance their fiscal deficits. The deficits are the results of many different situations including, but by no means limited to, productive inefficiencies. Governments borrow from foreigners to finance debts owed in both their own currencies and in foreign currencies.

Notation 8-5 describes the results of a domestic government's borrowing foreign currency to finance its foreign currency obligations to foreigners. The foreign currency exchange rate is 1D/1F and the interest rate is 10 percent. The superscripts are DG, domestic government, and FC, foreign creditor. The other notations are as previously defined.

/RSD/ $FTLM^{DG}_{-1}$ $FTLM^{FC}_{1}$ (8-5)

$FTLM^{DG}_{-1.1}$ $FTLM^{FC}_{1.1}$ FCM^{FC}_{-1} FCM^{DG}_{1} FCM^{DG}_{-1} FCM^{FC}_{1} $FTLM^{FC}_{-1}$ $FTLM^{DG}_{1}$

/RSD/ $FTLM^{DG}_{-1.1}$ $FTLM^{FC}_{1.1}$

Borrowing to finance fiscal deficits in foreign currency owed to foreigners decreases foreign currency reserves over time by the compounding interest.

Notation 8-6 describes borrowing foreign currency from foreign creditors to pay domestic creditors (DC) in foreign currency. This action increases the debt by the amount of interest and transfers the debt to foreign creditors.

/RSD/ $FTLM^{DG}_{-1}$ $FTLM^{DC}_{1}$ (8-6)

$FTLM^{DG}_{-1.1}$ $FTLM^{FC}_{1.1}$ FCM^{FC}_{-1} FCM^{DG}_{1} FCM^{DG}_{-1} FCM^{DC}_{1} $FTLM^{DC}_{-1}$ $FTLM^{DG}_{1}$

/RSD/ $FTLM^{DG}_{-1.1}$ $FTLM^{FC}_{1.1}$

Notation 8-7 describes printing domestic currency to finance a fiscal deficit in domestic currency owed domestically and by a domestic government. Superscript *DS* means domestic society, and the other notations are as previously defined.

/RSD/ $DTLM^{DG}_{-1}$ $DTLM^{DC}_{1}$ (8-7)

$DTLM^{DG}_{-1}$ $DTLM^{DS}_{1}$ DCM^{DS}_{-1} DCM^{DG}_{1} DCM^{DG}_{-1} DCM^{DC}_{-1} $DTLM^{DC}_{-1}$ $DTLM^{DG}_{1}$

/RSD/ $DTLM^{DG}_{-1}$ $DTLM^{DS}_{1}$ DCM^{DS}_{-1} DCM^{DC}_{1}

The debt obligation of the government has been transferred from a domestic creditor to the domestic society. Discretionary currency is left in the hands of the domestic creditor, who can spend it at will. If it is invested in new production, it will increase the overall availability of goods and services. If it is used to outbid others for existing products, society will bear its effect in inflation. No interest was involved in printing the money, so the amount of debt does not increase.

Fearing inflation, sometimes governments of developing nations borrow stronger foreign currency and print their weaker domestic currency against that coverage instead of just printing their own currency. That action is believed to strengthen the domestic currency in one of two ways. Either the foreign currency is held as increased foreign reserves or it is sold for domestic currency, neutralizing the increase of domestic currency. Notations 8-8 and 8-9 describe these ways in turn.

/RSD/ $DTLM^{DG}_{-1}$ $DTLM^{DC}_{1}$ (8-8)

$FTLM^{DG}_{-1.1}$ $FTLM^{FC}_{1.1}$ FCM^{FC}_{-1} FCM^{DG}_{1}

$DTLM^{DG}_{-1}$ $DTLM^{DS}_{1}$ DCM^{DS}_{-1} DCM^{DG}_{1} DCM^{DG}_{-1} DCM^{DC}_{1} $DTLM^{DC}_{-1}$ $DTLM^{DG}_{1}$

/RSD/ $FTLM^{DG}_{-1.1}$ $FTLM^{FC}_{1.1}$ FCM^{FC}_{-1} FCM^{DG}_{1} $DTLM^{DG}_{-1}$ $DTLM^{DS}_{1}$ DCM^{DS}_{-1}

DCM^{DC}_{1}

Increasing foreign currency reserves does not change the actual domestic situation at all. It obligates the domestic government to repay foreign currency in an amount equal to both principal and interest, however, while increasing foreign currency reserves by only the amount of the principal. The government is actually decreasing its reserves over time. If such action strengthens the domestic currency, it must do so by psychologically, not actually, influencing economic participants.

Selling the borrowed foreign currency for domestic currency has a different effect (8-9). The increased domestic currency is neutralized

/RSD/ $DTLM^{DG}_{-1}$ $DTLM^{DC}_{1}$ (8-9)

$FTLM^{DG}_{-1.1}$ $FTLM^{FC}_{1.1}$ FCM^{FC}_{-1} FCM^{DG}_{1}

$DTLM^{DG}_{-1}$ $DTLM^{DS}_{1}$ DCM^{DS}_{-1} DCM^{DG}_{1} DCM^{DG}_{-1} DCM^{DC}_{1} $DTLM^{DC}_{-1}$ $DTLM^{DG}_{1}$

FCM^{DG}_{-1} FCM^{DC}_{1} DCM^{DC}_{-1} DCM^{DG}_{1}

/RSD/ $FTLM^{DG}_{-1.1}$ $FTLM^{FC}_{1.1}$ FCM^{FC}_{-1} $FCM^{DC}_{1.0}$

and only discretionary foreign currency remains. The inflation potential has been transferred from domestic currency to foreign currency. The foreign debt has been increased by the principal and interest, however, without increasing the foreign currency reserves at all. Because it retained none of the foreign currency obtained, the domestic government will decrease its foreign currency reserves by the principal and interest when the debt comes due.

Apparently, neither of the ways in which developing nations use stronger foreign currency to fight the potential inflation of printing domestic currency is effective. The first way has no actual effect on inflation. The second one potentially deflates the domestic currency by removing more of it to pay foreign debt as falling foreign currency reserves force the domestic/foreign exchange rate up.

SUPRA-MONEY AS AN ACCOUNTING MEDIUM

Supra-money may be introduced to provide an accounting medium for determining how much discretionary currency is being introduced into foreign exchange and which societies are introducing it. A record of discretionary currency is needed because discretionary currency increases the overall currency MIM supply, causing global inflation. Supra-money is discussed with reference to the situations described in notations 8-10, 8-11, and 8-12.

Notation 8-10 describes society-initiated production similar to that described in 8-1 and 8-3. The symbols are the same. Supra-money information markers

(S), however, are introduced into the foreign currency exchange process by a supranational system (SS). As in 8-3, 8-10 assumes a fixed exchange rate. The price change, however, occurs in the foreign society instead of the domestic one.

The analysis shows that the introduction of supra-money information markers has no effect on the outcome of society-initiated production situations. The outcome is just like it would be without their introduction. The price change effect is passed through to the domestic customer without any filtering for inappropriately introduced foreign currency. All the problems that pressure changes in foreign currency exchange rates remain. Notwithstanding that outcome, supra-money introduces an important control. Supra-money can account for foreign currency exchange rates in obligatory, legal, negotiable money-information markers.

$$DTLM^{P1}_{-1} \quad DTLM^{S1}_{1} \quad DCM^{S1}_{-1} \quad DCM^{P1}_{1} \quad DCM^{P1}_{-1} \quad DCM^{C1}_{1} \quad DME^{C1}_{-1} \quad DME^{P1}_{1} (8-10)$$

$$FTLM^{P2}_{-2} \quad FTLM^{S2}_{2} \quad FCM^{S2}_{-2} \quad FCM^{P2}_{2} \quad FCM^{P2}_{-2} \quad FCM^{C2}_{2} \quad FME^{C2}_{-1} \quad FME^{P2}_{1}$$

$$DCM^{C1}_{-1} \quad DCM^{S1}_{1} \quad FTLM^{S1}_{-1} \quad FTLM^{C1}_{1} \quad DCM^{S1}_{-1} \quad DCM^{SS}_{1} \quad FLTM^{SS}_{-1} \quad FTLM^{S1}_{1}$$

$$SCM^{SS}_{-1} \quad SCM^{S2}_{1} \quad FCM^{S2}_{-1} \quad FCM^{SS}_{1} \quad FCM^{SS}_{-1} \quad FCM^{S1}_{1} \quad FLTM^{S1}_{-1} \quad FTLM^{SS}_{1}$$

$$FCM^{S1}_{-1} \quad FCM^{C1}_{1} \quad FTLM^{C1}_{-1} \quad FTLM^{S1}_{1}$$

$$FCM^{C2}_{-1} \quad FCM^{S2}_{1} \quad DTLM^{S2}_{-1} \quad DTLM^{C2}_{1} \quad FCM^{S2}_{-1} \quad FCM^{SS}_{1} \quad DTLM^{SS}_{-1} \quad DTLM^{S2}_{1}$$

$$SCM^{SS}_{-1} \quad SCM^{S1}_{1} \quad DCM^{S1}_{-1} \quad DCM^{SS}_{1} \quad DCM^{SS}_{-1} \quad DCM^{S2}_{1} \quad DTLM^{S2}_{-1} \quad DTLM^{SS}_{1}$$

$$DCM^{S2}_{-1} \quad DCM^{C2}_{1} \quad DTLM^{C2}_{-1} \quad DTLM^{S2}_{1}$$

$$FCM^{C1}_{-1} \quad FCM^{P2}_{1} \quad FME^{P2}_{-0.5} \quad FME^{C1}_{0.5}$$

$$DCM^{c2}_{-1} \quad DCM^{P1}_{1} \quad DME^{P1}_{-1} \quad DME^{C2}_{1}$$

$$FCM^{P2}_{-1} \quad FCM^{S2}_{1} \quad FTLM^{S2}_{-1} \quad FTLM^{P2}_{1}$$

$$DCM^{P1}_{-1} \quad DCM^{S1}_{1} \quad DTLM^{S1}_{-1} \quad DTLM^{P1}_{1}$$

$$/RSD/ \quad DME^{C1}_{-1} \quad FME^{C1}_{0.5} \quad FME^{C2}_{-1} \quad DME^{C2}_{1} \quad FME^{P2}_{0.5}$$

$$/RSD/ \quad FTLM^{P2}_{-1} \quad FTLM^{S2}_{1} \quad FCM^{S2}_{-1} \quad FCM^{C2}_{1}$$

The results of the foreign price change described in 8-10 are that the domestic consumer-labor entity gives up 1.0 value of goods/services for 0.5 value of foreign goods-services while the foreign consumer-labor entity's exchange is 1 for 1, the foreign producer holds 0.5 value of inventory and owes its society 1.0 value of debt, and the foreign consumer-labor entity holds 1 value of foreign discretionary currency.

The discretionary currency may be used to purchase the foreign producer's excess production or to buy more foreign product. If it is used to purchase the excess production, the foreign producer can repay foreign society, and the currency-debt circuit will close, leaving no discretionary MIM in either society. No global monetary inflation will occur. The only intersocietal effect is that sanctioned by the domestic consumer-labor entity paying the increased price of foreign product. Goods-services available in the domestic society nevertheless are decreased and those in the foreign society are increased.

A similar outcome is ultimately achieved if the foreign discretionary currency is used to purchase additional domestic product *and* the domestic consumer-labor entity in return purchases the excess production of the foreign producer. On the way to that end, however, discretionary currency is in the system and can inflate the prices of existing products rather than increase production. When the foreign consumer-labor entity purchases additional domestic product (8-11), the domestic currency is increased, and the increase may be used to buy the foreign product, to further increase domestic production, or to inflate domestic prices.

$$/RSD/ \ DME^{C1}_{-1} \ FME^{C1}_{0.5} \ FME^{C2}_{-1} \ DME^{C2}_{1} \ FME^{P2}_{0.5} \hspace{2cm} (8\text{-}11)$$

$$/RSD/ \ FTLM^{P2}_{-1} \ FTLM^{S2}_{1} \ FCM^{S2}_{-1} \ FCM^{C2}_{1}$$

$$FCM^{C2}_{-1} \ FCM^{S2}_{1} \ DTLM^{S2}_{-1} \ DTLM^{C2}_{1} \ FCM^{S2}_{-1} \ FCM^{SS}_{1} \ DTLM^{SS}_{-1} \ DTLM^{S2}_{1}$$

$$SCM^{SS}_{-1} \ SCM^{S1}_{1} \ DCM^{S1}_{-1} \ DCM^{SS}_{1} \ DCM^{SS}_{-1} \ DCM^{S2}_{1} \ DTLM^{S2}_{-1} \ DTLM^{SS}_{1}$$

$$DCM^{S2}_{-1} \ DCM^{C2}_{1} \ DTLM^{C2}_{-1} \ DTLM^{S2}_{1} \ DCM^{C2}_{-1} \ DCM^{P1}_{1} \ DTLM^{P1}_{-1} \ DTLM^{C2}_{1}$$

$$DCM^{P1}_{-1} \ DCM^{C1}_{1} \ DME^{C1}_{-1} \ DME^{P1}_{1} \ DME^{P1}_{-1} \ DME^{C2}_{1} \ DTLM^{C2}_{-1} \ DTLM^{P1}_{1}$$

$$/RSD/ \ DME^{C1}_{-2} \ FME^{C1}_{0.5} \ FME^{C2}_{-1} \ DME^{C2}_{2} \ FME^{P2}_{0.5}$$

$$/RSD/ \ FTLM^{P2}_{-1} \ FTLM^{S2}_{1} \ FCM^{S2}_{-1} \ FCM^{SS}_{1} \ SCM^{SS}_{-1} \ SCM^{S1}_{1} \ DCM^{S1}_{-1}$$

$$DCM^{C1}_{1}$$

The supra-money system provides information on the inflated currencies. The residuals of 8-11 indicate that the supranational system holds the inflation-initiating foreign currency and it has issued supra-currency to the domestic society. That information indicates where the inflation potential (discretionary currency) originated (in the foreign society) and where the inflation potential is at this time (in the domestic society).

Notation 8-12 continues the chain of exchanges to close the currency-debt circuit with the domestic consumer-labor entity's purchase of the excess production of the foreign producer. At the conclusion of those exchanges, only the different exchanged goods-services remain in the residuals. No money-information markers of any kind are left outstanding.

$$/RSD/ \ DME^{C1}_{-2} \ FME^{C1}_{0.5} \ FME^{C2}_{-1} \ DME^{C2}_{2} \ FME^{P2}_{0.5} \hspace{2cm} (8\text{-}12)$$

$$/RSD/ \ FTLM^{P2}_{-1} \ FTLM^{S2}_{1} \ FCM^{S2}_{-1} \ FCM^{SS}_{1} \ SCM^{SS}_{-1} \ SCM^{S1}_{1} \ DCM^{S1}_{-1}$$

$$DCM^{C1}_{1}$$

DCM^{C1}_{-1} DCM^{S1}_{1} $FTLM^{S1}_{-1}$ $FTLM^{C1}_{1}$ DCM^{S1}_{-1} DCM^{SS}_{1} FCM^{SS}_{-1} FCM^{S1}_{1}

FCM^{S1}_{-1} FCM^{C1}_{1} $FTLM^{C1}_{-1}$ $FTLM^{S1}_{1}$

FCM^{C1}_{-1} FCM^{P2}_{1} $FME^{P2}_{-0.5}$ $FME^{C1}_{0.5}$ FCM^{P2}_{-1} FCM^{S2}_{1} $FTLM^{S2}_{-1}$ $FTLM^{P2}_{1}$

SCM^{S1}_{-1} SCM^{SS}_{1} DCM^{SS}_{-1} DCM^{S1}_{1}

/RSD/ DME^{C1}_{-2} FME^{C1}_{1} FME^{C2}_{-1} DME^{C2}_{2}

Consequently, no global inflation of either currency has occurred. It is important to observe, however, that twice as much product has been produced and given by the domestic society to the foreign one. The full price increase that occurred in the foreign society has been realized in goods-services by that society.

The supramoney signal occurs in the supranational system only when there is an imbalance between the currencies exchanged by two societies. The currency causing the imbalance is actually held by the supranational system during the time it is being used to increase the other society's currency supply. That accounting is in legal tender, fully negotiable for value. Without supra-money administered in a supranational system, such an accounting is not possible. The information is buried in private exchanges within the two societies and among their components.

The accounting record (the residual money-information markers) in the supranational system forms a basis for determining whether foreign currency exchange rates should be changed. The record is automatically formed when an imbalance is introduced into foreign exchange and automatically eliminated when no imbalance remains. The record concerns only that portion of a society's discretionary currency introduced into the foreign exchange process. Any other discretionary currency introduced within a society remains unidentified—the prerogative of that society. The relative independence of individual societies can thus be maintained.

An important characteristic of this particular pattern of transmission of money-information markers to the supranational system is that *no* societal debt is transmitted. The supranational system has no legal right to claim the excess inventory of the foreign producers. That right remains with the society. A policy of widely dispersing the societal decider subsystem to prevent any single organization from controlling the society would require that the organization designated to issue currency money-information markers for the society should not be empowered to claim excess goods-services against which any debt it holds was issued. Supra-money could be introduced in a way to honor that information disconnect. All currency-issuing organizations should be limited by regulations decided by a society's legal system.

SUMMARY

This chapter has extended the methods of macro accounting to intersocietal exchanges. The analyses have shown how actual foreign exchange rates emerge from prices within societies, how different levels of economic development can cause price differentials between developed and developing countries, and the effects of fixed and changing foreign currency exchange rates. It has suggested that the current monetary system fosters an international privileged class of individuals at the expense of society members. Some pitfalls of fiscal deficit financing by governments with foreign debts were discussed, and the introduction of supra-money as an accounting device was suggested.

REFERENCE

Swanson, G. A. and Miller, James Grier. *Measurement and Interpretation in Accounting– A Living Systems Theory Approach.* New York: Quorum Books, 1989.

Figure 8-1
How Societies Can React to Price Change (Inflation/Deflation)

	Inflationary Domestic	Deflationary Domestic	Inflationary Foreign	Deflationary Foreign
Domestic Can Issue D	no incentive	X	X	no incentive
Foreign Can Issue F	X	no incentive	no incentive	X

Figure 8-2
Inticed Reactions to Monetary Policies

	Loose Policy	Tight Policy
Domestic	F_L	D_L
Foreign	D_L	F_L

9

Conclusions

This final chapter pulls together important insights into modern economic processes discussed throughout the book. They primarily concern concrete processes and structures, but some extend to current policies as well.

THE DOMINANT FORM OF MODERN MONEY: ACCOUNTING DOCUMENTATION OF DEBT

By far, the largest volume of modern money is debt instrumentation. Although monies by fiat, precious commodities, and so on exist to some extent, the dominant form is debt money. Debt monetary economies emerge as debt instruments (time-lagged money-information markers) are introduced into exchange processes to document executory contracts that require the future delivery of matter-energy forms (goods-services).

Debt instruments are negotiable accounting documents. They are negotiable because they are exchanged at the value of certain goods-services that they legally command when the contracts they document are executed. The value that they document is determined by agreement of the particular participants in specific market exchanges. It is the specific exchange value of actual goods-services being traded. It is value in exchange measured by the participants on a monetary scale.

Debt instruments must be executed at a specified time or they are defaulted. When defaulted, they no longer have value, but the holder can seek redress at law. Because they are negotiable, the risk of default may be transmitted to someone other than the original creditor. Whoever is holding the debt instrument at the moment of default suffers the loss.

DEBT MONEY EMERGES FROM LEGAL SYSTEMS

Legal systems consist of concrete, conceptual, and abstracted systems. An evolving code of law is an abstracted system. It is stored and communicated in public media outside private human brains. Conceptual systems of various persons such as lawyers, legislators, judges, police, and the citizenry influence the code's evolution. The most important element of a legal system is the concrete system element, however. That element includes physical power. Whether the power is exercised through enticement or coercion, it must be exercisable for a legal system to exist.

The behavior required by the executory contract documented by a debt instrument must be enforceable if the instrument is to be exchanged for value. Without the physical force of law—the police function—the instrument would only account, not negotiate.

The legal systems that introduce debt money need not be societal. The legal systems of groups, organizations, communities, and supranational systems can introduce debt instrumentation as well. In fact, an important cause of the emerging higher levels of living systems may be the need for higher-level legal systems to enforce executory contracts among relatively independent lower-level systems.

THE IRREDUCIBLE UNIT OF MODERN ECONOMIC PROCESSES: THE EXCHANGE

An exchange consists of reciprocating transactions that motivate each other. It is the smallest (least complex) economic process incorporating a dynamic that makes modern economic systems work. Although a single transaction may be physically observed, a transaction by itself contains no dynamic to make it happen.

Modern economic processes are exchange processes. They are self-motivating at the most fundamental unit of process. As such, they widely disperse decider functions of higher-order human systems among identifiable components. At the fundamental process level, they approximate ideal democratic process more closely than any other human institution.

Administered economic processes are motivated by coercion and enticement. They specialize components to enforce behaviors decided by administrations (specialized decider subsystems). The decision process is not widely dispersed among identifiable components.

The wide dispersion of their decider subsystems among societal elements makes exchange-based societies very strong. Wide participation in the decision-making process appeals to a certain sense of fairness and freedom. It enhances individual creativity, increasing the probability of a society's survival by adjusting to environmental stresses and societal strains.

Models of exchange economies should include the coupling relationships among the transactions of particular exchanges. Selecting sets of transactions without regard to which transactions are reciprocals of others ignores the dynamic that makes the system work. A requirement to limit economic models to those incorporating entire exchanges, termed the *quadratic constraint,* should be imposed by macro economists. Such constraint forces attention to the dynamics that cause the concrete economic processes to occur.

MONEY-INFORMATION MARKERS

Concrete systems consist of matter and energy forms arranged in space and ordered in time by information. Information in concrete systems is retained over time or relocated in space by relatively small bundles of matter termed *information markers.* Concrete monetary information is borne on money-information markers. Such money-information markers account for and motivate the economic activities of money-based societies. These markers communicate the fundamental economic information among the various physical components of an economy.

Money-information markers are concrete system elements. Consequently, they may be studied by scientific means that concern concrete systems. Macro accounting is a methodology for studying certain concrete processes of modern money-based societies by mapping the flows of money-information markers among societal components.

ACCOUNTING MEASUREMENT

Money-information markers that flow across boundaries of societal components are measurements of economic activity on the variable specific exchange value. Goods, services, and other forms of money-information markers are exchanged for the values encoded on the money-information markers. The information about the specific exchange value of the goods, services, and other money-information markers is contained in the flow of the encoded values of money-information markers. The exchange process effectively places a monetary scale in spatiotemporal proximity to real economic activity and assigns monetary values to that activity by comparing the scale values to the activities. The assigned values ordinarily have high validity because the markers have taken on economic values themselves.

The accounting double-entry method records the measurements in terms of both the money-information marker flows and the real economic activity. The economic activity may also be recorded on variables other than specific exchange value. The double-entry model, however, always records the monetary measurements of the variable specific exchange value.

The accounting measurement method records flows across boundaries as they are observed in exchanges. Flows are processes, and all processes occur over time. Higher-level living systems process information more slowly than lower-level ones. Critical process periods are consequently longer for higher-level living systems than for lower-level ones. The accounting measurement scale incorporates a temporal function as well as a spatial one. What period of time contains a particular exchange is as important as the monetary values assigned in the exchange. Reassigning monetary values to periods other than when the exchange occurred obscures the measurement record.

Macro accounting methodology extends certain aspects of double-entry accounting from the organization level of living systems to the societal level. The methodology is concerned more, however, with analytical procedures of tracing the effects of typical introductions of money-information markers into societies than with actually accounting for societies. The extended methodology can be used to account for societies as well, however.

MACRO ACCOUNTING

Macro accounting is a set of concepts, theory, and procedures that may be used to investigate the concrete processes of higher-order human systems such as societies and supranational systems. It extends accounting measurement and recording logic developed at the organization level of living systems to those higher levels.

Macro accounting procedures model chains of linked exchanges with notations and study the alternative patterns that may occur within the restrictions of an exchange economy. How societies should introduce various forms of money-information markers may be studied using such notations. The notations are also useful for studying foreign exchange processes.

BASIC ECONOMIC PROCESSES

Economic processes are complex chains of exchanges. Exchanges are the basic links that compose economic processes. Trades are one-link chains.

The most fundamental unit of exchange processes is a trade—reciprocating transfers of goods-services (matter-energy forms). It is the most condensed and simplest exchange process. The dynamic that causes a trade is the widely held preference among societal components for different forms of goods and services. The constraint that consummates a trade is a perceived equilibrium of value. The traders believe that the goods-services traded have equal values. The act of trading determines the economic value of the exchanged goods-services in terms of each other.

More complex chains are introduced by splitting trades into their component transfers. Time-lagged money-information markers are the splitting agents. The markers are legal instruments that document executory debt contracts between parties to an exchange. The markers are transmitted in exchange for transfers of goods-services at different moments—separating the reciprocating transfers of trades in time.

During the periods in which the executory contracts are in force, the money-information markers documenting them may be transmitted in exchanges for the value of the goods-services they command when executed. They are negotiable because the goods-services value is legally imputed to them.

The complex chains that result from separating the transfers of trades are composed of links of exchanges consisting of reciprocating transactions that may be transfers of matter-energy forms or transmissions of various sorts of money-information markers. Each transaction is composed of two accounts. Although transactions and accounts may be separately observed, they cannot occur independently of exchanges because no dynamic to motivate them exists. Complex economic processes, therefore, emerge as expansions of trades into chains of exchanges. The complexity of the chains is limited by the executory contract period of the debt instrument transmitted in the initial and terminal exchanges of each chain.

The emergence of debt-money does not depend on higher-order living systems (such as societies and supranational systems). Their legal systems nevertheless facilitate its emergence. Debt-money originates in the trust of recipients of time-lagged money-information markers. Some means of enforcement of the executory contracts underlying the markers is needed, however, for a debt-monetary system to become robust. That need likely is a major impetus in the evolutionary emergence of higher-order living systems, particularly societies.

The emergence of modern currency money-information markers does depend, however, on higher-order living systems. Currency money-information markers are societal emergents.

Debt-based economic processes may be broadly classified into determinate processes and dynamic processes. Determinate processes are composed of chains of exchanges that close on themselves, forming complete circuits. Money-information markers are introduced into the economy in the initial link and are removed in the final link. Dynamic processes are composed of chains of exchanges that do not close on themselves but require a following chain to close them. The connected chains form dynamic processes of recurring cycles. The open circuit of a prior cycle motivates the processes of a following one.

The negotiability characteristic of debt money-information markers allows them to be disconnected from the specific activities in which they were originated. The introduction of currency money-information markers further disconnects them. The disconnects allow the amounts of money given for a product or service and the money originated in the production of the product or service to differ. Such differences can cause the originator of the money-initiating debt instrument not to have enough currency to repay the instrument when due. In that case, a determinate circuit cannot be closed. Pending defaults may be avoided by initiating an additional circuit and using some of the money of that circuit to pay the overdue debt of the previous one. That action closes the previous circuit and initiates a dynamic process of recurring cycles. Initiating additional circuits to obtain currency money-information markers to avoid defaults (such as consumer loans to purchase residual production of a previous cycle) may be a stronger signal than necessary to turn determinate circuits into dynamic cycles. A more manageable signal may be accomplished with the introduction of interest charged on executory contracts held by society.

Discretionary currency money-information markers are left in the hands of societal components when money-initiating debt instruments are defaulted. Whoever holds the instrument at the due date suffers the default. If a societal component is holding the debt instrument on default, that component suffers the loss; the discretionary currency in the hands of another component is termed *local discretionary currency*. Such currency does not increase the overall money supply, but it redistributes economic value among societal components. If society is holding the defaulted instrument, however, the discretionary currency is termed *global discretionary currency* and increases the overall money supply.

DYNAMICS OF INTEREST, TAXES, RENT, AND PROFIT

Fundamental market economies are driven by a preference for multiple, different goods-services that is prevalent among individual persons and groups such as families, organizations, communities, and societies. That trade dynamic is sufficient to motivate extensive economic activity. The introduction of money-information markers refines the basic dynamic by facilitating specialization and integration by division of labor.

Certain additional dynamics commonly believed to expedite economic processes have emerged in modern economies. Whether the additional dynamics in fact motivate a higher level of economic process depends on how the money-information markers documenting them are introduced into an economy.

Interest, taxes, rent, royalties, and dividends motivate the production and export of goods-services. They signal the desires of producers. The introduction of money-information markers to include production signals can be orderly. Debt originated to finance production can include them and, consequently, the money-information markers documenting the debt can cover their costs. When this is done, the money flow introduced can form a determinant circuit—the most orderly process.

Alternatively, introducing profit into an economy perturbs an already initiated process and, consequently, its introduction cannot be orderly. Profit is the only motivator introduced into modern economies by consumer-importers. It signals the preferences of consumption.

Profit may be as necessary in the economies of free societies as democratic processes are in their political systems. That possibility has been neither confirmed nor denied by human history up to now. The turn of the twenty-first century may provide the opportunity to test the hypothesis that profit is necessary.

As they legitimatize certain dynamics such as those being discussed, societies should include the dynamics in the amount of money-information markers they introduce into their economies. If they do not, the amount of markers will be insufficient to negotiate fully the production-distribution stipulated by the executory contracts underlying the markers. There will not be enough money to complete the required exchanges.

Introducing insufficient markers can have several different consequences, depending on how the markers are introduced. Common outcomes, however, are defaults on executory contracts that result in either society or societal components suffering losses and corresponding discretionary currency money-information markers being left in the hands of societal components not party to the defaulted contracts. The discretionary currency is global and is left in the economy perpetually if society holds the defaulted contract—the general money supply is perpetually increased. The default is shared by all societal components in some fashion through additional production or inflation of the prices of existing goods-services. If a societal component holds the defaulted contract, it suffers the entire loss of the redistributed money-information markers that now constitute discretionary currency. No increase in the general money supply is effected, however.

Societies may charge interest on the executory contracts they hold and introduce currency money-information markers to cover the interest in a manner that changes a determinate production-distribution circuit into orderly recurring dynamic cycles. The process involves coercing additional production loans to repay previously unfunded interest with currency from them.

In effect, societies introduce an economic ion (an incomplete exchange), and the exchange system repeatedly attempts to complete the exchange. They violate the quadratic constraint of the system by introducing a transaction without a reciprocating one. The system supplies the reciprocating transaction from an exchange in a following chain only to cause that chain to leave a residual transaction, an incomplete exchange that must be completed by a following chain. The economic ion may be introduced in a manner that requires societies to hold increasingly more debt to cover increasing interest amounts or in a manner that requires holding a constant increment of debt to support a recurring interest amount.

Connecting circuits into recurring cycles with interest charged by society requires society to hold far less debt than connecting them with consumer loans to avoid defaults. A much less intense signal accomplishes much the same thing. Nevertheless, the process requires societies to continuously hold debt equal to the interest imposed. The dynamic processes activated by societal interest-bearing debt are degenerative with reference to production and consumption if societies do not hold debt equal to the interest they impose.

Interest imposed by one societal component lending to another also should be covered by the amount of currency MIM introduced into an economy. If a level of currency MIM equal to the level of interest in an economy is not maintained in excess of that needed for production and consumption, they will decline.

Other accepted dynamics such as rent, dividends, and royalties should be included in the amount of currency MIM recurringly introduced into economies. As with interest, failure to cover these dynamics will leave an economy without sufficient currency MIM to negotiate completely a production-distribution circuit. Because they motivate production-exportation, those dynamics may be included in the economic circuits or cycles at their initiation, resulting in orderly processes.

RECURRING EFFECTS OF CERTAIN DYNAMICS

The recurring effects of introducing different motivators in different ways vary, depending on how they are introduced and in what combinations. The effects are sometimes counterintuitive because economic systems are complex and interacting.

When debt instruments and currency are introduced without interest, profits, or changes in costs of factors of production such as labor, an incremental level of production can be motivated in repeated circuits. The process can be very orderly, removing from each circuit all debt instruments and currency MIM introduced. The debt instruments and currency cause no inflation or deflation, no excess inventory, and no discretionary currency MIM. A circuit may be initiated for any amount of product demanded. Sufficient currency MIM may be introduced to produce and distribute the product and may be retrieved at the conclusion of those activities.

Introducing interest into economic processes provides an additional motivation for economic activity. Although it can connect otherwise independent production-distribution circuits into recurring cycles, interest charged by a society introduces a positive feedback that moves the process in recurring cycles increasingly away from equilibrium in terms of residual debt to society held by producers. Nevertheless, no discretionary currency MIM are left in any cycle, and the initiated production remains stable over recurring cycles. The process is neither inflationary nor deflationary as long as society holds debt in the amount of interest it is charging.

The recurring effects of introducing profit into economic processes are more complex than those of interest. Profit causes positive feedback on production and discretionary currency MIM as well as on residual debt. Negative feedback that intermittently dampens the positive feedback also is coincidently initiated. The positive feedback is dominant, however, moving the processes away from equilibrium on both money-information marker and matter-energy forms (products and services).

The feed processes occur despite society's willingness to monetize the activities fully. They are caused by the quadratic constraint of market economies and the need to introduce profits into already initiated processes, thus perturbing them. Even though it attempts to cover the profit signal with additional currency MIM, society can receive the profit signal only after the fact. The perturbance caused by the profit signals various actions of societal components. By the time a signal reaches society, it is too late to provide currency MIM to avoid the actions already signaled.

When some producers receive profit and the others do not, society must hold proportionately more debt than the profit level as the process recurs. The increasing incremental debt is borne by the unprofitable producers. Discretionary currency in the amount of the increasing debt is given to the profitable producers, signaling preference for their products. Nevertheless, production is not increased. In fact, overall production decreases dramatically. The decrease is caused by lack of available currency MIM to complete each cycle.

When all producers receive profit, the processes are dramatically more orderly. The debt instruments and currency MIM clear with each cycle. Nevertheless, even more residual production is left after each cycle. The downward spiral of production, again, is caused by currency MIM being unavailable at the right times and places to complete the distribution of the product.

When the profits of some producers equal the losses of others, production is not decreased over time. That condition follows the common wisdom. The debt instruments and currency MIM required to maintain production increase over recurring cycles, however. The increasing MIM redistribute wealth dramatically. For example, profitable producers can receive discretionary currency and the consumers-laborers buying the unprofitable products and producing the profitable ones can be required to hold debt in order for the cycles to clear their production.

When wages or other factors of production increase after a production cycle is initiated, the producer suffering the increased wages owes society increasingly more money. Discretionary currency accumulates in the hands of the benefited consumer-laborer entity. Production is not decreased, however. When everyone receives a raise, the condition is compounded, leaving inflationary discretionary currency in the hands of consumer-labor entities.

The combined effects of introducing multiple motivators is not intuitively obvious. Adding profit to an interest-motivated economy might be expected to require currency MIM and debt instruments equal to the sum of the requirements of each motive introduced alone. That is not necessarily the case. Profits may drag production down so much that not nearly as many MIM are required for interest on production loans.

The recurring effects of introducing different motivators into economic processes can be dramatic and variable. The limited simulations provided in this book suggest that extensive macro accounting simulations of economic processes may increase our understanding of them.

SUPRANATIONAL SYSTEM: INTER-SOCIETAL EXCHANGES

Modern debt-monetary economies are societal emergents. At that level of living systems, currency MIM emerge from legal instruments, documenting debt-executory contracts agreed to by societal components. Currency MIM socialize the risk of default that characterizes individual executory contracts.

Foreign currency exchange rates are emergents of supranational systems. Nevertheless, their composition can be understood with reference to the society-level currencies that make them possible. A foreign exchange rate is composed of a ratio relationship between two ratios. The compound ratio consists ideally of the ratio of all currency in one society to that in another *to* the ratio of all matter-energy forms in the first society to that of the second. It is unlikely that methods can be developed to measure an ideal rate due to the complexity of modern economies.

Actual foreign currency exchange rates emerge from actual prices in different economies. Because societies usually export a mix of goods-services different from the overall mix produced, an actual exchange rate would be expected to differ from the ideal rate.

The difference between the overall average price and that of exports provides an opportunity for societies to benefit from certain trades with countries that have different goods-services mixes. Ricardo's comparative trade advantage is a result of such differentials. He identified comparative trade advantage in terms of labor value only, however, not in terms of all the values synthesized in modern currency MIM.

Comprehensive price differentials can be caused by many different conditions, including both legitimate charges and illegitimate distortions and manipulations of the money-information markers themselves. Legitimate charges include introducing more kinds of economic motivators as economies develop (become more complex). Such motivators usually improve technology and the quality of life.

As economic motivators—that are themselves MIM forms and not goods-services—are monetized, the costs of production and distribution of goods-services increase to incorporate them. The rising costs increase monetary inefficiencies as economies develop.

The monetary inefficiencies of more developed societies can provide an exchange advantage to less developed societies. The advantage arises from fewer costs associated with economic motivation in less developed societies. Such a comparative exchange advantage is different from the comparative trade advantage described by Ricardo. It can occur only between two relatively independent currency MIM systems, but trade advantage can occur between any arbitrarily identified divisions of a producing-consuming whole. Although the underdevelopment of a less developed society causes a comparative exchange advantage, the advantage may be exploited by either trading society or by both societies.

Foreign exchange rates may be held constant or changed. Fixed foreign exchange rates pass a producing society's price increases through to the consuming society. Changing foreign exchange rates can keep the effects of price changes occurring in one society from being transmitted to another. They can also introduce price changes in an importing society that did not occur in the exporting society.

Societies are not unlimited in the control they can exercise over changing exchange rates. Because currency MIM are issued on demand of economic participants and are retrieved on completion of an executory contract, societies ultimately can control only their introduction, not their retrieval. Although a society can protect itself from external price increases, the protective action is always inflationary. This society must act to increase its currency proportionately. It cannot remove the foreign currency.

Supply-demand forces have been introduced into the currency exchange–rate-setting process. The process permits different societies and societal components to hold reserves of currencies other than their own. If a society perceives that a particular exchange rate is moving contrary to its best interest, the society may buy or sell the other society's currency, as well as its own currency reserves. That action can have a local, and often temporary, effect on the offending exchange rate.

Because the supply-demand process is local and temporary, societies may attempt to break the internal-external consistency of reasonable global actions to achieve less than global effects favoring some faction of its economy or some perceived social purpose or goal. Viewing a society's internal benefits and consequences of a trade action independently from its external benefits and consequences permits an internationally sensitive privileged class to emerge. Such a class can eventually control societies, collapsing them into a world organization–level living system.

The most important characteristic of the organization level of human systems is the hierarchical structure of its decider subsystem. Modern pluralistic societies are approaching knowledge and technology to disperse widely societal decider subsystems among their components. Human civilization has repeatedly travailed to give birth to such a system only to have it snatched away by an organization's powerful hierarchical decider subsystem. The paramount question of human history in the twenty-first century is: Will human civilization finally reject the rule of privileged classes with its attendant cycles of economic boom and bust and political benevolence and despotism? This century can produce the knowledge and technology to introduce just systems of interaction with widely dispersed decider subsystems. Refining the world monetary system is an important aspect of those advances.

Societies benefit by increasing the amount of their currency MIM outstanding if other societies' outstanding currency MIM are unchanged. The analyses of this book have shown that the amount of currency MIM outstanding is increased by defaults on the executory debt contracts underlying it—leaving global discretionary currency MIM in an economy. Fixed foreign exchange rates pass the price increases (the inflation) of discretionary currency through to trading partners.

Supra-money may be introduced to provide an accounting medium for determining how much discretionary currency is being introduced into foreign exchange and what societies are introducing it. Supra-money information markers can be introduced in a manner so that they do not affect the outcome of society-initiated production situations—maintaining the relative independence of the societies. Societal decider subsystems can function as dispersed elements of the supranational system decider subsystem in addition to performing their own societal functions. Without infringing on societies, supra-money information markers can account for foreign currency exchange rates in obligatory, legal, negotiable money-information markers.

SUMMARY

This book has presented a new methodology for examining certain economic aspects of modern societies and supranational systems. The author has termed the methodology *macro accounting* because it concerns global economic effects and recognizes the central position of accounting documentation of executory debt contracts in modern exchange economies. The book presents enough analyses for a serious scholar of higher-order human systems to evaluate its usefulness. It also reveals numerous insights that should interest policymakers at various levels of government and industry. The insights suggest that extensive macro accounting analysis of modern economic processes may contribute to their evolutionary refinement.

Annotated Bibliography

Burkhardt, Helmut. "System Physics: A Uniform Approach to Branches of Classical Physics." *American Journal of Physics* 55, 4 (April 1987), pp. 344–50.

In this article, Burkhardt demonstrates a generalization of the accounting input-output algorithm. Burkhardt believes the model is universal and may be used from physics through the biological sciences to the social ones.

Ifrah, Georges. *From One to Zero: A Universal History of Numbers.* New York: Penguin Books, 1987.

Beginning with archaeological evidence of how early man kept track of his sheep and cattle, Georges Ifrah traces the development of numerical systems in Sumerian, Egyptian, Greek, Roman, Chinese, Babylonian, and Mayan cultures. He supports the thesis that written accounting preceded the transcription of language and identifies a Near East token system existing from 8,000 B.C. to 5,000 B.C. as the remote ancestor of our present monetary conventions.

Miller, James Grier. *Living Systems.* New York: McGraw-Hill, 1978.

Living Systems is the seminal work on living systems theory (LST). That theory conceives of all existence as systems—sets of related and interacting elements—and distinguishes among concrete, conceptual, and abstracted systems. Living systems are concrete systems, existing in physical space, that possess certain characteristics that can be measured and studied. They may be found at seven levels of complexity and each type of living system is composed of nineteen critical subsystems that are similar across levels. LST recognizes money as a form of information that emerged in society-level living systems.

Miller, James Grier. (1986). "Can Systems Theory Generate Testable Hypotheses?: From Talcott Parsons to Living Systems Theory." *Systems Research* 3, 2 (1986), pp. 73–84.

In this article, Miller discusses the difference between conceptual systems frameworks that concern concrete systems and those that describe abstracted systems. Theories based on concrete systems can be tested empirically while those based on abstracted systems generally cannot be tested in that manner.

Parsons, Talcott. *The Structure of Social Action.* New York: Free Press, 1968.

This book is probably the most influential conceptual framework of sociology in the twentieth century. It conceptualizes social systems as abstracted systems rather than concrete systems. While highly influential, the theory has produced little quantitative research. In the development of living systems theory, the great influence of Parson's theory made it necessary to clearly distinguish the concrete processes in social systems from conceptual aspects. Thus, those processes that are measurable may be identified and studied by scientific measures.

Schmandt-Besserat, Denise. *Before Writing: Volume I, From Counting to Cuneiform; Volume II, A Catalog of Near Eastern Tokens.* Austin, TX: University of Texas Press, 1992.

Professor Schmandt-Besserat asserts that written language developed from a system of counters (tokens) that appeared in the Near East about 8,000 B.C. following the rise of agriculture. This system was used to count and account for various agricultural products—it was a prehistoric accounting information system. It also contributed to the development of abstract numbering from objective numbering and to the eventual development of monetary systems.

Swanson, G. A. and Miller, James Grier. *Measurement and Interpretation in Accounting: A Living Systems Theory Approach.* Westport, CT: Greenwood Press, 1989.

This book extends the general concepts of living systems theory (LST) to the field of accounting. It provides a conceptual framework for identifying measurements of concrete processes of organizations in their accounting records and public statements. The measurements are made on the attribute specific exchange value and in terms of monetary values. The system provides a cosmic view on a common attribute of the many different forms of matter-energy in organization processes. The book also proposes that organizational accounting input-output procedures be adapted to societal accounting.

Stevens, S. S. "On the theory of measurement." *Science* 103 (1946), pp. 677–80; "Mathematics, Measurement, and Psychophysics" in S. S. Stevens, ed., *Handbook of Experimental Psychology.* New York: Wiley, 1946.

Stevens' ideas about measurement theory have become known as modern measurement theory. Acknowledging that certain limitations are inherent in particular and different methods of observation, modern measurement theory encourages developing scales that do not violate the limits of emerging observation methods.

Whitehead, Alfred North. *Science and the Modern World*. New York: Free Press, 1967.

Philosopher Whitehead's conceptualization of science influenced diverse theoretical developments in the social sciences. His clear perception of physical reality and his theory of organisms (systems) that exist on a hierarchy of increasing size and complexity directly influenced James Grier Miller's synthesis of living systems theory.

Guide to Financial Instruments. New York: Coopers and Lybrand, 1988.

This booklet describes many emerging forms of money-information markers that are hybrids between ownership and credit documents. These instruments are evidence of the continuing evolution of modern monetary systems.

Index

About the Author

G. A. SWANSON is a Professor of Accounting at Tennessee Technological University. His more than 50 articles have appeared in such journals as *Systems Research, Behavior Science, The Accounting Review, Internal Auditor Advances in Accounting, Accounting Historians Journal,* and *The Journal of Business Education.* He is coauthor of *Measurement and Interpretation in Accounting: A Living Systems Theory Approach* (Quorum, 1989), *Internal Auditing Theory—A Systems View* (Quorum, 1991), and *Management Observation and Communication Theory* (Quorum, 1992).